UNDERWORLD™

Underworld Movie Adaptation

Based on the Screenplay by DANNY MCBRIDE

Story by KEVIN GREVIOUX AND LEN WISEMAN & DANNY MCBRIDE

Adaptation by KRIS OPRISKO

Flashback Panels 2 & 3 on page 25 inspired
by the art of SALVATI DESIGN

Underworld: Red in Tooth and Claw
Story by KRIS OPRISKO AND DANNY MCBRIDE

Art: NICK POSTIC AND NICK MARINKOVICH

Lettering: ROBBIE ROBBINS

Design: CINDY CHAPMAN

Editor: JEFF MARIOTTE

Compilation Editor: ALEX GARNER

ISBN: 1-932382-26-7
07 06 05 04   1 2 3 4 5

Ted Adams, Publisher
Jeff Mariotte, Editor-in-Chief
Robbie Robbins, Design Director
Kris Oprisko, Vice President
Alex Garner, Art Director
Cindy Chapman, Designer
Beau Smith, Sales & Marketing
Chance Boren, Editorial Assistant
Jeremy Corps, Editorial Assistant
Yumiko Miyano, Business Development
Rick Privman, Business Development

www.idwpublishing.com

UNDERWORLD

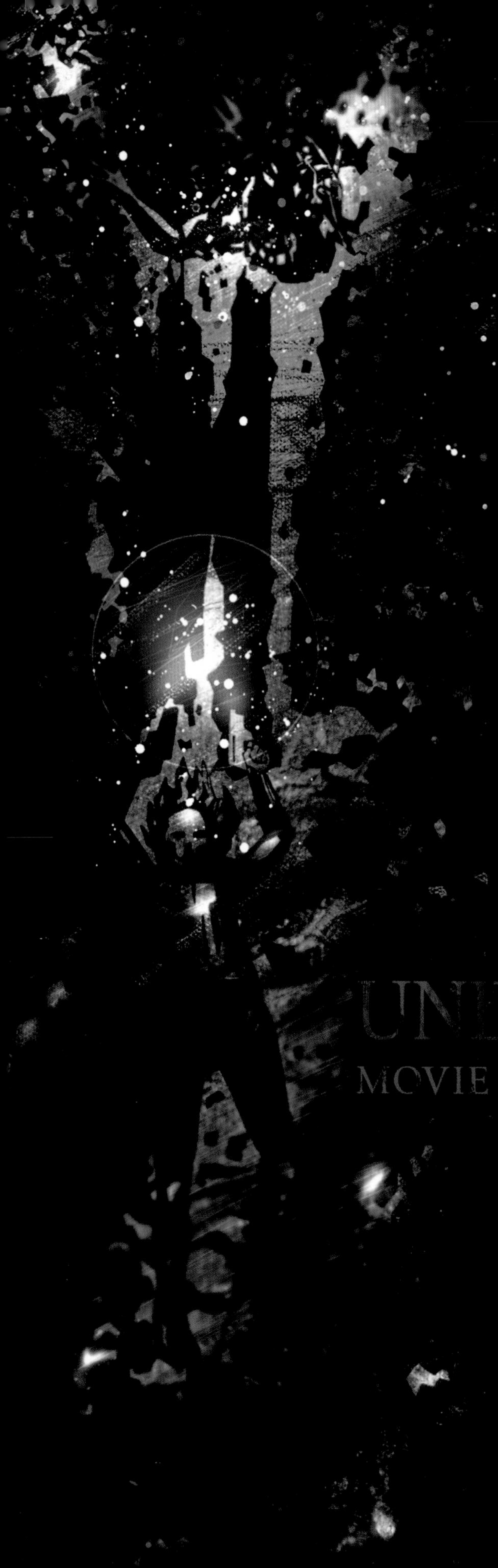

UNDERWORLD™

MOVIE ADAPTATION

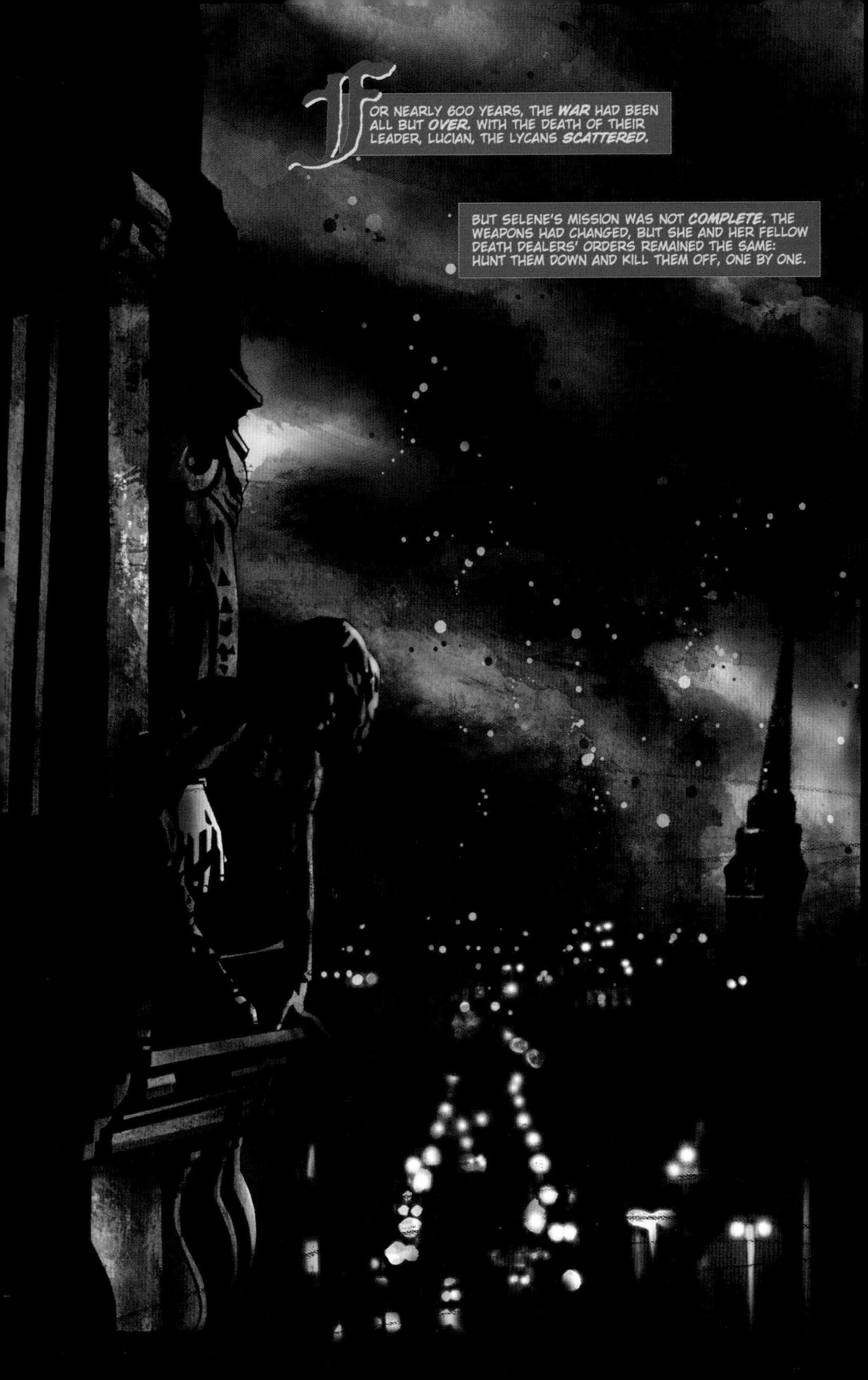
FOR NEARLY 600 YEARS, THE WAR HAD BEEN ALL BUT OVER. WITH THE DEATH OF THEIR LEADER, LUCIAN, THE LYCANS SCATTERED.
BUT SELENE'S MISSION WAS NOT COMPLETE. THE WEAPONS HAD CHANGED, BUT SHE AND HER FELLOW DEATH DEALERS' ORDERS REMAINED THE SAME: HUNT THEM DOWN AND KILL THEM OFF, ONE BY ONE.

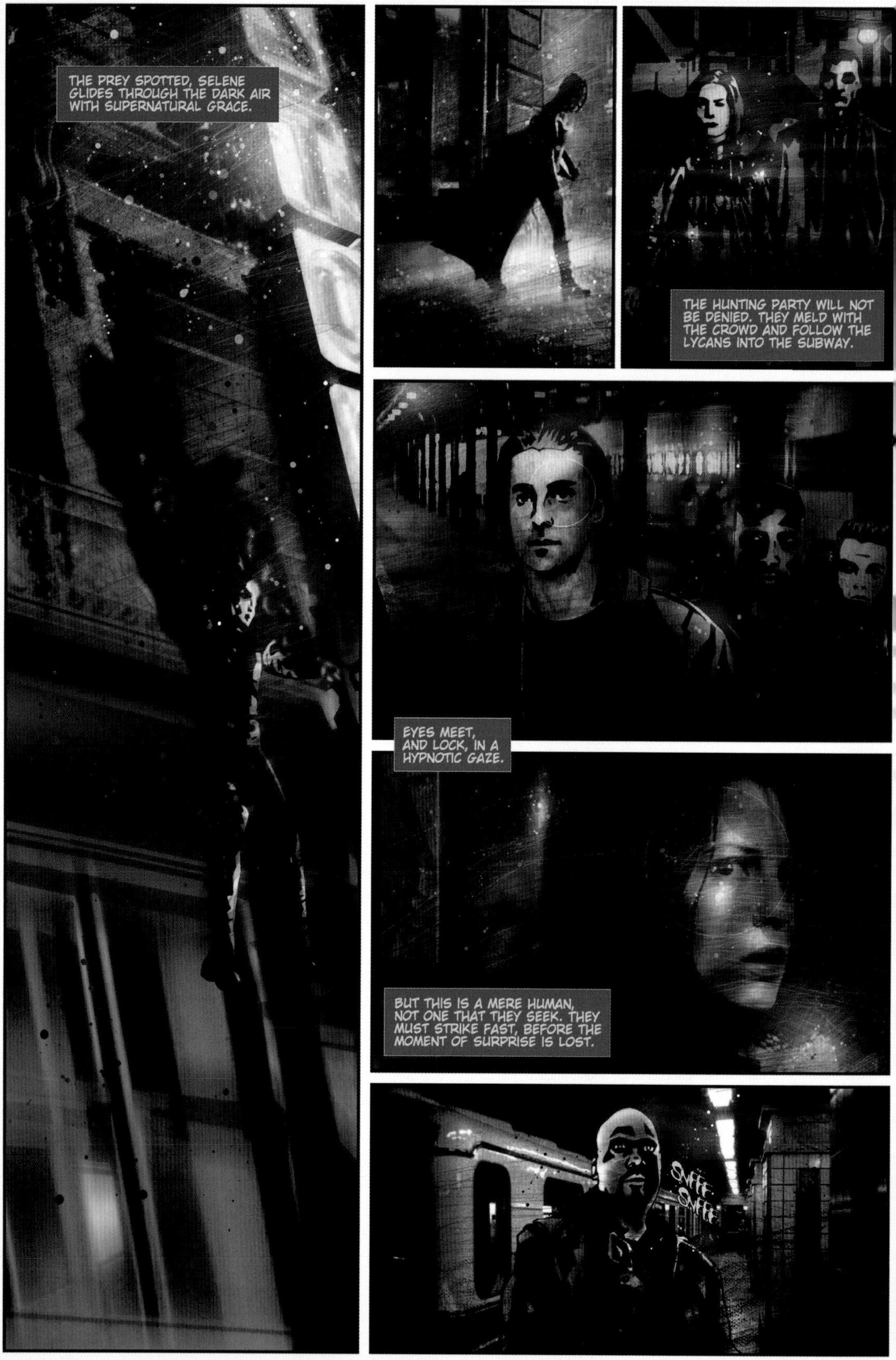
THE PREY SPOTTED, SELENE GLIDES THROUGH THE DARK AIR WITH SUPERNATURAL GRACE.
THE HUNTING PARTY WILL NOT BE DENIED. THEY MELD WITH THE CROWD AND FOLLOW THE LYCANS INTO THE SUBWAY.
EYES MEET, AND LOCK, IN A HYPNOTIC GAZE.
BUT THIS IS A MERE HUMAN, NOT ONE THAT THEY SEEK. THEY MUST STRIKE FAST, BEFORE THE MOMENT OF SURPRISE IS LOST.
SNFFF SNFFF

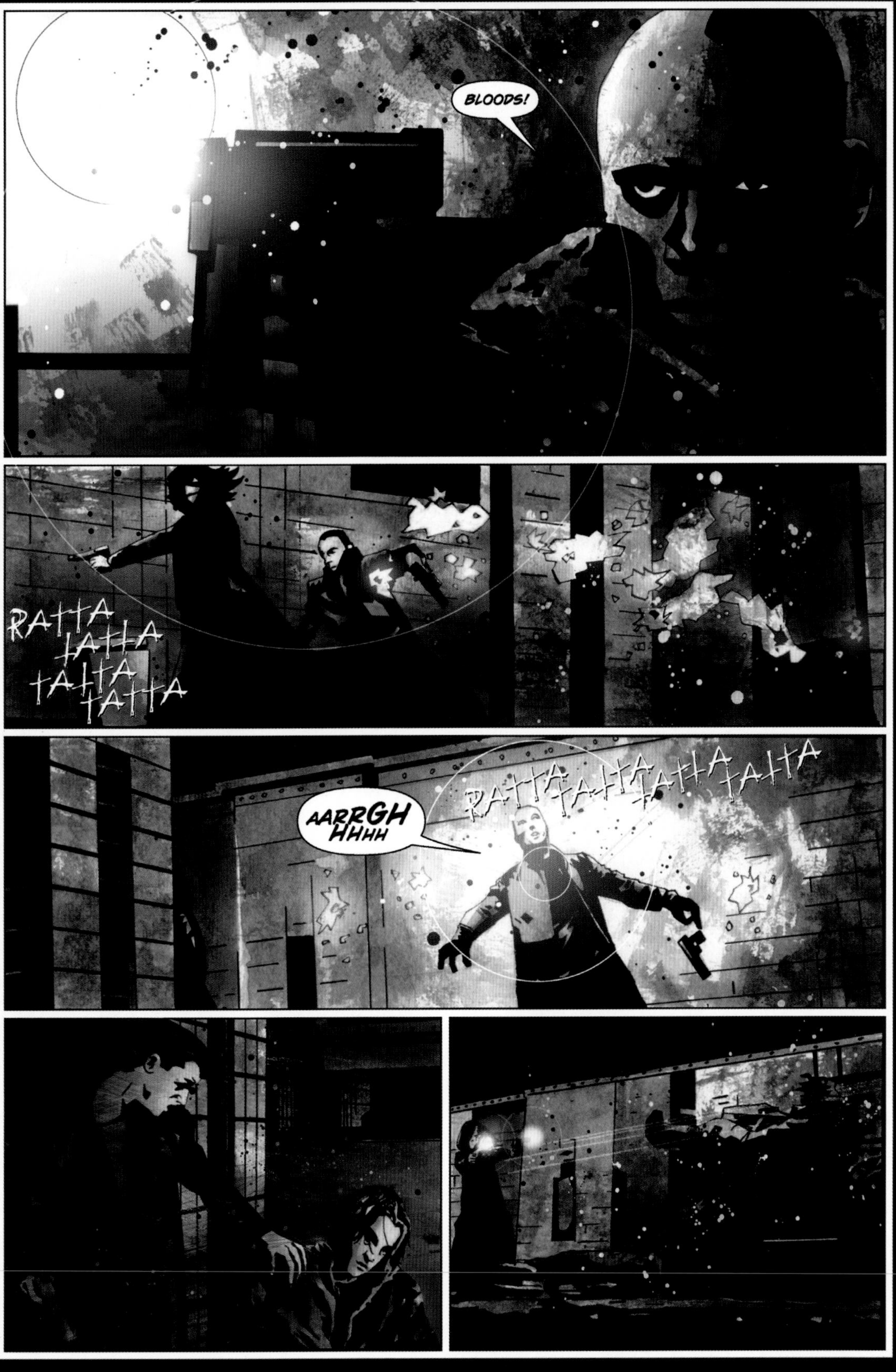
BLOODS!
RATTA TATTA TATTA TATTA
AARRGH HHHH
RATTA TATTA TATTA TATTA

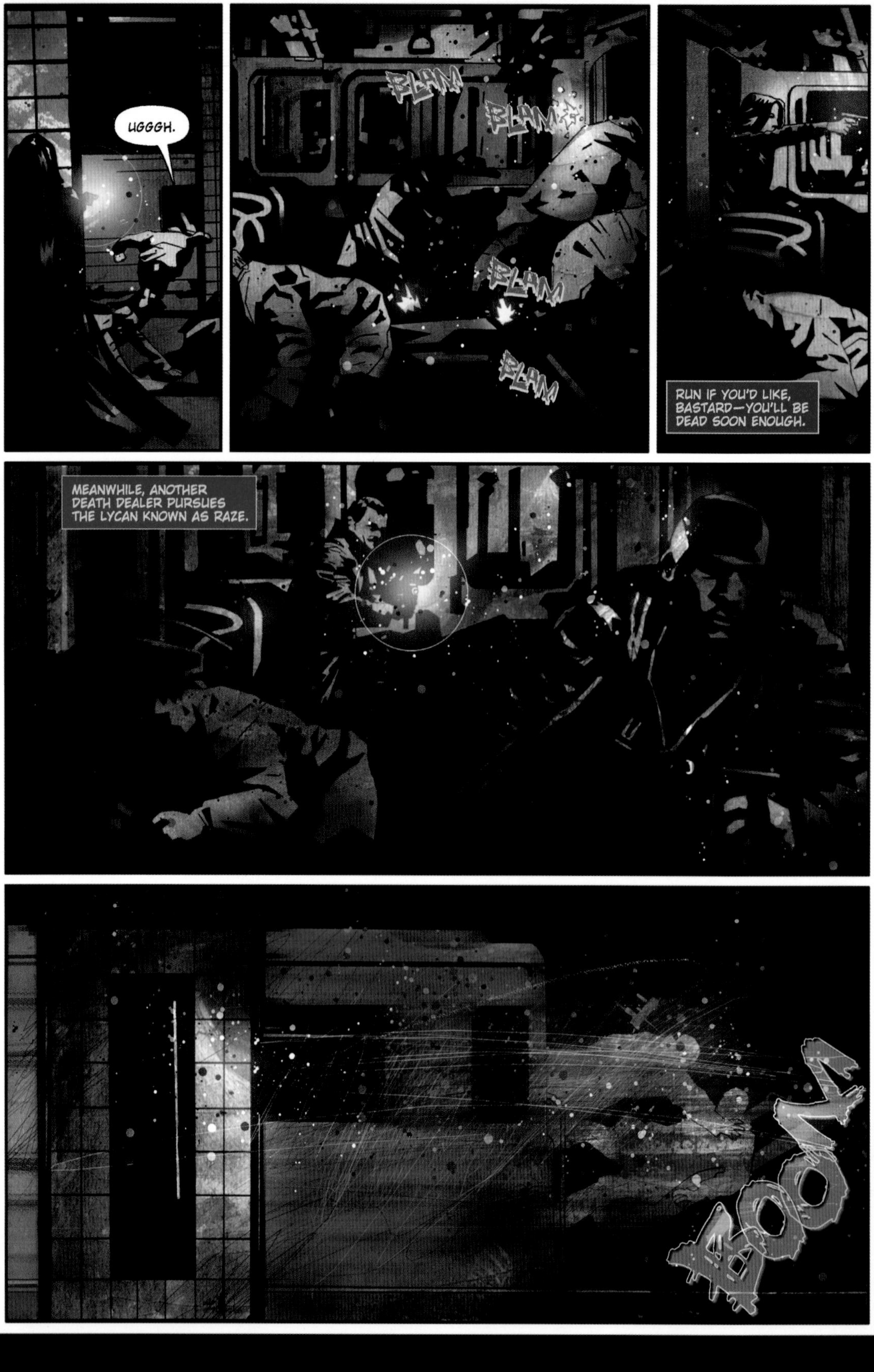
UGGGH.
BLAM
BLAM
BLAM
BLAM
RUN IF YOU'D LIKE, BASTARD—YOU'LL BE DEAD SOON ENOUGH.
MEANWHILE, ANOTHER DEATH DEALER PURSUES THE LYCAN KNOWN AS RAZE.
BOOM

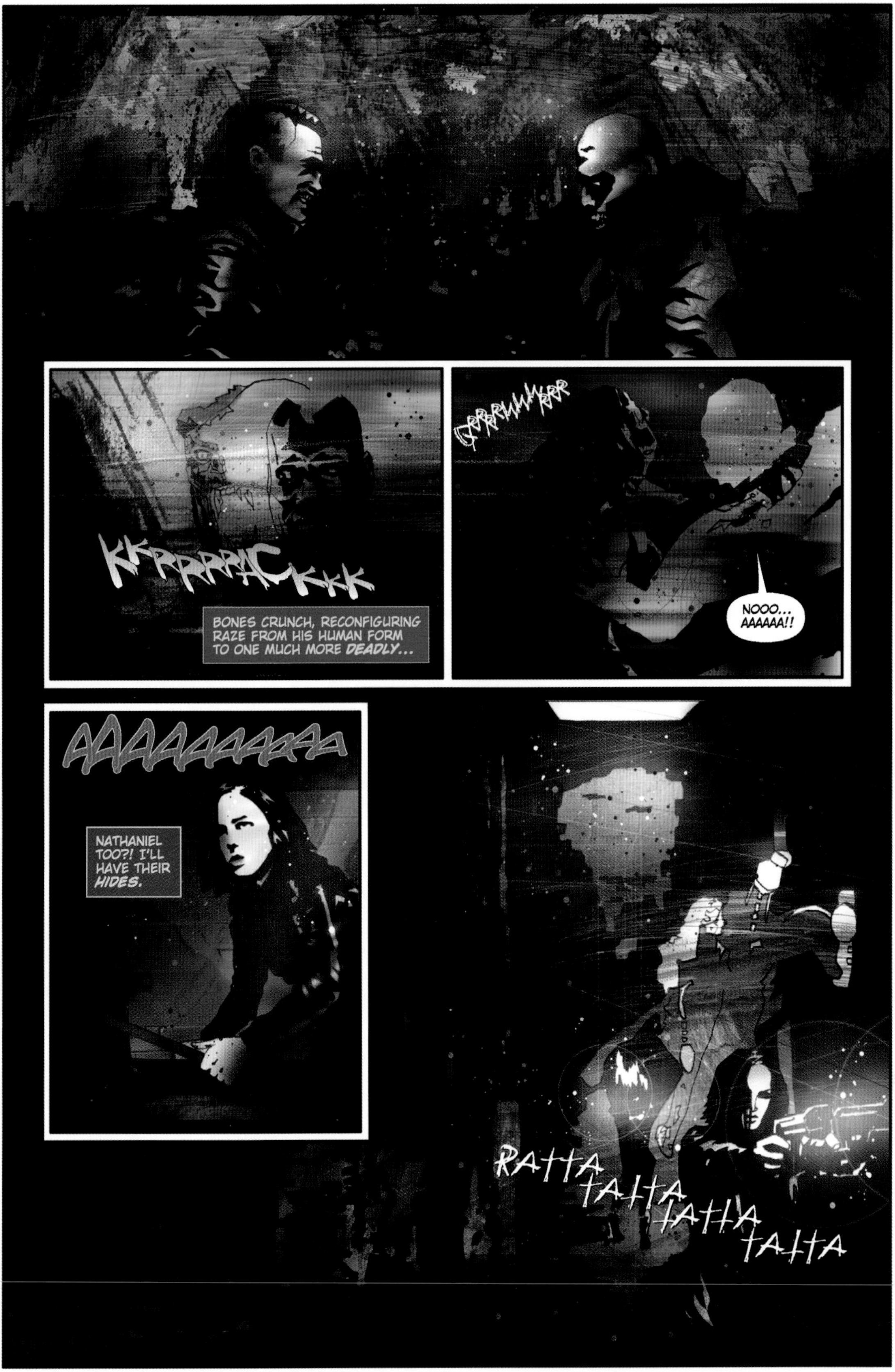
KKRRRRACKKK
BONES CRUNCH, RECONFIGURING RAZE FROM HIS HUMAN FORM TO ONE MUCH MORE DEADLY...
NOOO... AAAAAA!!
AAAAAAAAAA
NATHANIEL TOO?! I'LL HAVE THEIR HIDES.
RATTA TATTA TATTA TATTA

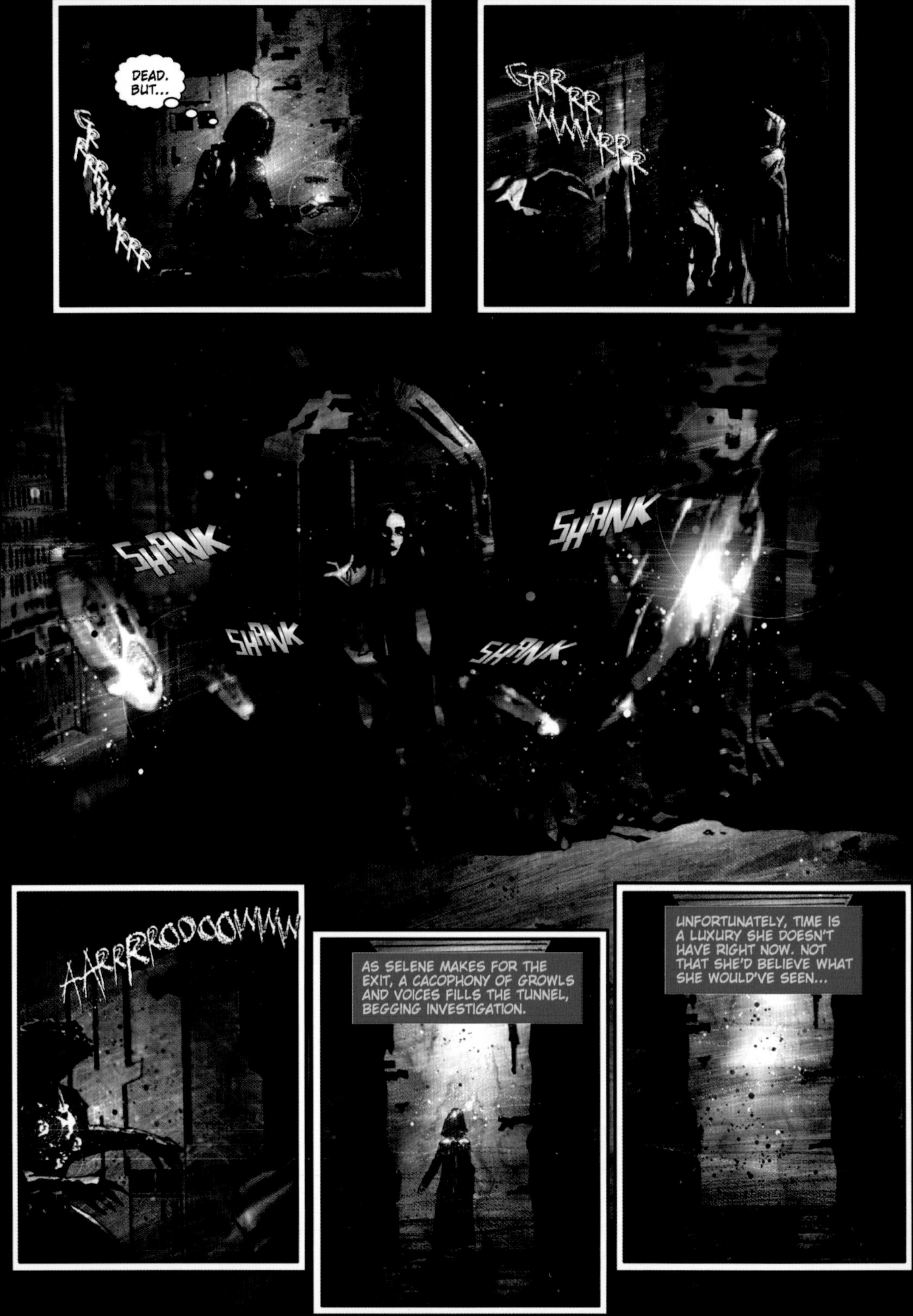
DEAD. BUT...
GRRRRNWWRRR
GRRRRR WWWRRR
SHANK
SHANK
SHANK
SHANK
AARRRROOOOWWW
AS SELENE MAKES FOR THE EXIT, A CACOPHONY OF GROWLS AND VOICES FILLS THE TUNNEL, BEGGING INVESTIGATION.
UNFORTUNATELY, TIME IS A LUXURY SHE DOESN'T HAVE RIGHT NOW. NOT THAT SHE'D BELIEVE WHAT SHE WOULD'VE SEEN...

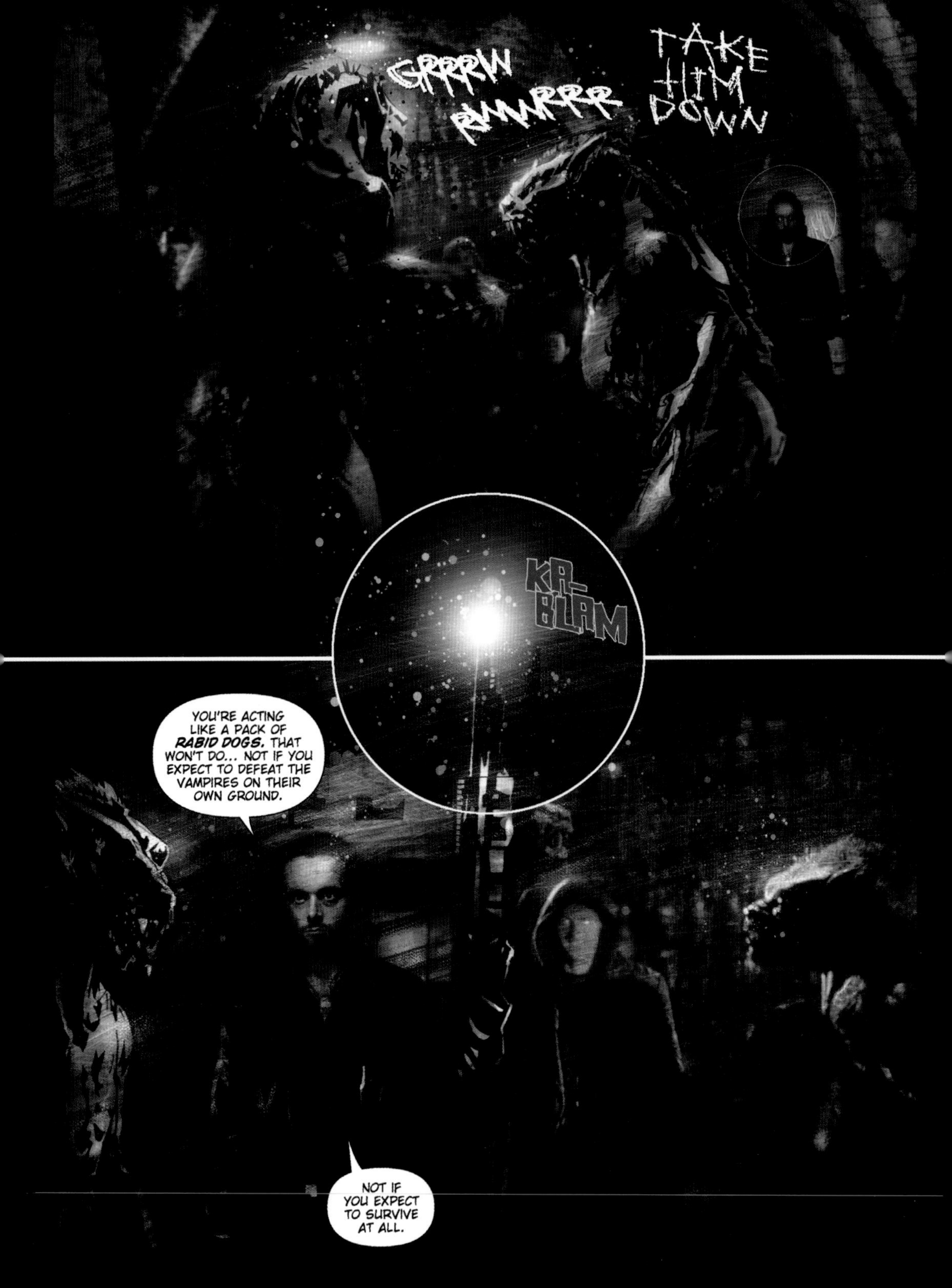
GRRRW RWWRRR
TAKE HIM DOWN
KA-BLAM
YOU'RE ACTING LIKE A PACK OF **RABID DOGS.** THAT WON'T DO... NOT IF YOU EXPECT TO DEFEAT THE VAMPIRES ON THEIR OWN GROUND.
NOT IF YOU EXPECT TO SURVIVE AT ALL.

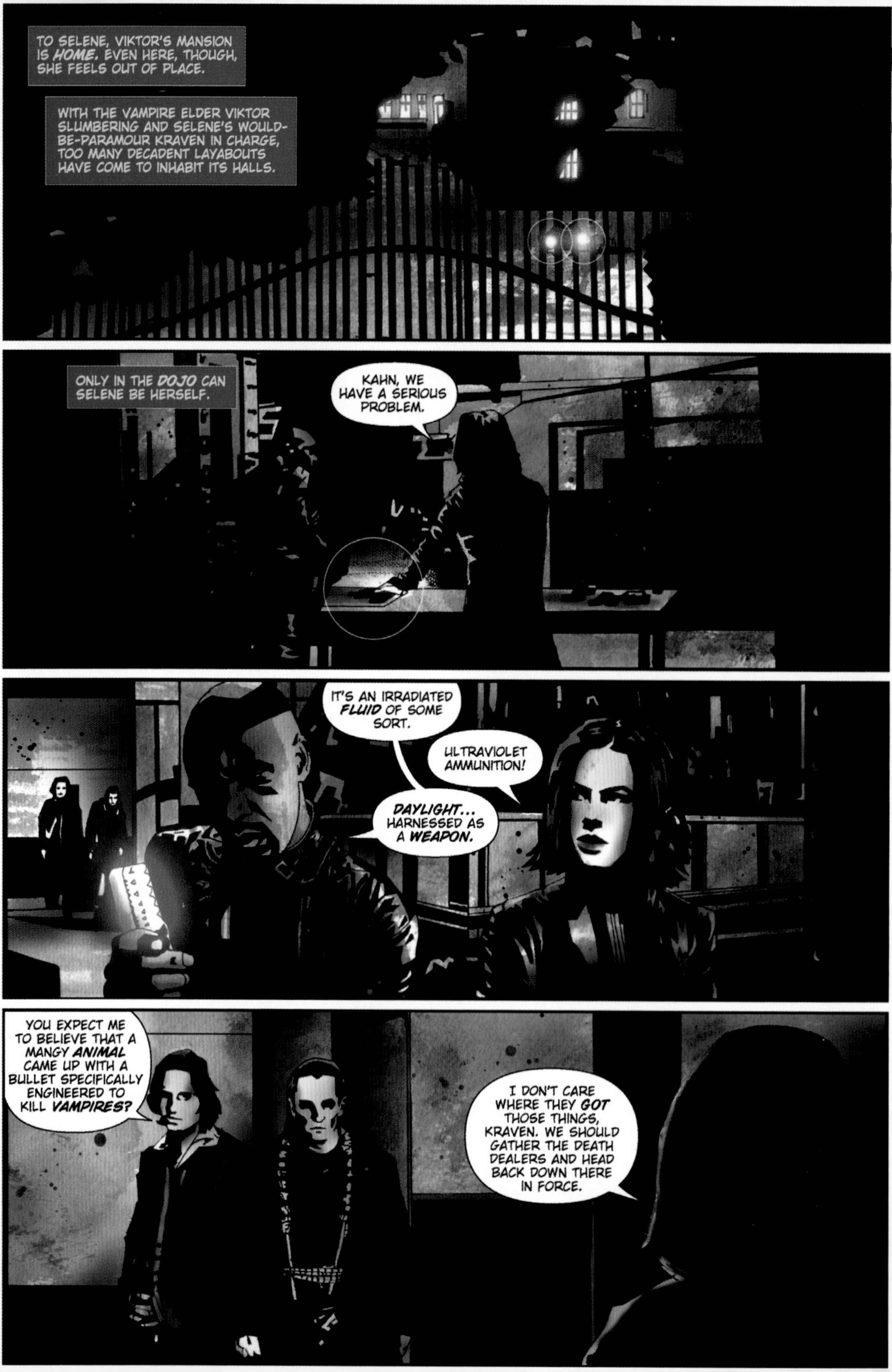
TO SELENE, VIKTOR'S MANSION IS HOME. EVEN HERE, THOUGH, SHE FEELS OUT OF PLACE.
WITH THE VAMPIRE ELDER VIKTOR SLUMBERING AND SELENE'S WOULD-BE-PARAMOUR KRAVEN IN CHARGE, TOO MANY DECADENT LAYABOUTS HAVE COME TO INHABIT ITS HALLS.
ONLY IN THE DOJO CAN SELENE BE HERSELF.
KAHN, WE HAVE A SERIOUS PROBLEM.
IT'S AN IRRADIATED FLUID OF SOME SORT.
ULTRAVIOLET AMMUNITION!
DAYLIGHT... HARNESSED AS A WEAPON.
YOU EXPECT ME TO BELIEVE THAT A MANGY ANIMAL CAME UP WITH A BULLET SPECIFICALLY ENGINEERED TO KILL VAMPIRES?
I DON'T CARE WHERE THEY GOT THOSE THINGS, KRAVEN. WE SHOULD GATHER THE DEATH DEALERS AND HEAD BACK DOWN THERE IN FORCE.

OUT OF THE QUESTION! NOT WITH THE *AWAKENING* ONLY A FEW DAYS OFF!

I'M TELLING YOU, I HEARD DOZENS OF LYCANS DOWN THERE— MAYBE *HUNDREDS!*

WE'VE HUNTED THEM TO THE BRINK OF *EXTINCTION.*

KRAVEN'S RIGHT, SELENE. THERE HASN'T BEEN A DEN OF THAT MAGNITUDE SINCE THE DAYS OF LUCIAN. BUT I'LL CHECK IT OUT.

NO, KAHN. SOREN HERE WILL HANDLE IT. HUNDREDS, REALLY!

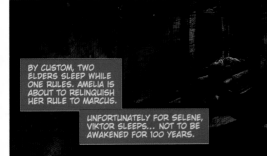

"VIKTOR WOULD BELIEVE ME."

BY CUSTOM, TWO ELDERS SLEEP WHILE ONE RULES. AMELIA IS ABOUT TO RELINQUISH HER RULE TO MARCUS.

UNFORTUNATELY FOR SELENE, VIKTOR SLEEPS... NOT TO BE AWAKENED FOR 100 YEARS.

THEY WERE AFTER *YOU.*

LATER.

COME ON, WE NEED YOU TO GET READY FOR THE PARTY. AMELIA'S ENVOY WILL BE HERE ANY TIME NOW.

WHY AREN'T YOU DRESSED, SELENE? YOU KNOW I WAS PLANNING TO HAVE YOU AT MY SIDE THIS EVENING.

DO YOU SEE THIS *HUMAN?*

WHAT OF HIM?

I THINK THE LYCANS WERE AFTER HIM.

OTHER THAN FOOD, WHY WOULD LYCANS STALK A HUMAN?

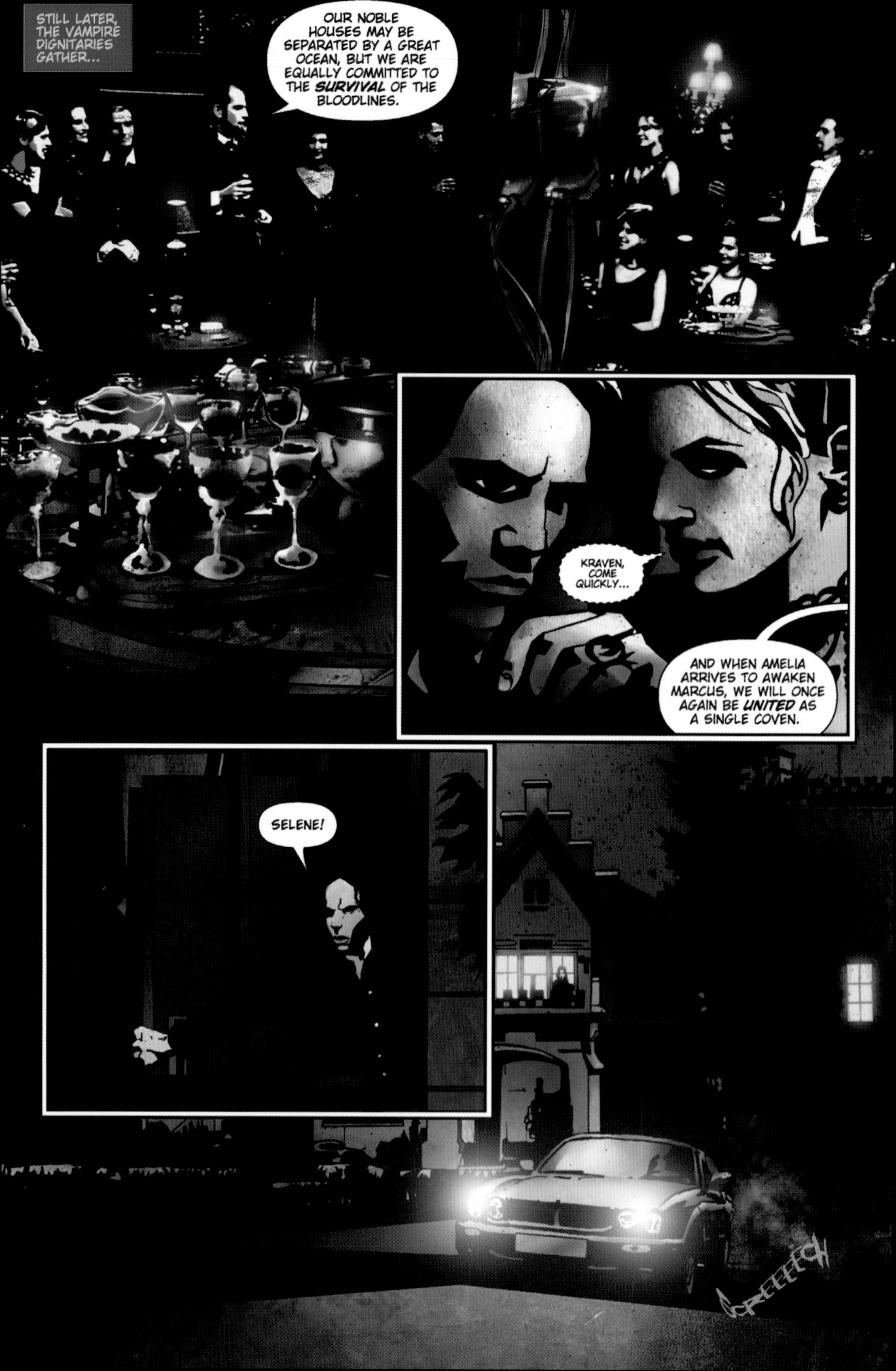
STILL LATER, THE VAMPIRE DIGNITARIES GATHER...
OUR NOBLE HOUSES MAY BE SEPARATED BY A GREAT OCEAN, BUT WE ARE EQUALLY COMMITTED TO THE SURVIVAL OF THE BLOODLINES.
KRAVEN, COME QUICKLY...
AND WHEN AMELIA ARRIVES TO AWAKEN MARCUS, WE WILL ONCE AGAIN BE UNITED AS A SINGLE COVEN.
SELENE!
SCREEEECH

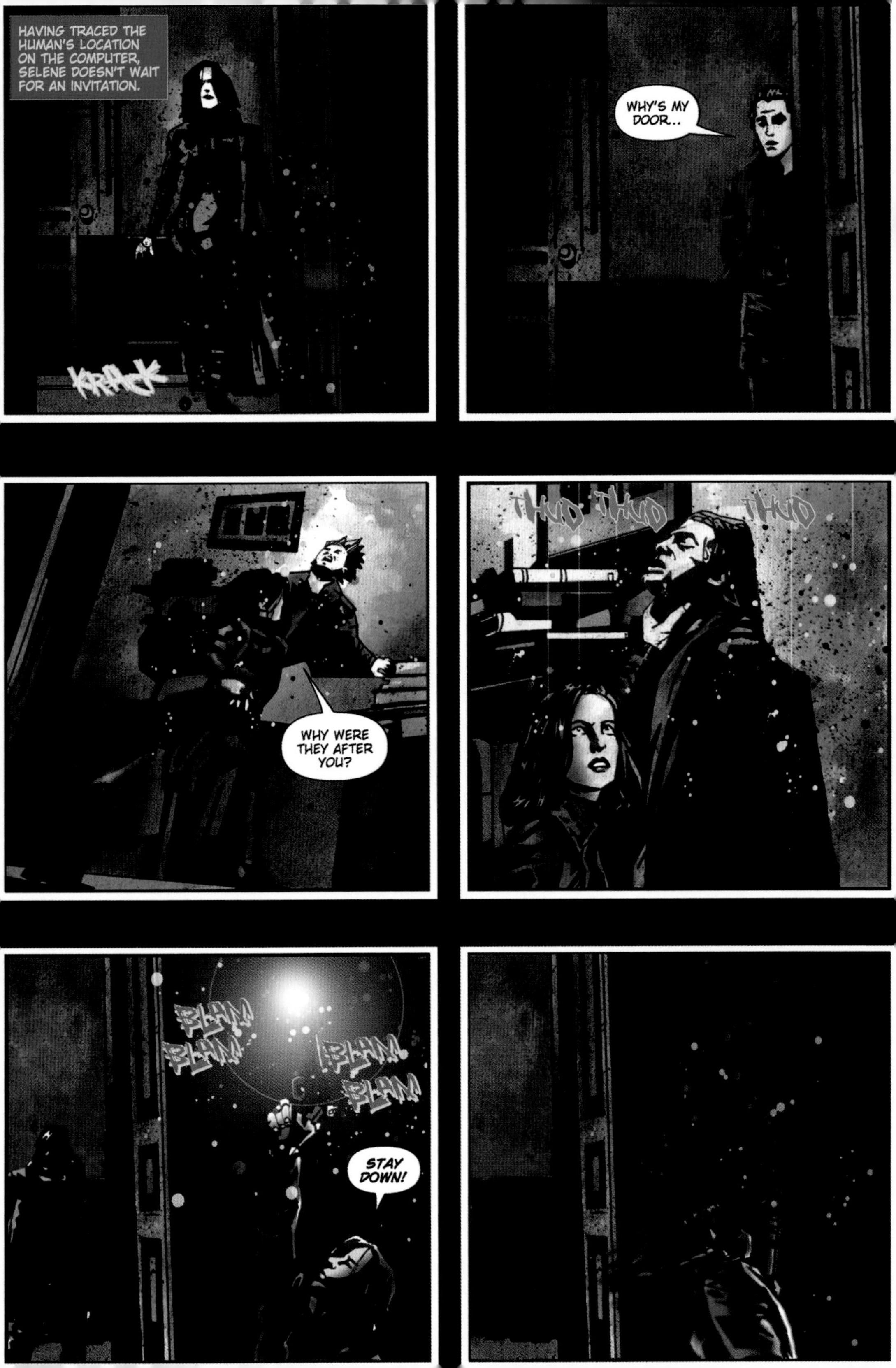
HAVING TRACED THE HUMAN'S LOCATION ON THE COMPUTER, SELENE DOESN'T WAIT FOR AN INVITATION.
KRAACK
WHY'S MY DOOR...
WHY WERE THEY AFTER YOU?
THUD THUD THUD
BLAM BLAM
BLAM BLAM
STAY DOWN!

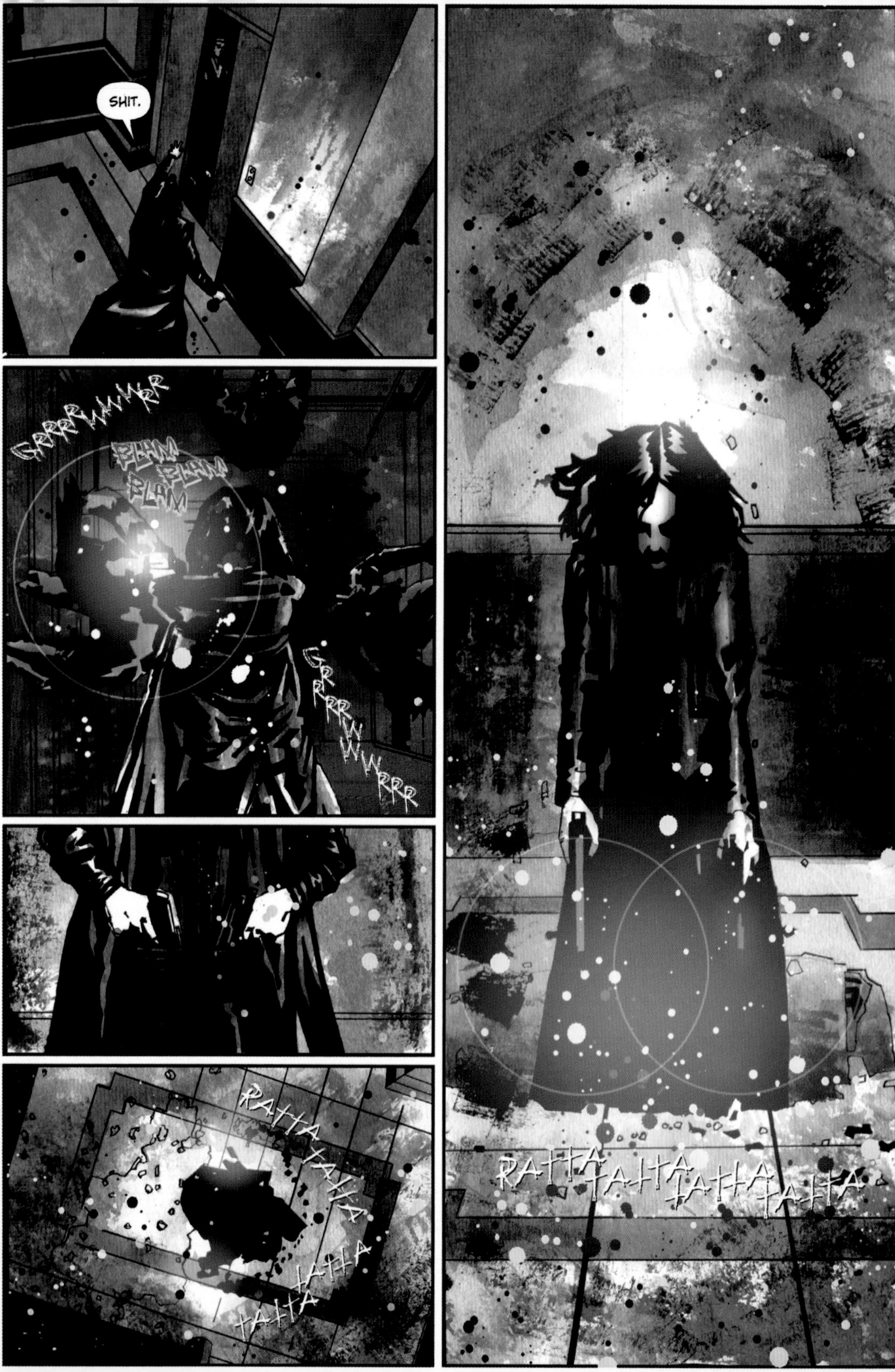
SHIT.
GRRRRWWWRR
BLAM BLAM BLAM
GRRRRWWWRRR
RATTATATTA
TATTA
TATTA
RATTA TATTA TATTA TATTA

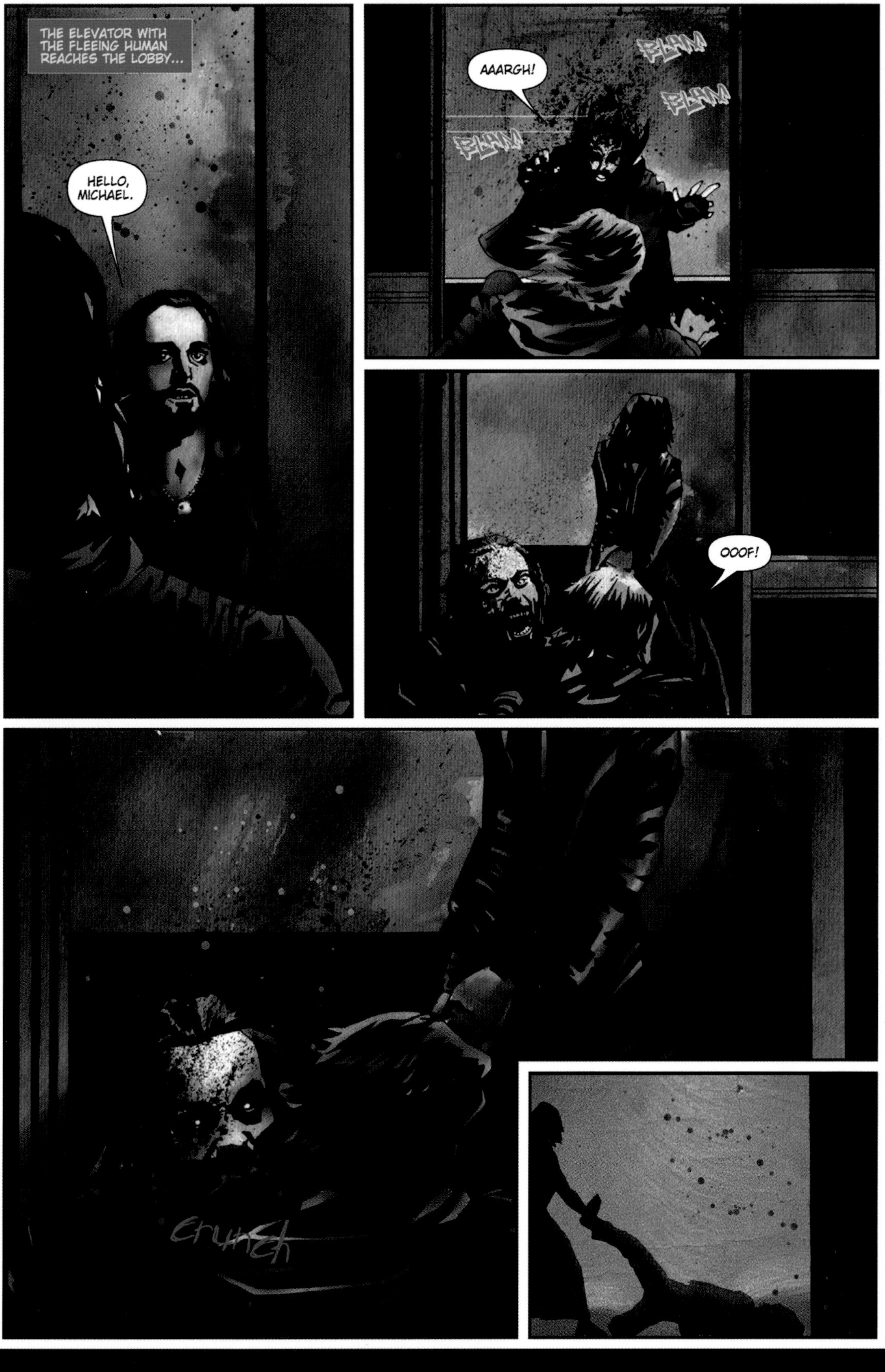
THE ELEVATOR WITH THE FLEEING HUMAN REACHES THE LOBBY...
HELLO, MICHAEL.
AAARGH!
BLAM
BLAM
BLAM
OOOF!
crunch

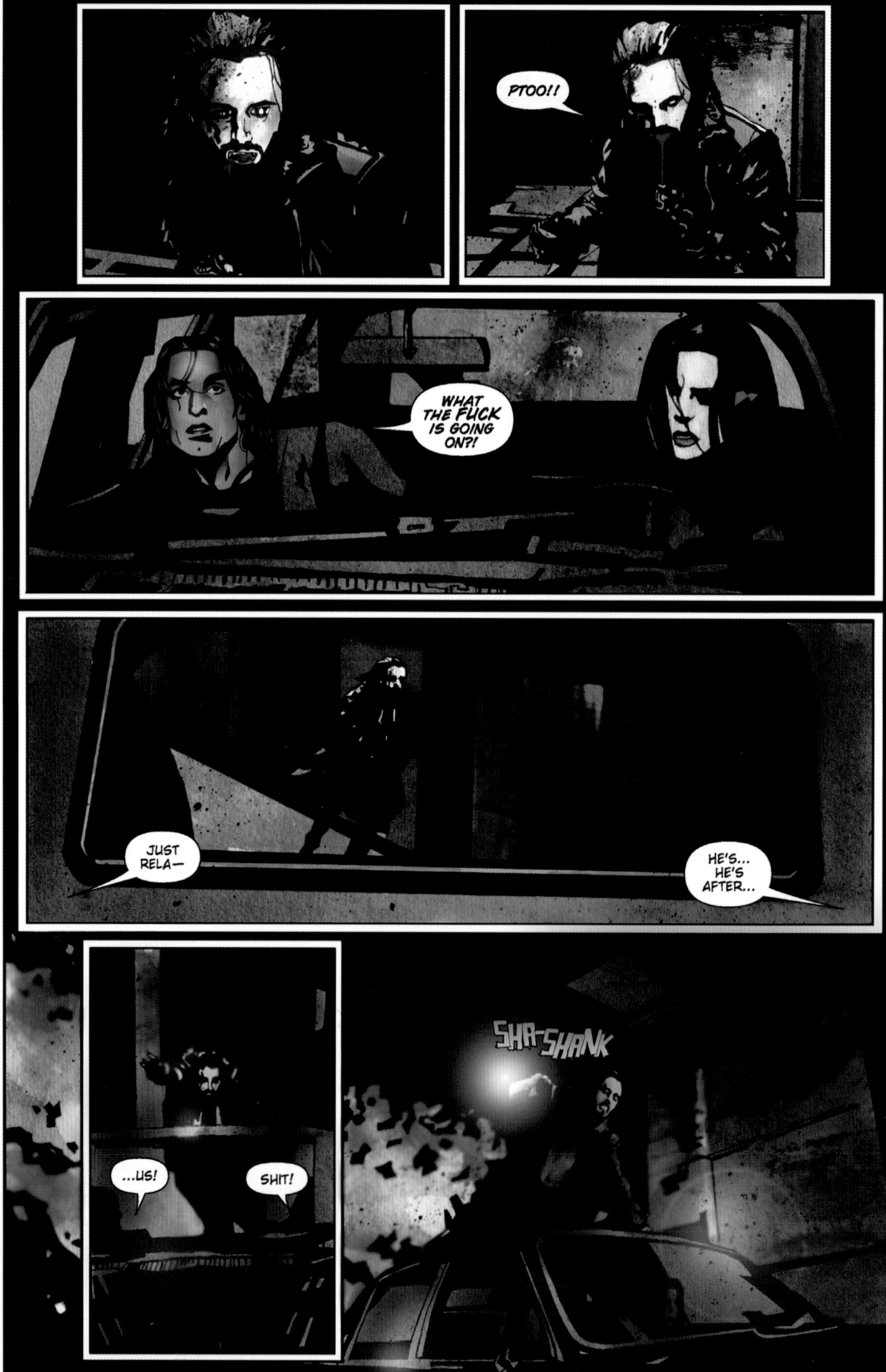
PTOO!!
WHAT THE FUCK IS GOING ON?!
JUST RELA—
HE'S... HE'S AFTER...
...US!
SHIT!
SHA-SHANK

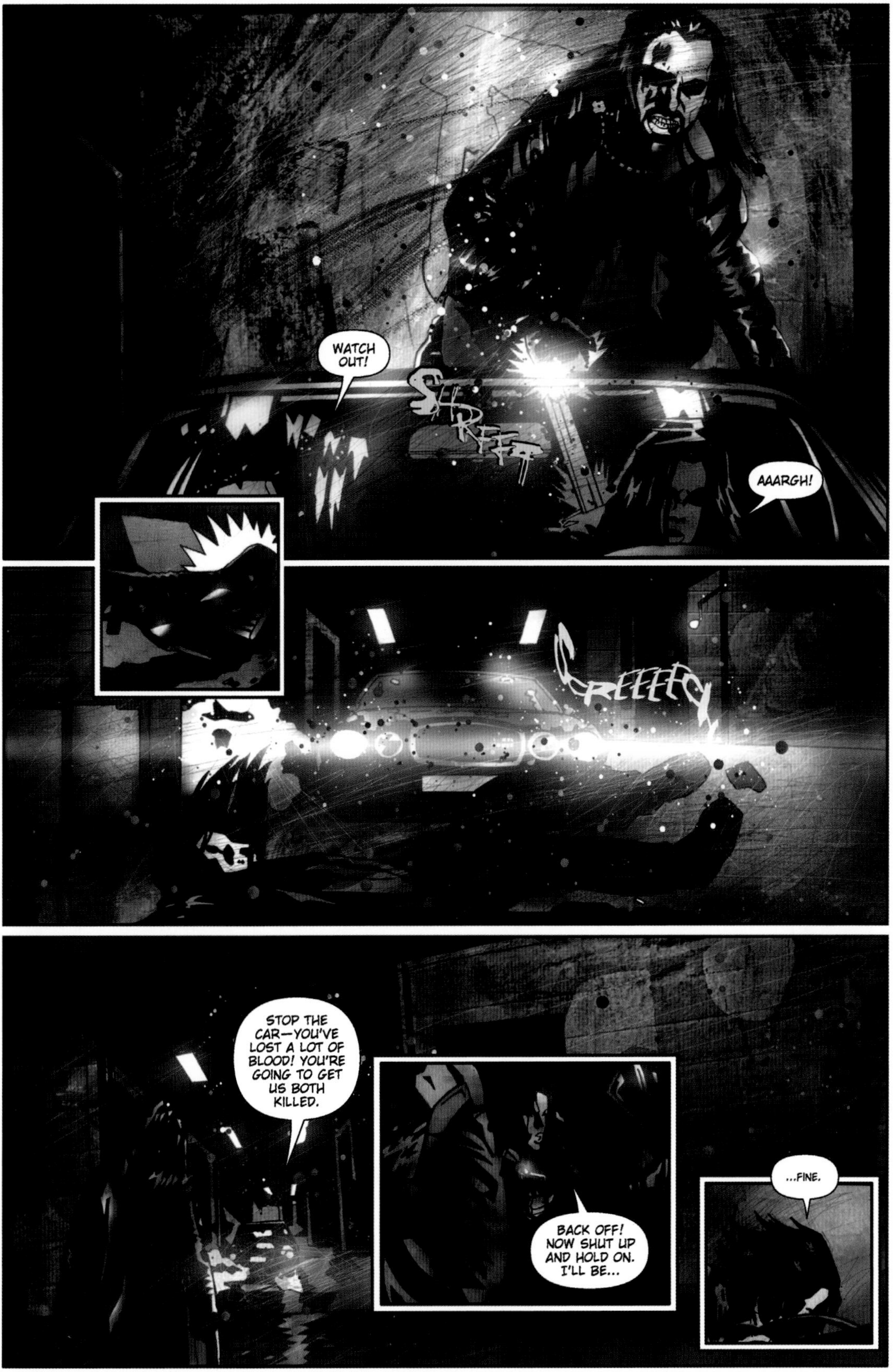

WATCH OUT!
AAARGH!
STOP THE CAR—YOU'VE LOST A LOT OF BLOOD! YOU'RE GOING TO GET US BOTH KILLED.
BACK OFF! NOW SHUT UP AND HOLD ON. I'LL BE...
...FINE.

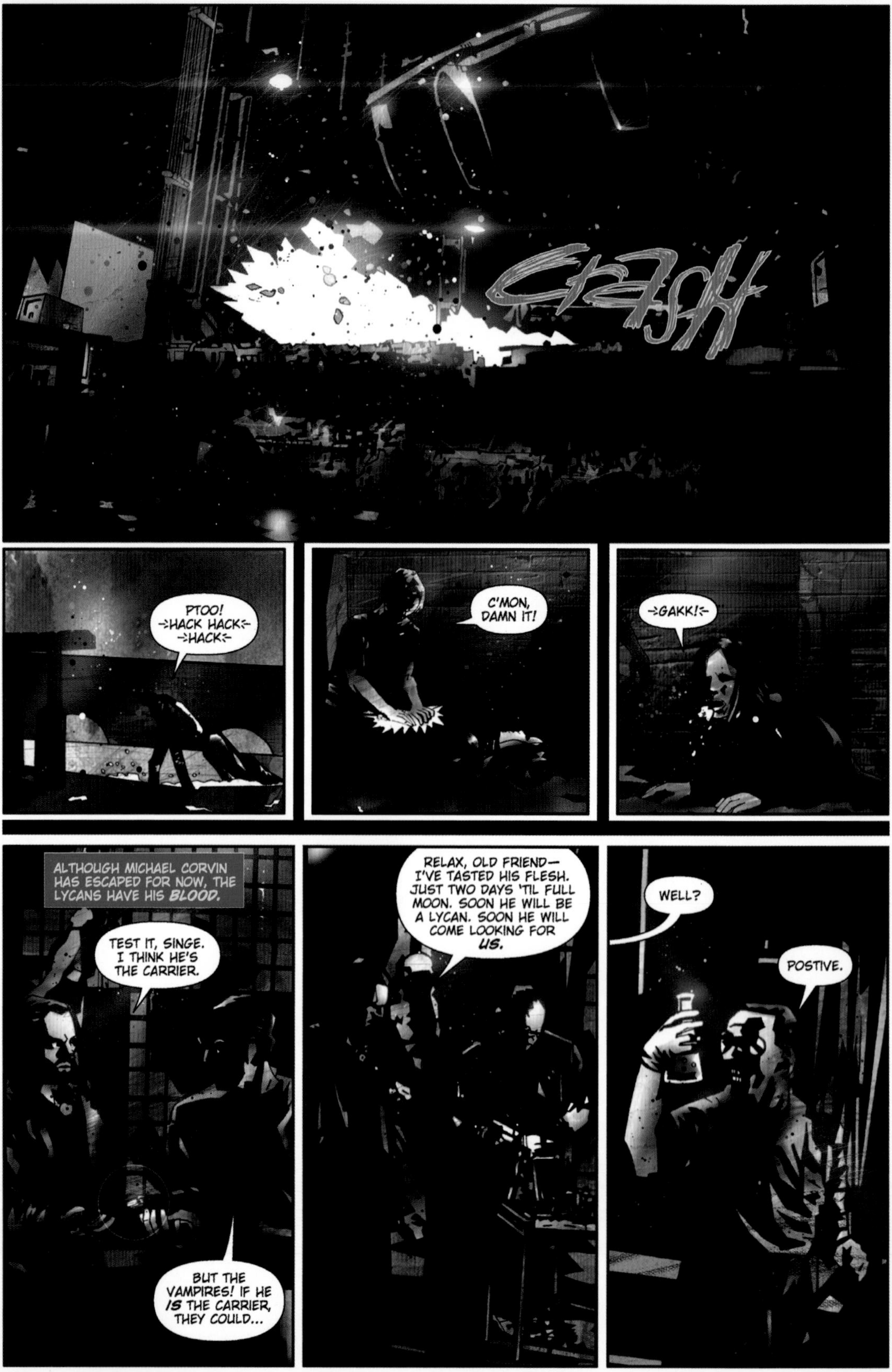
CRASH
PTOO! ⇾HACK HACK⇽ ⇾HACK⇽
C'MON, DAMN IT!
⇾GAKK!⇽
ALTHOUGH MICHAEL CORVIN HAS ESCAPED FOR NOW, THE LYCANS HAVE HIS *BLOOD.*
TEST IT, SINGE. I THINK HE'S THE CARRIER.
BUT THE VAMPIRES! IF HE *IS* THE CARRIER, THEY COULD...
RELAX, OLD FRIEND— I'VE TASTED HIS FLESH. JUST TWO DAYS 'TIL FULL MOON. SOON HE WILL BE A LYCAN. SOON HE WILL COME LOOKING FOR *US.*
WELL?
POSTIVE.

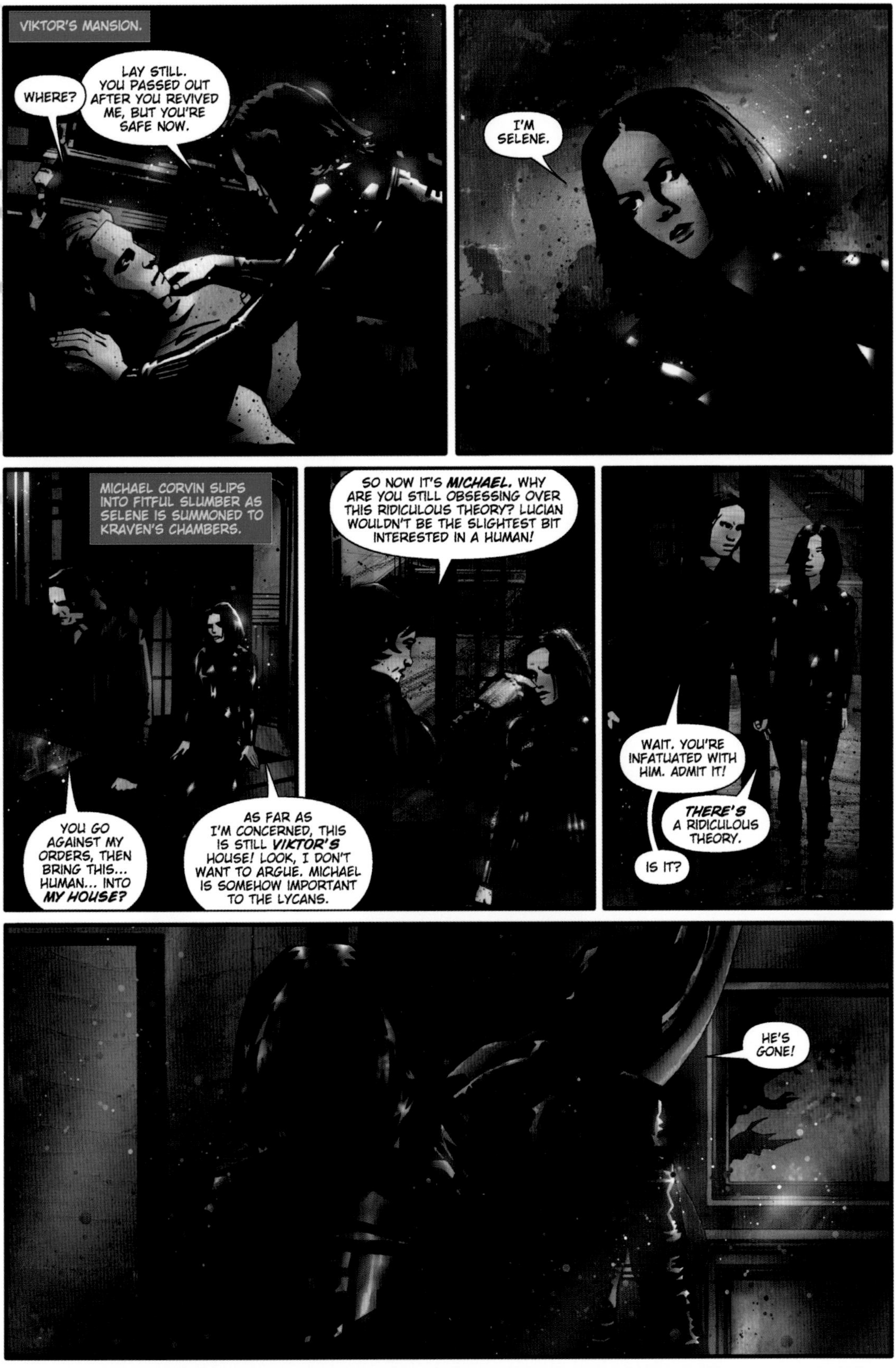
VIKTOR'S MANSION.
WHERE?
LAY STILL. YOU PASSED OUT AFTER YOU REVIVED ME, BUT YOU'RE SAFE NOW.
I'M SELENE.
MICHAEL CORVIN SLIPS INTO FITFUL SLUMBER AS SELENE IS SUMMONED TO KRAVEN'S CHAMBERS.
YOU GO AGAINST MY ORDERS, THEN BRING THIS... HUMAN... INTO MY HOUSE?
AS FAR AS I'M CONCERNED, THIS IS STILL VIKTOR'S HOUSE! LOOK, I DON'T WANT TO ARGUE. MICHAEL IS SOMEHOW IMPORTANT TO THE LYCANS.
SO NOW IT'S MICHAEL. WHY ARE YOU STILL OBSESSING OVER THIS RIDICULOUS THEORY? LUCIAN WOULDN'T BE THE SLIGHTEST BIT INTERESTED IN A HUMAN!
WAIT. YOU'RE INFATUATED WITH HIM. ADMIT IT!
THERE'S A RIDICULOUS THEORY.
IS IT?
HE'S GONE!

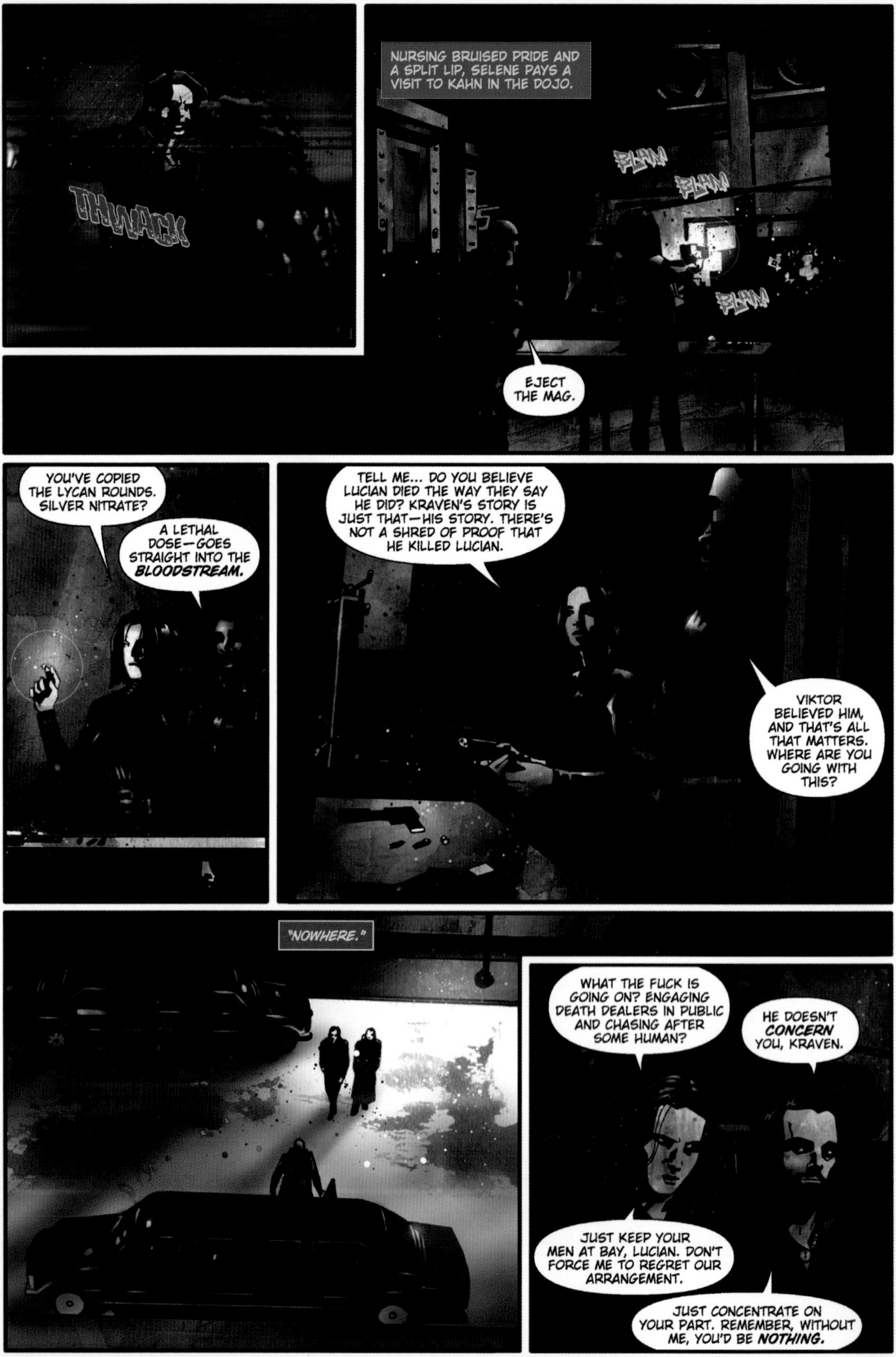
THWACK
NURSING BRUISED PRIDE AND A SPLIT LIP, SELENE PAYS A VISIT TO KAHN IN THE DOJO.
BLAM
BLAM
BLAM
EJECT THE MAG.
YOU'VE COPIED THE LYCAN ROUNDS. SILVER NITRATE?
A LETHAL DOSE—GOES STRAIGHT INTO THE *BLOODSTREAM.*
TELL ME... DO YOU BELIEVE LUCIAN DIED THE WAY THEY SAY HE DID? KRAVEN'S STORY IS JUST THAT—HIS STORY. THERE'S NOT A SHRED OF PROOF THAT HE KILLED LUCIAN.
VIKTOR BELIEVED HIM, AND THAT'S ALL THAT MATTERS. WHERE ARE YOU GOING WITH THIS?
"NOWHERE."
WHAT THE FUCK IS GOING ON? ENGAGING DEATH DEALERS IN PUBLIC AND CHASING AFTER SOME HUMAN?
HE DOESN'T *CONCERN* YOU, KRAVEN.
JUST KEEP YOUR MEN AT BAY, LUCIAN. DON'T FORCE ME TO REGRET OUR ARRANGEMENT.
JUST CONCENTRATE ON YOUR PART. REMEMBER, WITHOUT ME, YOU'D BE *NOTHING.*

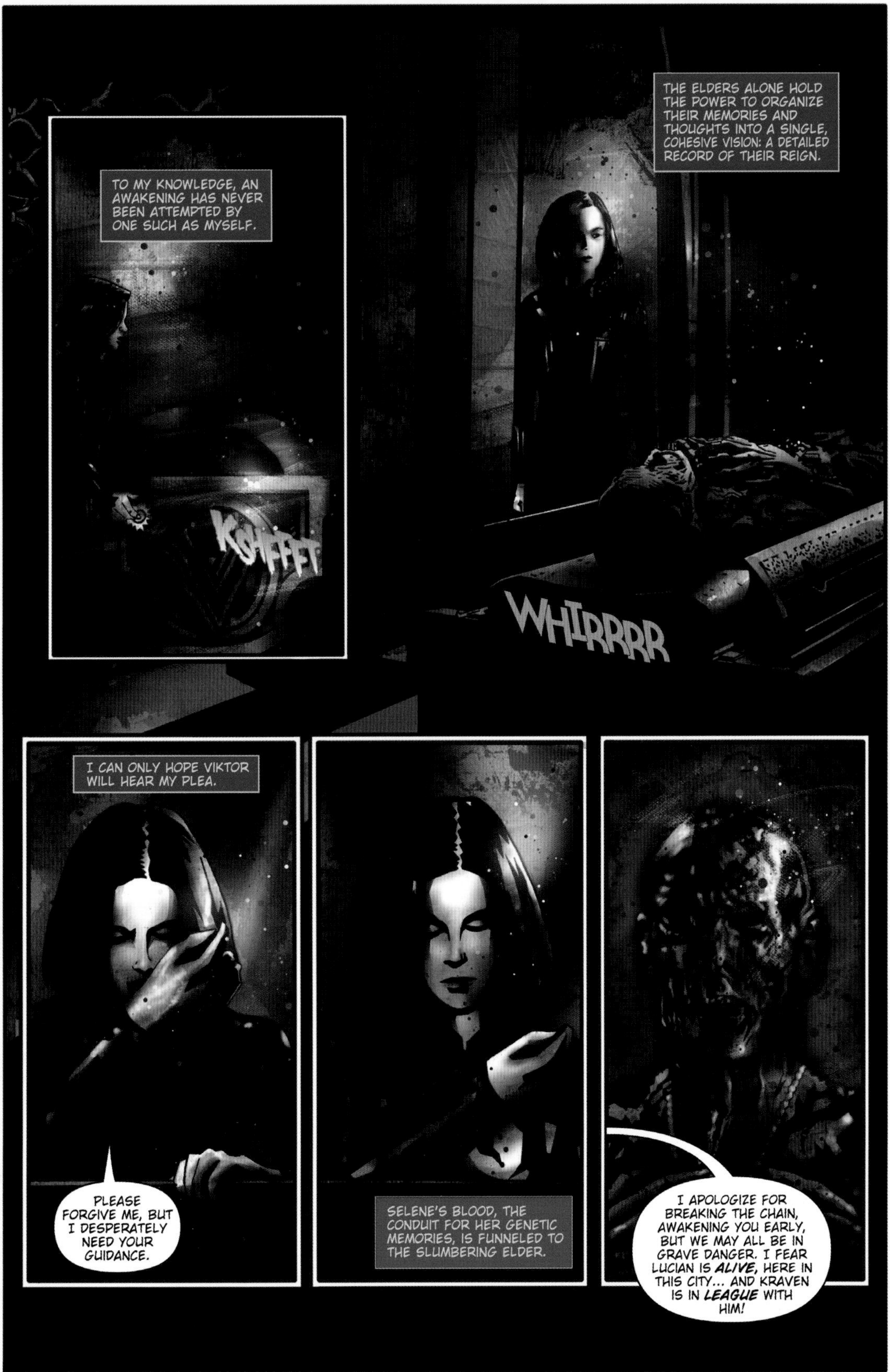
TO MY KNOWLEDGE, AN AWAKENING HAS NEVER BEEN ATTEMPTED BY ONE SUCH AS MYSELF.
KSHFFFT
THE ELDERS ALONE HOLD THE POWER TO ORGANIZE THEIR MEMORIES AND THOUGHTS INTO A SINGLE, COHESIVE VISION: A DETAILED RECORD OF THEIR REIGN.
WHIRRRR
I CAN ONLY HOPE VIKTOR WILL HEAR MY PLEA.
PLEASE FORGIVE ME, BUT I DESPERATELY NEED YOUR GUIDANCE.
SELENE'S BLOOD, THE CONDUIT FOR HER GENETIC MEMORIES, IS FUNNELED TO THE SLUMBERING ELDER.
I APOLOGIZE FOR BREAKING THE CHAIN, AWAKENING YOU EARLY, BUT WE MAY ALL BE IN GRAVE DANGER. I FEAR LUCIAN IS *ALIVE,* HERE IN THIS CITY... AND KRAVEN IS IN *LEAGUE* WITH HIM!

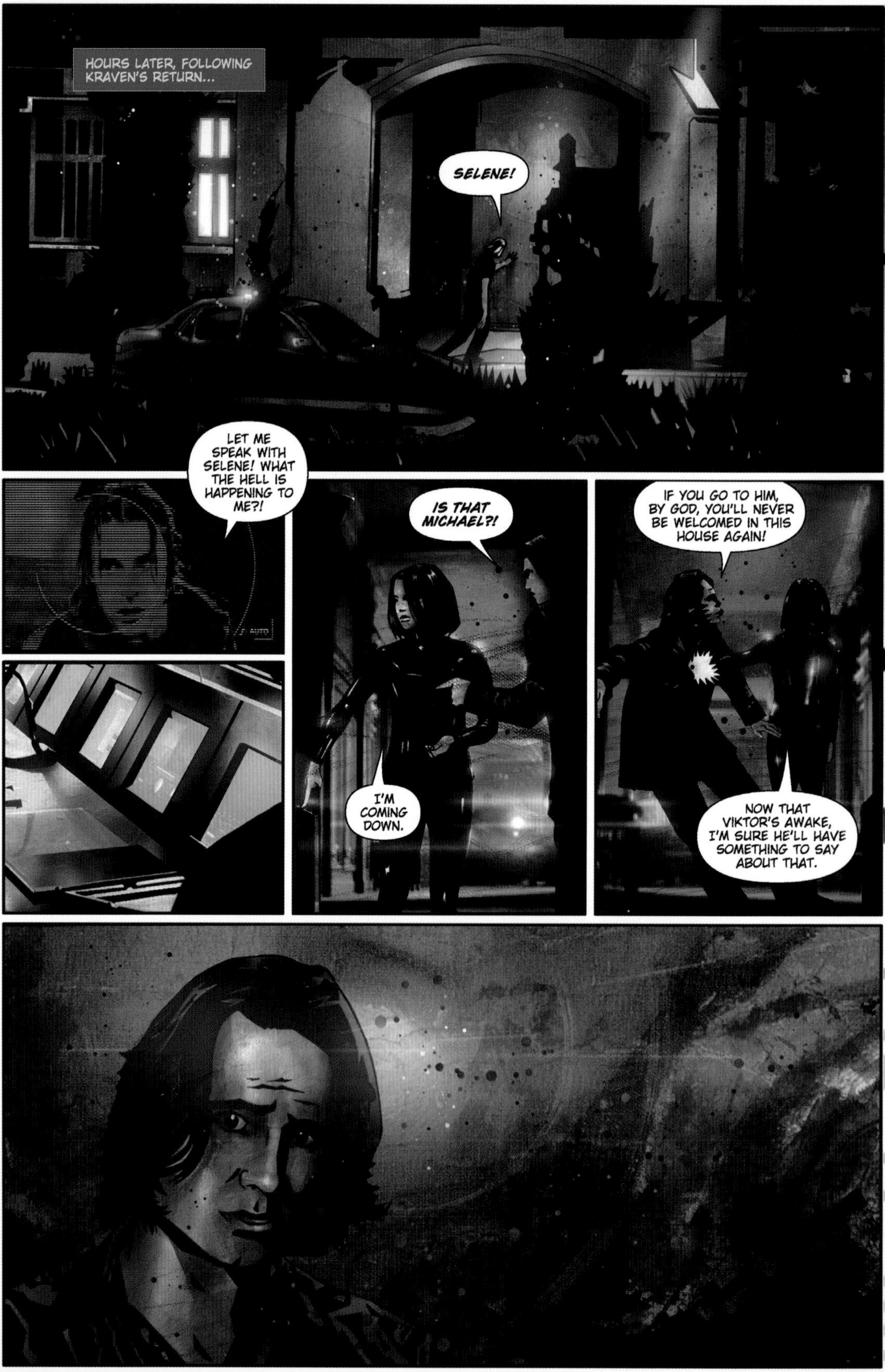
HOURS LATER, FOLLOWING KRAVEN'S RETURN...
SELENE!
LET ME SPEAK WITH SELENE! WHAT THE HELL IS HAPPENING TO ME?!
IS THAT MICHAEL?!
I'M COMING DOWN.
IF YOU GO TO HIM, BY GOD, YOU'LL NEVER BE WELCOMED IN THIS HOUSE AGAIN!
NOW THAT VIKTOR'S AWAKE, I'M SURE HE'LL HAVE SOMETHING TO SAY ABOUT THAT.

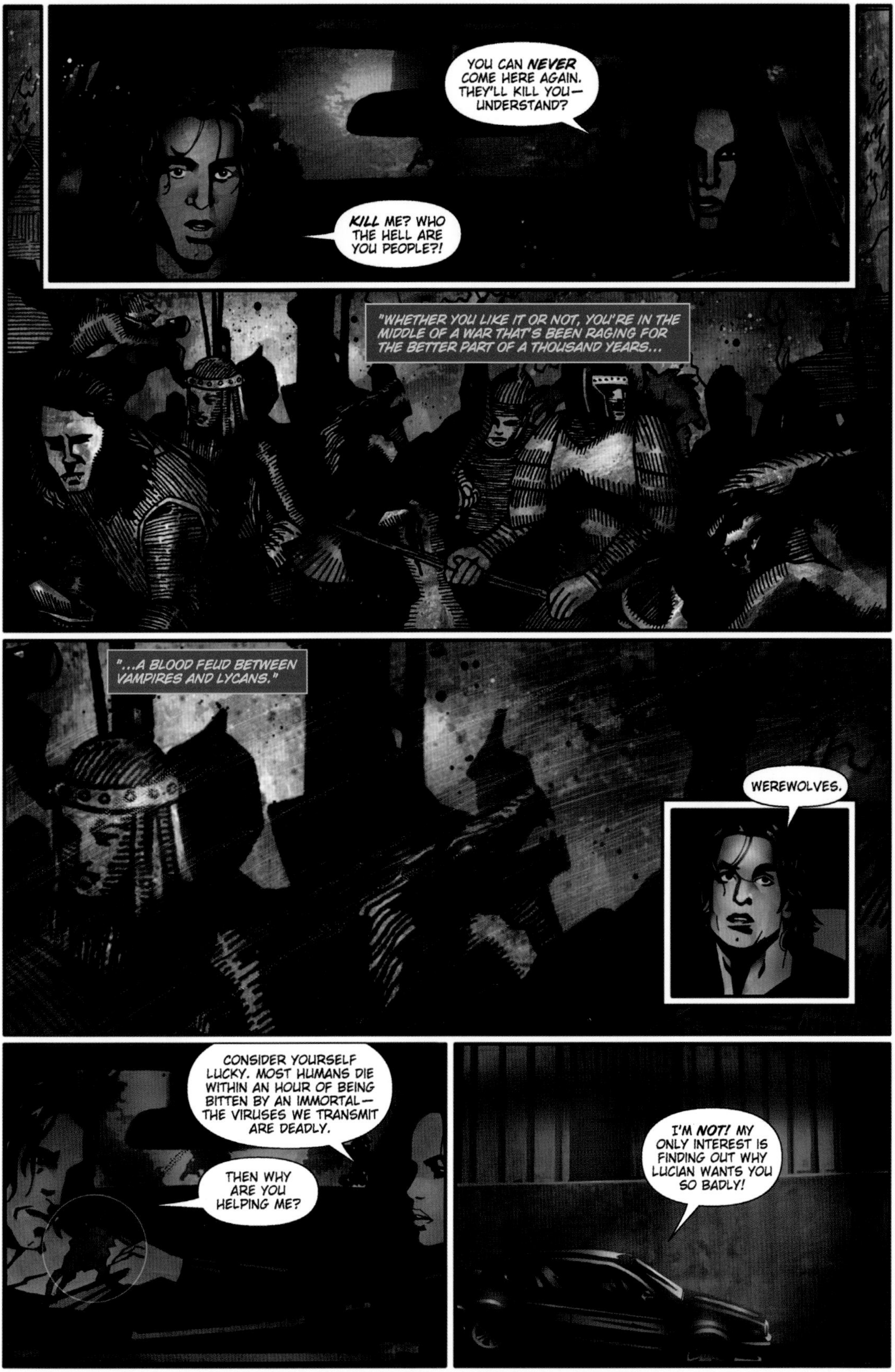
YOU CAN NEVER COME HERE AGAIN. THEY'LL KILL YOU— UNDERSTAND?
KILL ME? WHO THE HELL ARE YOU PEOPLE?!
"WHETHER YOU LIKE IT OR NOT, YOU'RE IN THE MIDDLE OF A WAR THAT'S BEEN RAGING FOR THE BETTER PART OF A THOUSAND YEARS...
"...A BLOOD FEUD BETWEEN VAMPIRES AND LYCANS."
WEREWOLVES.
CONSIDER YOURSELF LUCKY. MOST HUMANS DIE WITHIN AN HOUR OF BEING BITTEN BY AN IMMORTAL— THE VIRUSES WE TRANSMIT ARE DEADLY.
THEN WHY ARE YOU HELPING ME?
I'M NOT! MY ONLY INTEREST IS FINDING OUT WHY LUCIAN WANTS YOU SO BADLY!

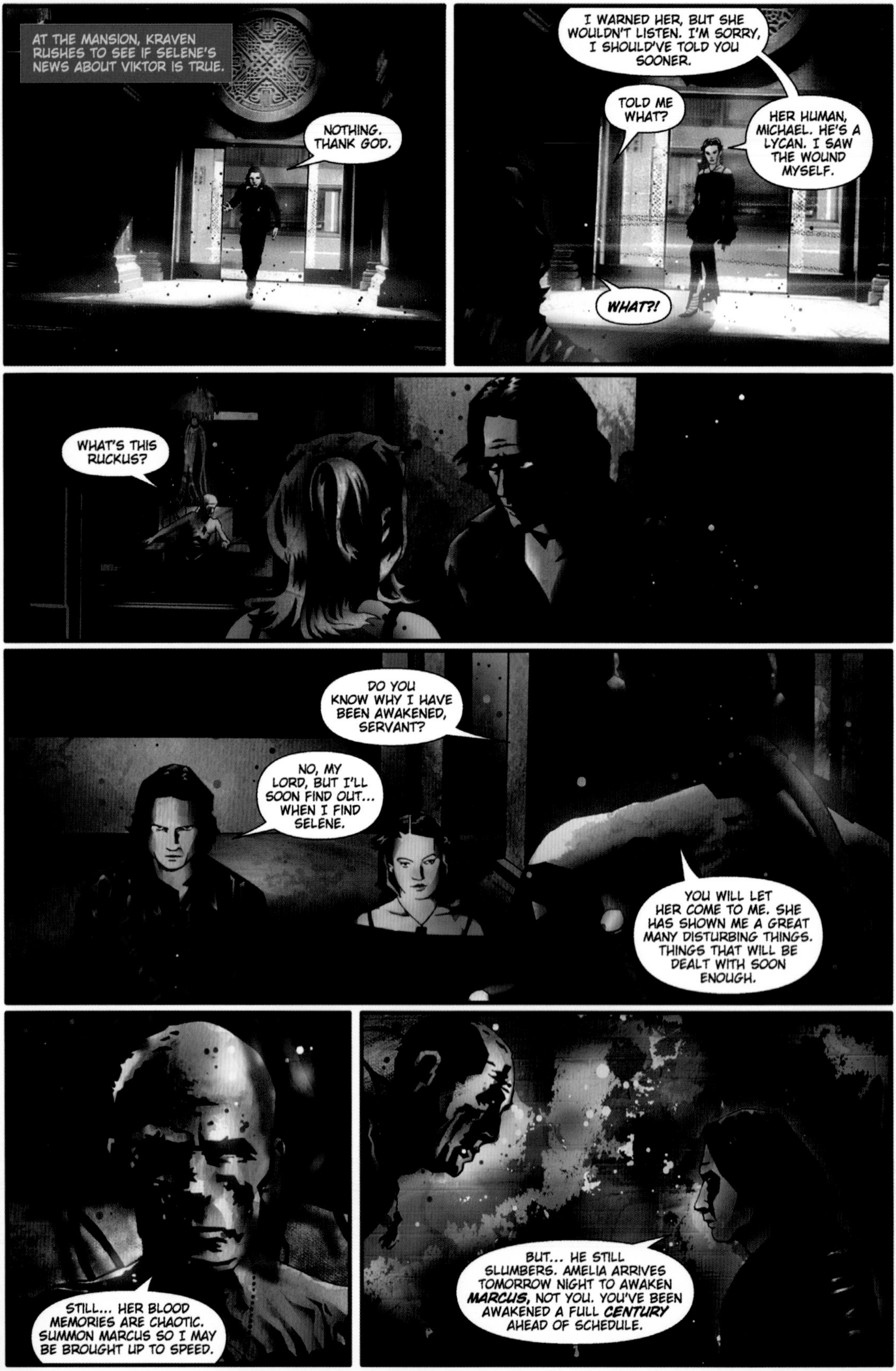
AT THE MANSION, KRAVEN RUSHES TO SEE IF SELENE'S NEWS ABOUT VIKTOR IS TRUE.
NOTHING. THANK GOD.
I WARNED HER, BUT SHE WOULDN'T LISTEN. I'M SORRY, I SHOULD'VE TOLD YOU SOONER.
TOLD ME WHAT?
HER HUMAN, MICHAEL. HE'S A LYCAN. I SAW THE WOUND MYSELF.
WHAT?!
WHAT'S THIS RUCKUS?
DO YOU KNOW WHY I HAVE BEEN AWAKENED, SERVANT?
NO, MY LORD, BUT I'LL SOON FIND OUT... WHEN I FIND SELENE.
YOU WILL LET HER COME TO ME. SHE HAS SHOWN ME A GREAT MANY DISTURBING THINGS. THINGS THAT WILL BE DEALT WITH SOON ENOUGH.
STILL... HER BLOOD MEMORIES ARE CHAOTIC. SUMMON MARCUS SO I MAY BE BROUGHT UP TO SPEED.
BUT... HE STILL SLUMBERS. AMELIA ARRIVES TOMORROW NIGHT TO AWAKEN MARCUS, NOT YOU. YOU'VE BEEN AWAKENED A FULL CENTURY AHEAD OF SCHEDULE.

ACROSS TOWN...

THIS IS ONE OF THE PLACES WE USE FOR INTERROGATIONS. YOU'LL BE SAFE HERE.

THE LYCANS... WHY DO YOU HATE THEM SO MUCH?

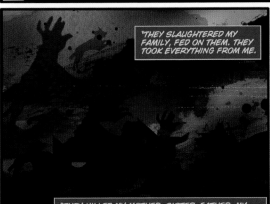

"THEY SLAUGHTERED MY FAMILY, FED ON THEM. THEY TOOK EVERYTHING FROM ME.

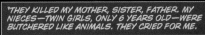

"THEY KILLED MY MOTHER, SISTER, FATHER. MY NIECES—TWIN GIRLS, ONLY 6 YEARS OLD—WERE BUTCHERED LIKE ANIMALS. THEY CRIED FOR ME.

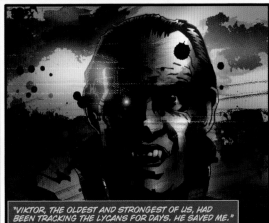

"VIKTOR, THE OLDEST AND STRONGEST OF US, HAD BEEN TRACKING THE LYCANS FOR DAYS. HE SAVED ME."

THAT NIGHT, HE MADE ME A VAMPIRE. HIS BLOOD GAVE ME THE STRENGTH TO AVENGE MY FAMILY.

ALMOST 5 AM— I SHOULD BE HEADING BACK. VIKTOR WILL KNOW WHAT TO DO WITH YOU. I'LL BE BACK TOMORROW.

NO, I WANT TO GO WITH YOU!

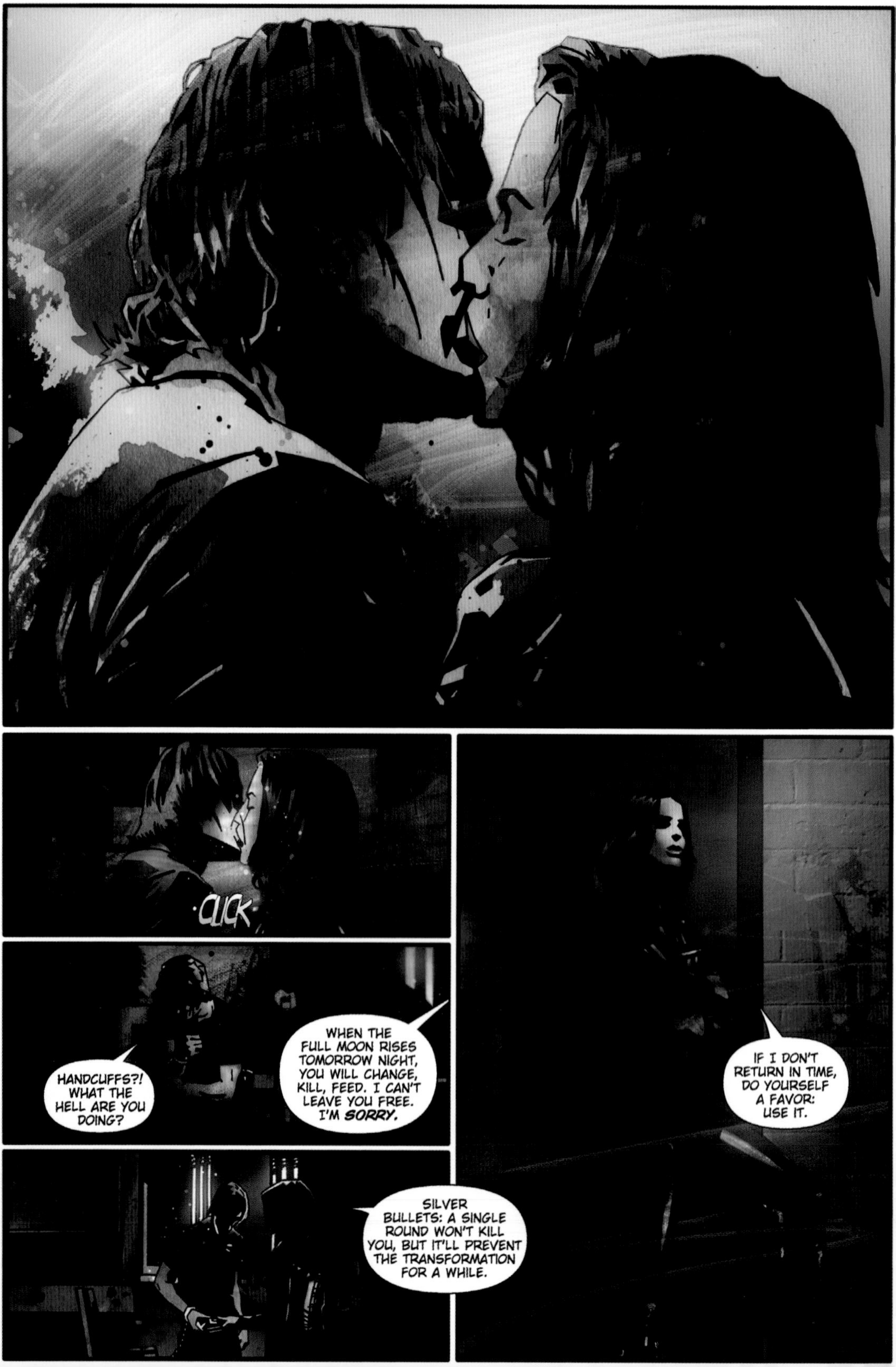
CLICK
HANDCUFFS?! WHAT THE HELL ARE YOU DOING?
WHEN THE FULL MOON RISES TOMORROW NIGHT, YOU WILL CHANGE, KILL, FEED. I CAN'T LEAVE YOU FREE. I'M *SORRY.*
SILVER BULLETS: A SINGLE ROUND WON'T KILL YOU, BUT IT'LL PREVENT THE TRANSFORMATION FOR A WHILE.
IF I DON'T RETURN IN TIME, DO YOURSELF A FAVOR: USE IT.

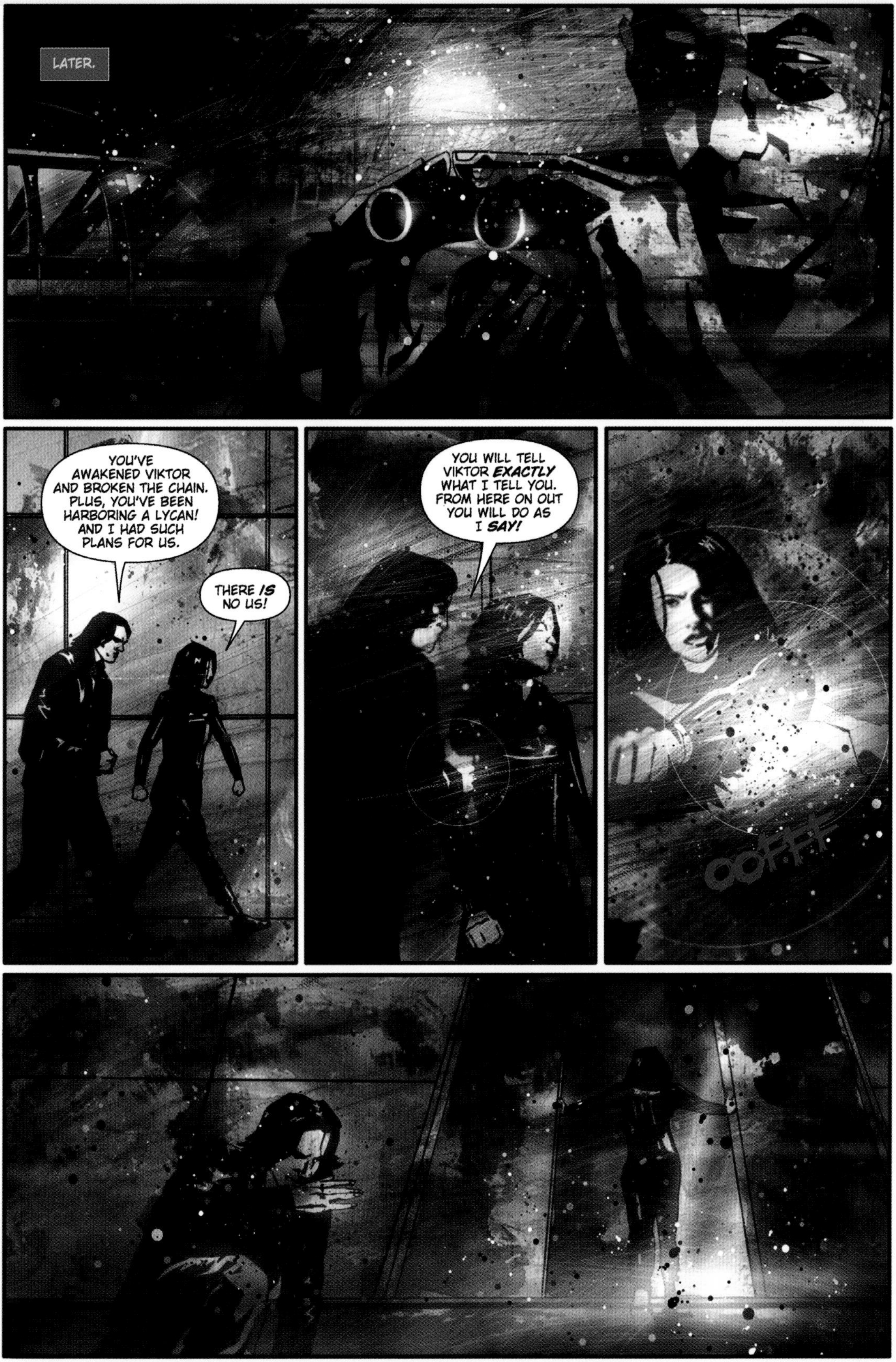
LATER.
YOU'VE AWAKENED VIKTOR AND BROKEN THE CHAIN. PLUS, YOU'VE BEEN HARBORING A LYCAN! AND I HAD SUCH PLANS FOR US.
THERE *IS* NO US!
YOU WILL TELL VIKTOR ***EXACTLY*** WHAT I TELL YOU. FROM HERE ON OUT YOU WILL DO AS I ***SAY!***
OOFFF

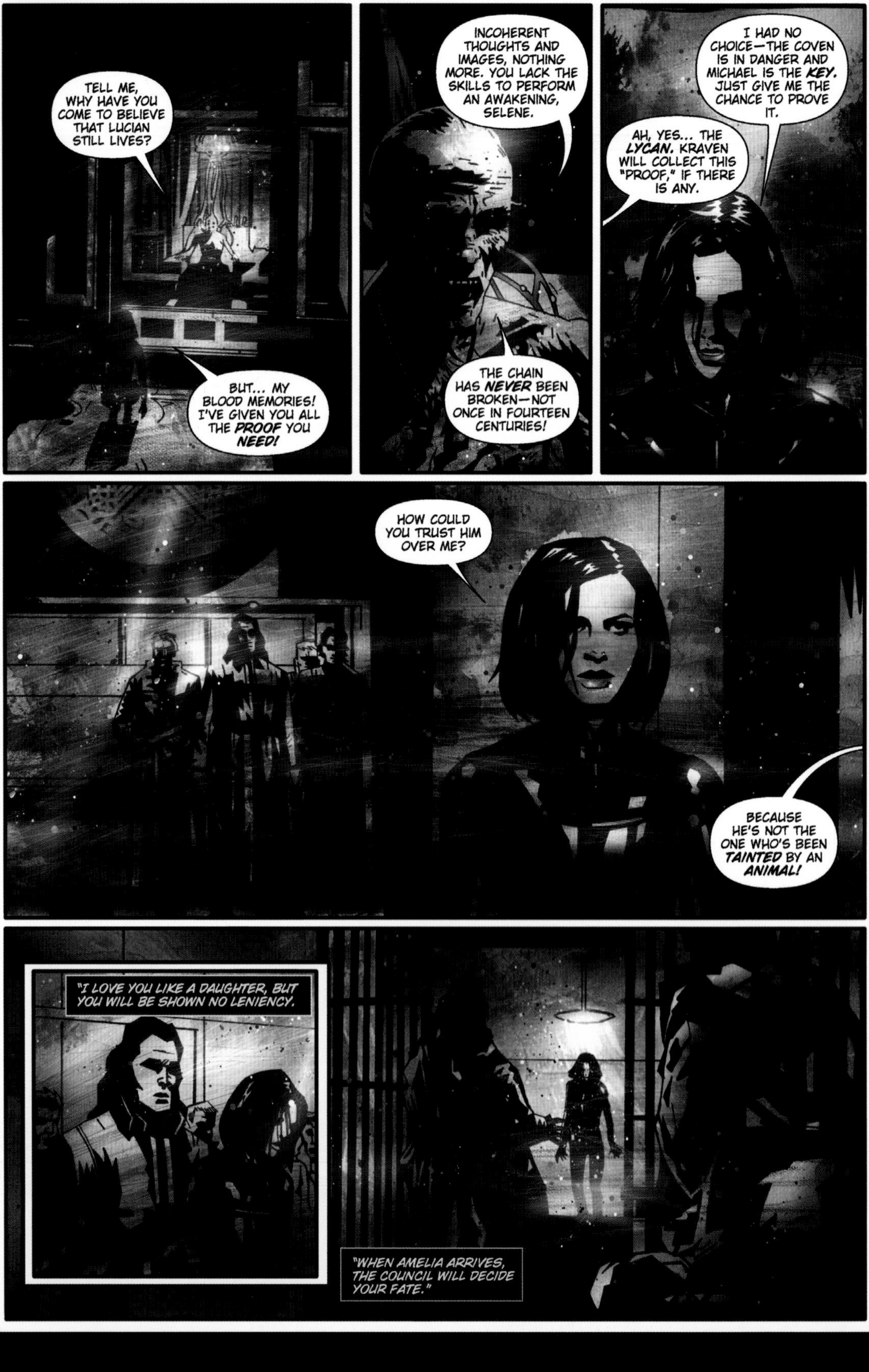
TELL ME, WHY HAVE YOU COME TO BELIEVE THAT LUCIAN STILL LIVES?
BUT... MY BLOOD MEMORIES! I'VE GIVEN YOU ALL THE PROOF YOU NEED!
INCOHERENT THOUGHTS AND IMAGES, NOTHING MORE. YOU LACK THE SKILLS TO PERFORM AN AWAKENING, SELENE.
THE CHAIN HAS NEVER BEEN BROKEN—NOT ONCE IN FOURTEEN CENTURIES!
I HAD NO CHOICE—THE COVEN IS IN DANGER AND MICHAEL IS THE KEY. JUST GIVE ME THE CHANCE TO PROVE IT.
AH, YES... THE LYCAN. KRAVEN WILL COLLECT THIS "PROOF," IF THERE IS ANY.
HOW COULD YOU TRUST HIM OVER ME?
BECAUSE HE'S NOT THE ONE WHO'S BEEN TAINTED BY AN ANIMAL!
"I LOVE YOU LIKE A DAUGHTER, BUT YOU WILL BE SHOWN NO LENIENCY.
"WHEN AMELIA ARRIVES, THE COUNCIL WILL DECIDE YOUR FATE."

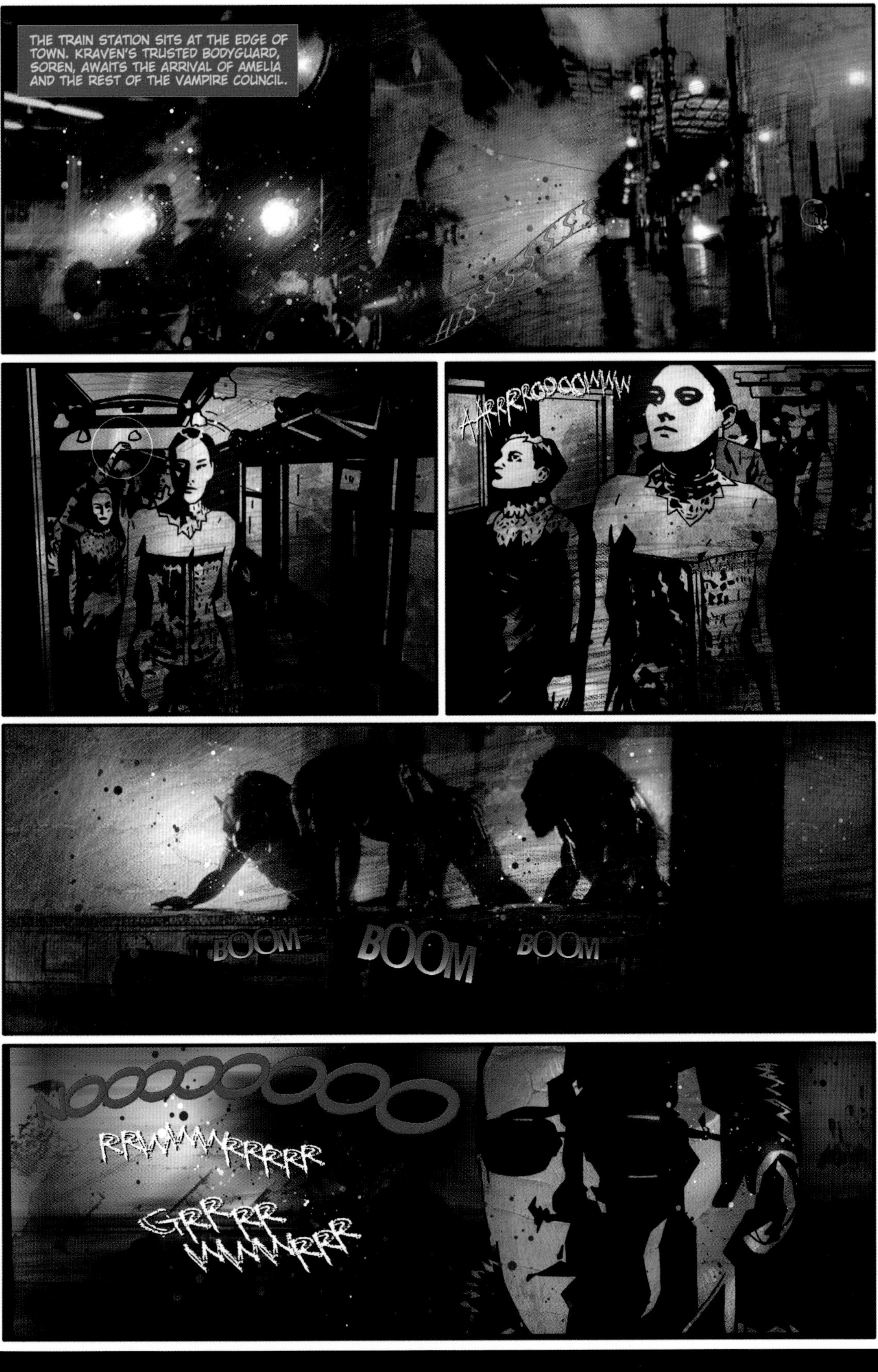
THE TRAIN STATION SITS AT THE EDGE OF TOWN. KRAVEN'S TRUSTED BODYGUARD, SOREN, AWAITS THE ARRIVAL OF AMELIA AND THE REST OF THE VAMPIRE COUNCIL.
HISSSSSSSS
AARRRROOOOWWW
BOOM
BOOM
BOOM
NOOOOOOOOO
RRWWWRRRRRR
GRRRR
WWWRRR

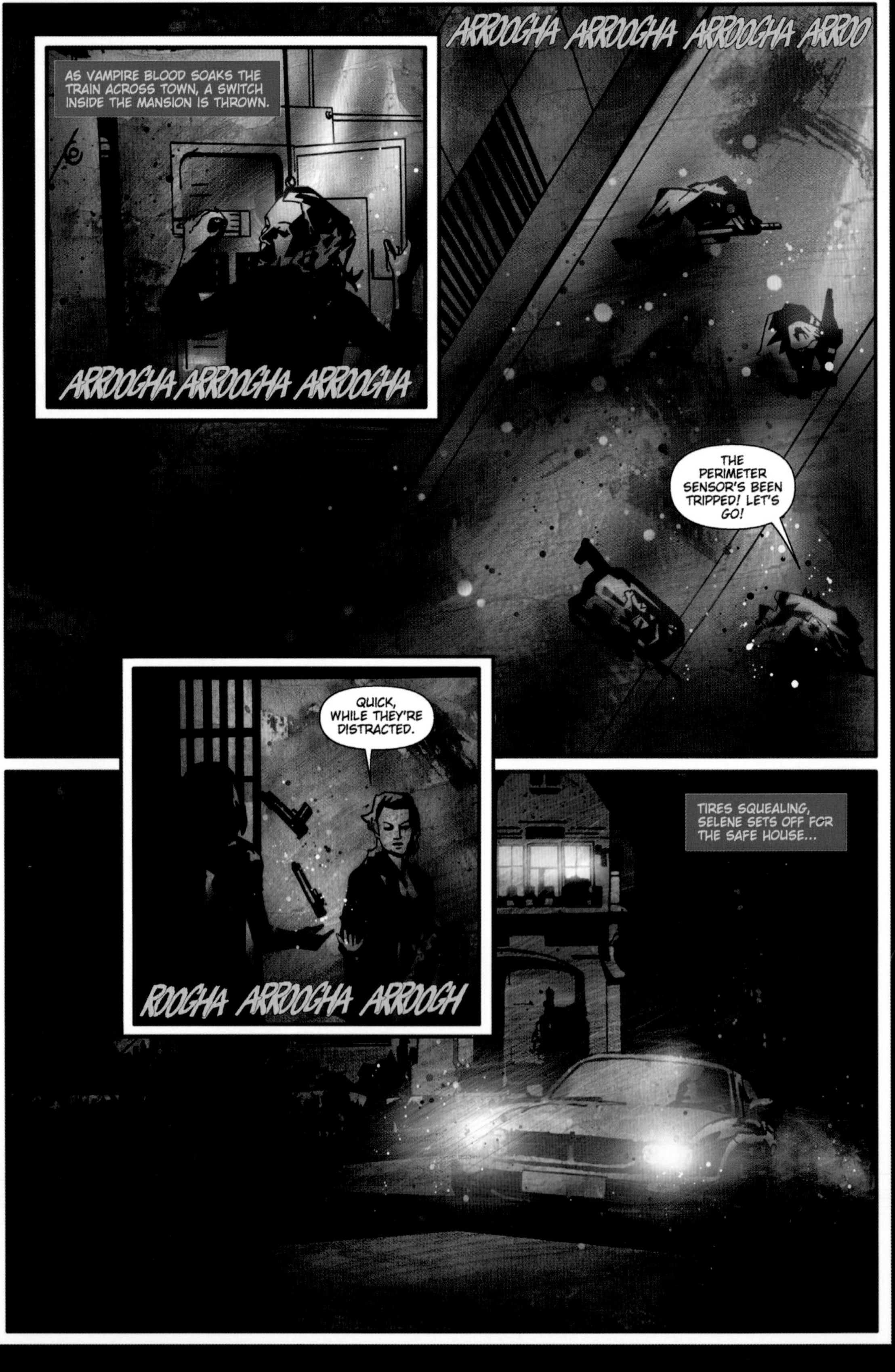

AS VAMPIRE BLOOD SOAKS THE TRAIN ACROSS TOWN, A SWITCH INSIDE THE MANSION IS THROWN.
ARROOGHA ARROOGHA ARROOGHA
ARROOGHA ARROOGHA ARROOGHA ARROO
THE PERIMETER SENSOR'S BEEN TRIPPED! LET'S GO!
QUICK, WHILE THEY'RE DISTRACTED.
ROOGHA ARROOGHA ARROOGH
TIRES SQUEALING, SELENE SETS OFF FOR THE SAFE HOUSE...

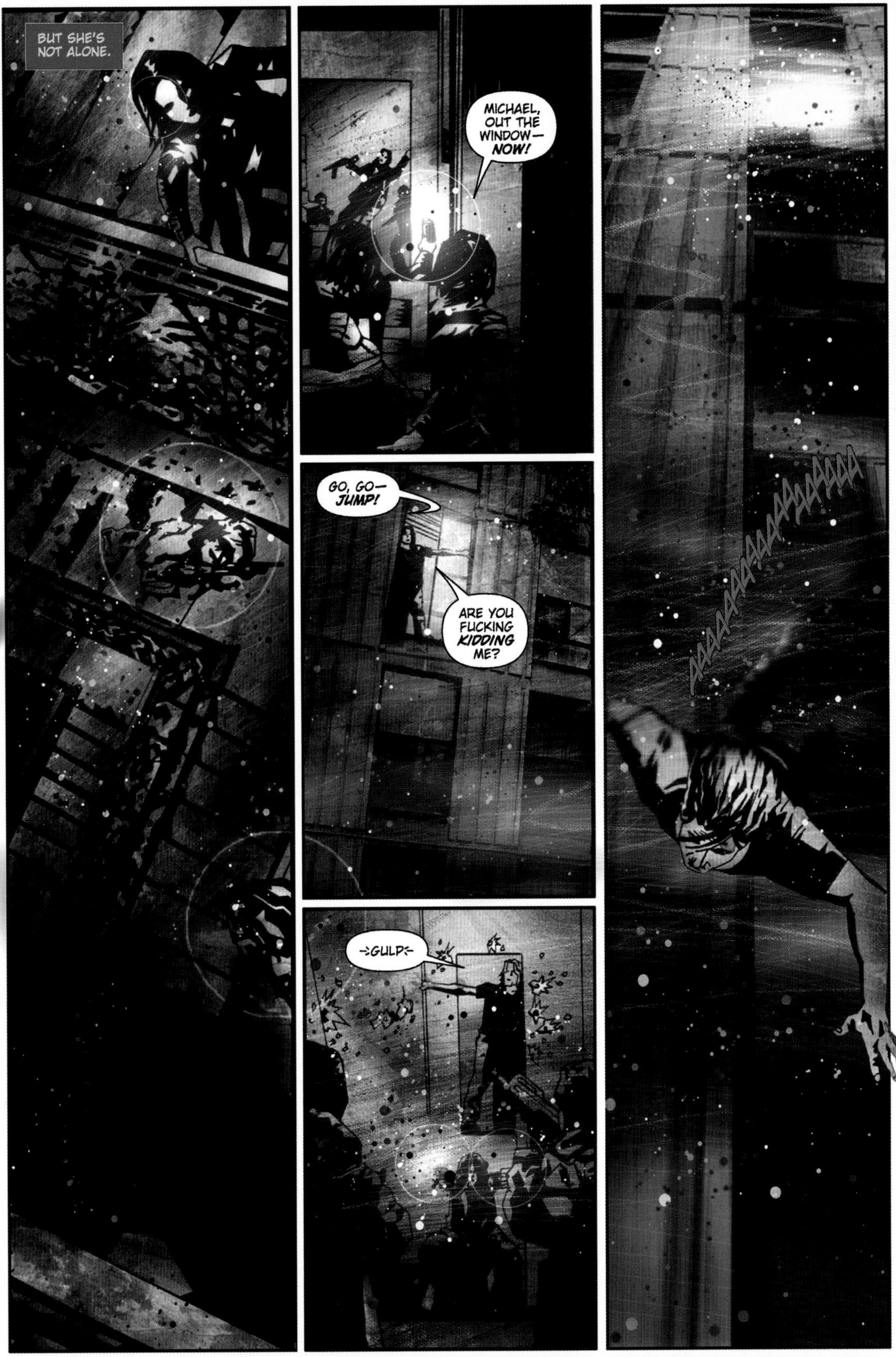
BUT SHE'S NOT ALONE.
MICHAEL, OUT THE WINDOW— NOW!
GO, GO— JUMP!
ARE YOU FUCKING KIDDING ME?
-GULP-
AAAAAAAAAAAAAAAAAAAA

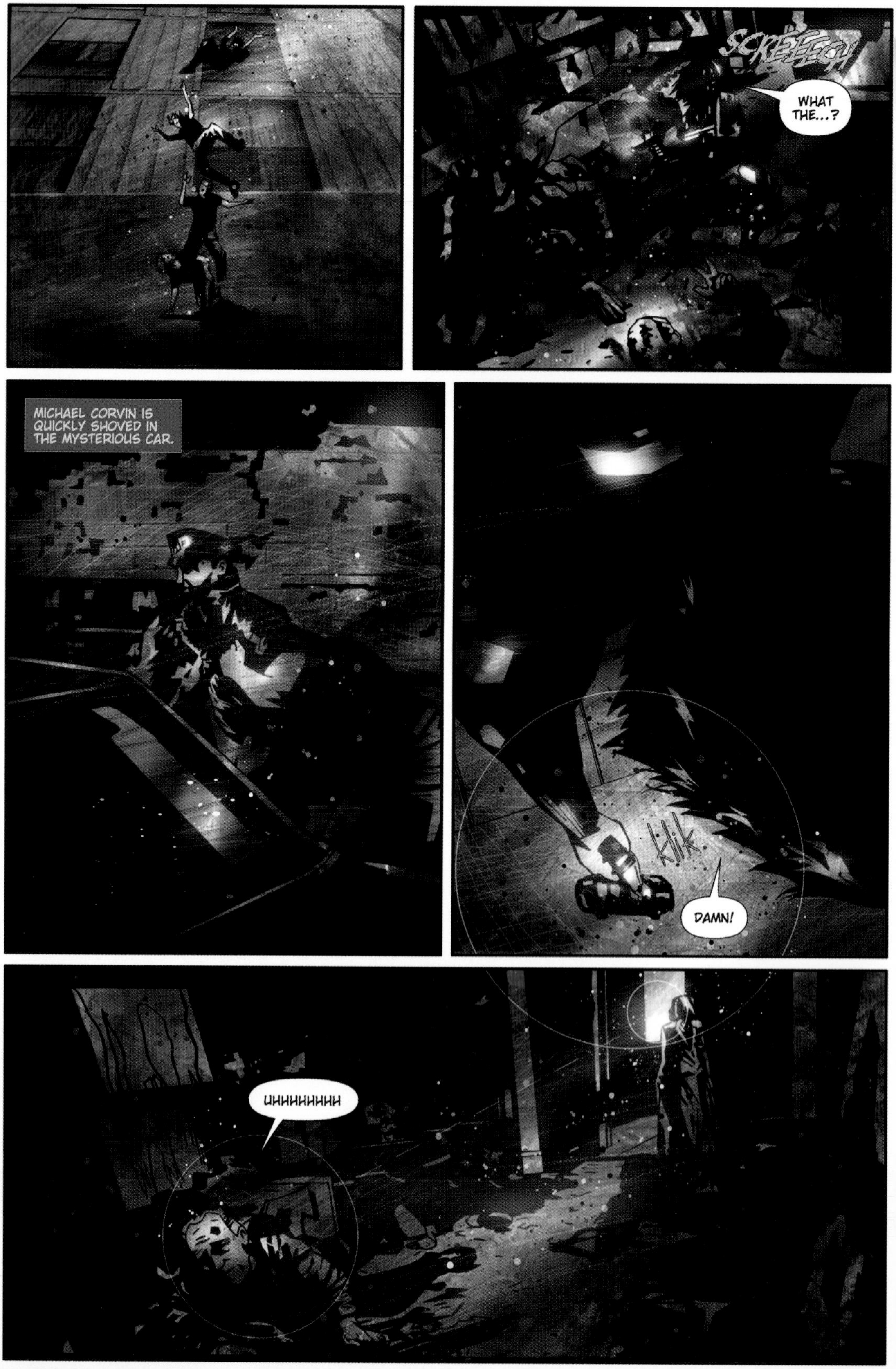
SCREEECH
WHAT THE...?
MICHAEL CORVIN IS QUICKLY SHOVED IN THE MYSTERIOUS CAR.
klik
DAMN!
UHHHHHHHH

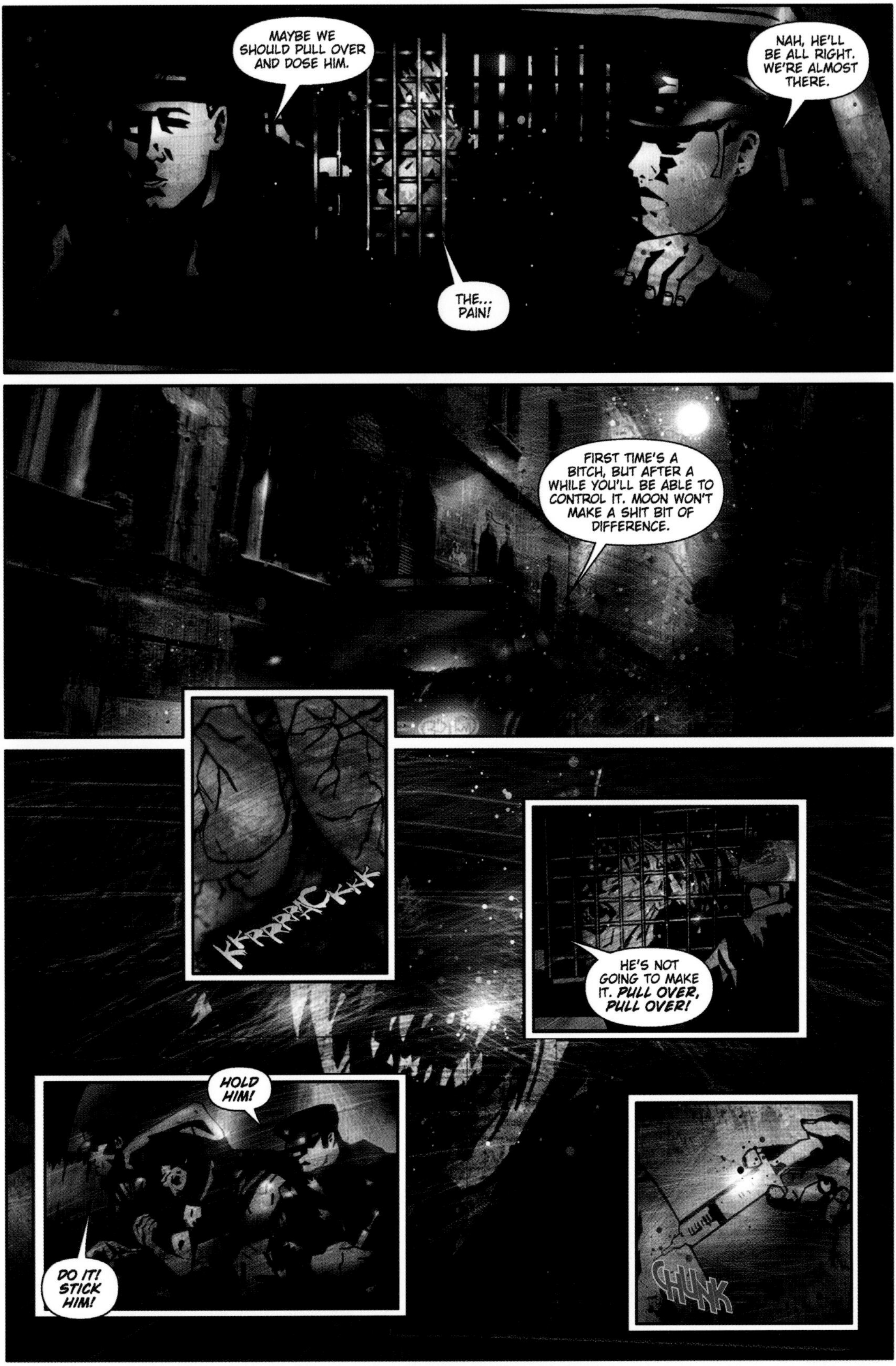
MAYBE WE SHOULD PULL OVER AND DOSE HIM.
NAH, HE'LL BE ALL RIGHT. WE'RE ALMOST THERE.
THE... PAIN!
FIRST TIME'S A BITCH, BUT AFTER A WHILE YOU'LL BE ABLE TO CONTROL IT. MOON WON'T MAKE A SHIT BIT OF DIFFERENCE.
KRRRRACKKK
HE'S NOT GOING TO MAKE IT. PULL OVER, PULL OVER!
HOLD HIM!
DO IT! STICK HIM!
CHUNK

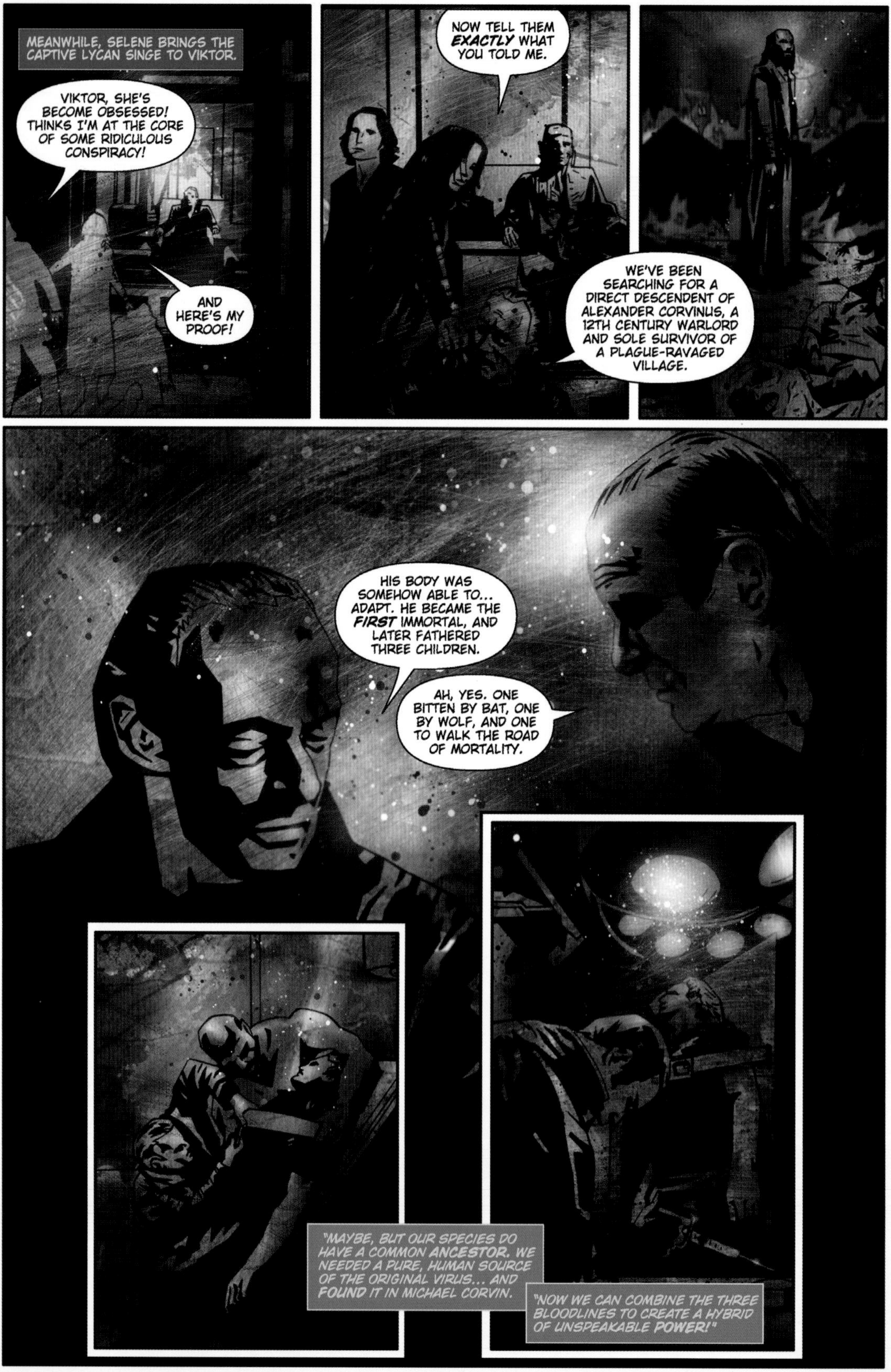
MEANWHILE, SELENE BRINGS THE CAPTIVE LYCAN SINGE TO VIKTOR.
VIKTOR, SHE'S BECOME OBSESSED! THINKS I'M AT THE CORE OF SOME RIDICULOUS CONSPIRACY!
AND HERE'S MY PROOF!
NOW TELL THEM EXACTLY WHAT YOU TOLD ME.
WE'VE BEEN SEARCHING FOR A DIRECT DESCENDENT OF ALEXANDER CORVINUS, A 12TH CENTURY WARLORD AND SOLE SURVIVOR OF A PLAGUE-RAVAGED VILLAGE.
HIS BODY WAS SOMEHOW ABLE TO... ADAPT. HE BECAME THE FIRST IMMORTAL, AND LATER FATHERED THREE CHILDREN.
AH, YES. ONE BITTEN BY BAT, ONE BY WOLF, AND ONE TO WALK THE ROAD OF MORTALITY.
"MAYBE, BUT OUR SPECIES DO HAVE A COMMON ANCESTOR. WE NEEDED A PURE, HUMAN SOURCE OF THE ORIGINAL VIRUS... AND FOUND IT IN MICHAEL CORVIN.
"NOW WE CAN COMBINE THE THREE BLOODLINES TO CREATE A HYBRID OF UNSPEAKABLE POWER!"

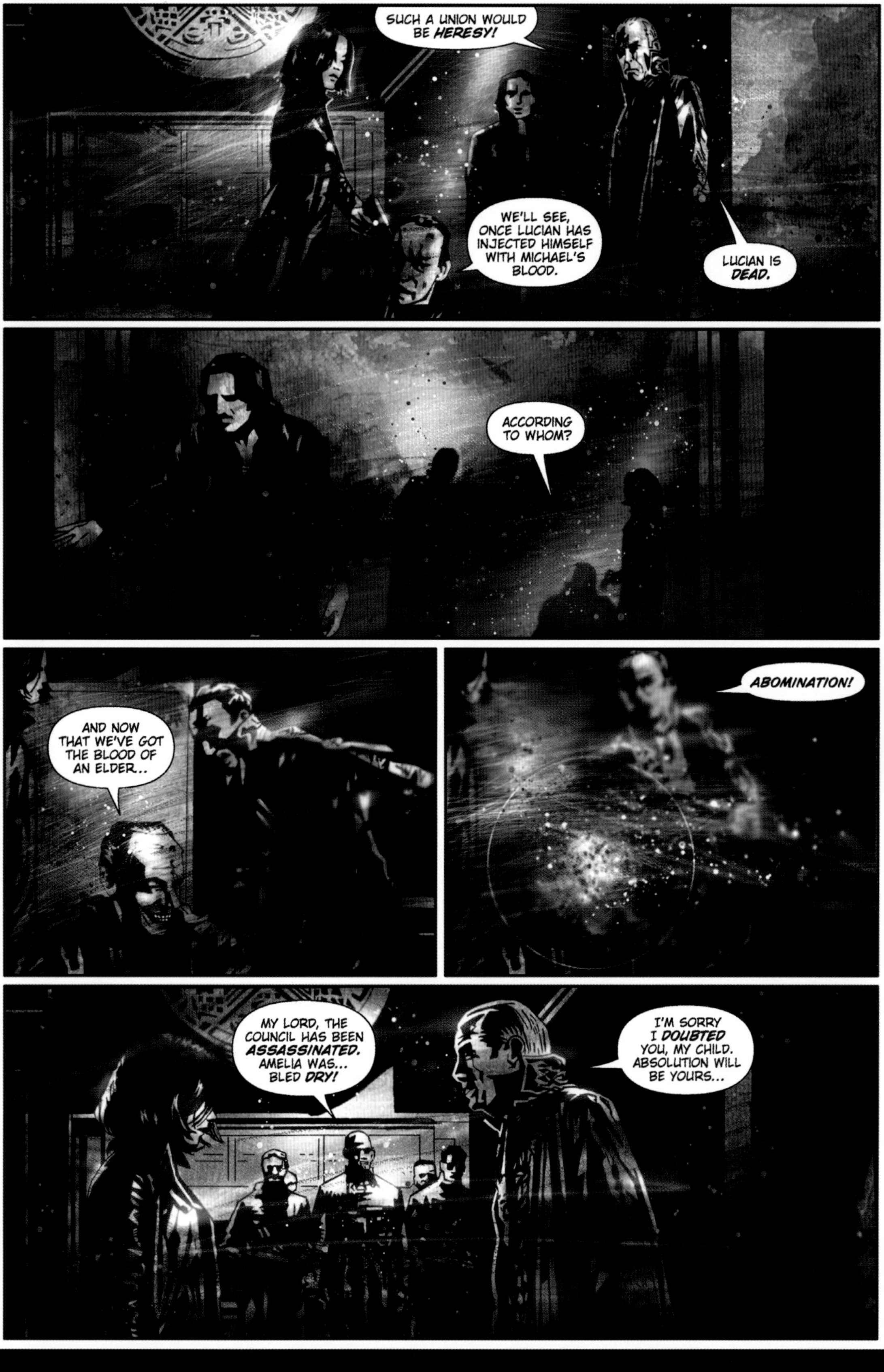
SUCH A UNION WOULD BE HERESY!
WE'LL SEE, ONCE LUCIAN HAS INJECTED HIMSELF WITH MICHAEL'S BLOOD.
LUCIAN IS DEAD.
ACCORDING TO WHOM?
AND NOW THAT WE'VE GOT THE BLOOD OF AN ELDER...
ABOMINATION!
MY LORD, THE COUNCIL HAS BEEN ASSASSINATED. AMELIA WAS... BLED DRY!
I'M SORRY I DOUBTED YOU, MY CHILD. ABSOLUTION WILL BE YOURS...

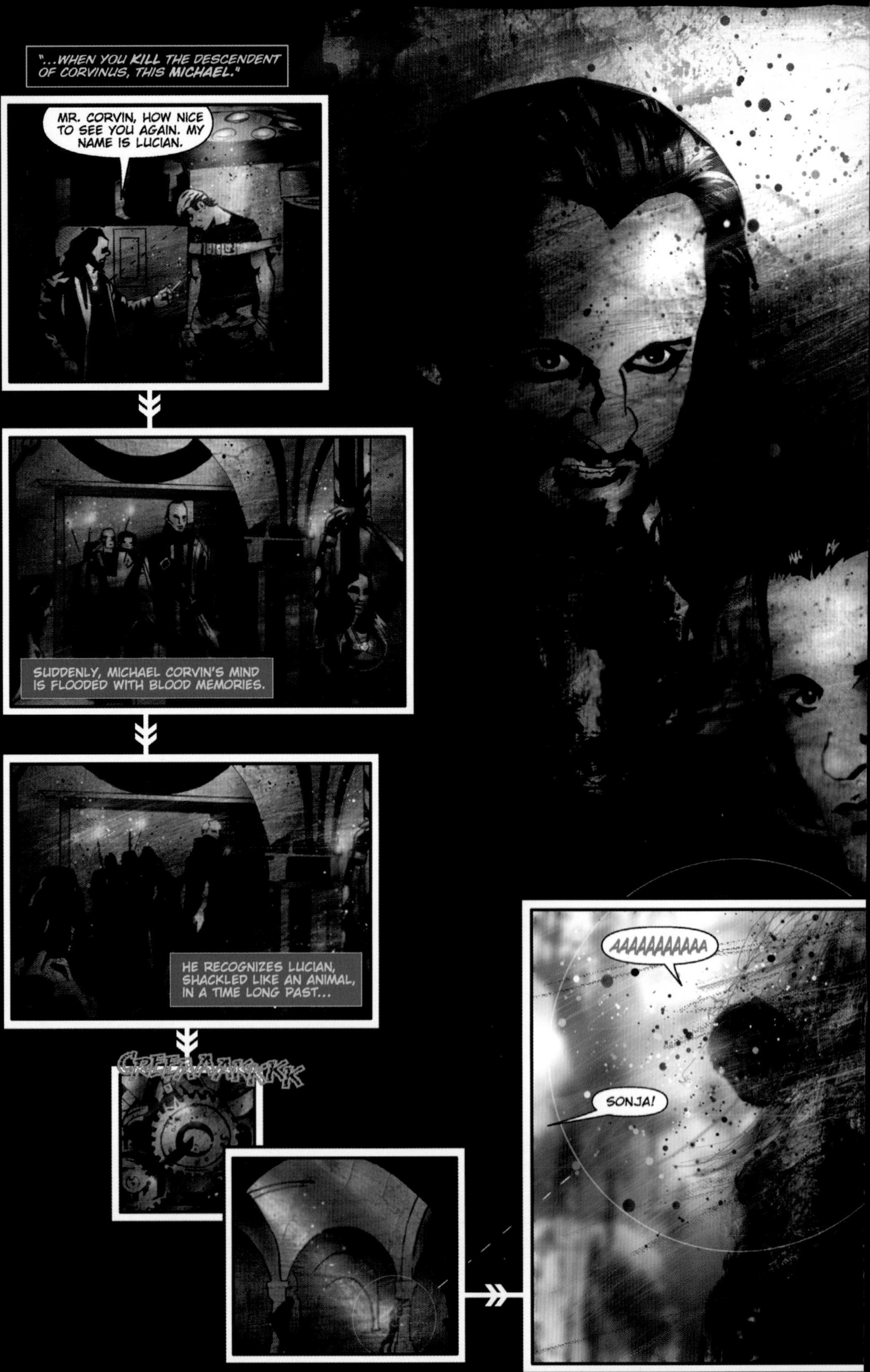
"...WHEN YOU KILL THE DESCENDENT OF CORVINUS, THIS MICHAEL."
MR. CORVIN, HOW NICE TO SEE YOU AGAIN. MY NAME IS LUCIAN.
SUDDENLY, MICHAEL CORVIN'S MIND IS FLOODED WITH BLOOD MEMORIES.
HE RECOGNIZES LUCIAN, SHACKLED LIKE AN ANIMAL, IN A TIME LONG PAST...
GREEAAAARKKK
AAAAAAAAAAA
SONJA!

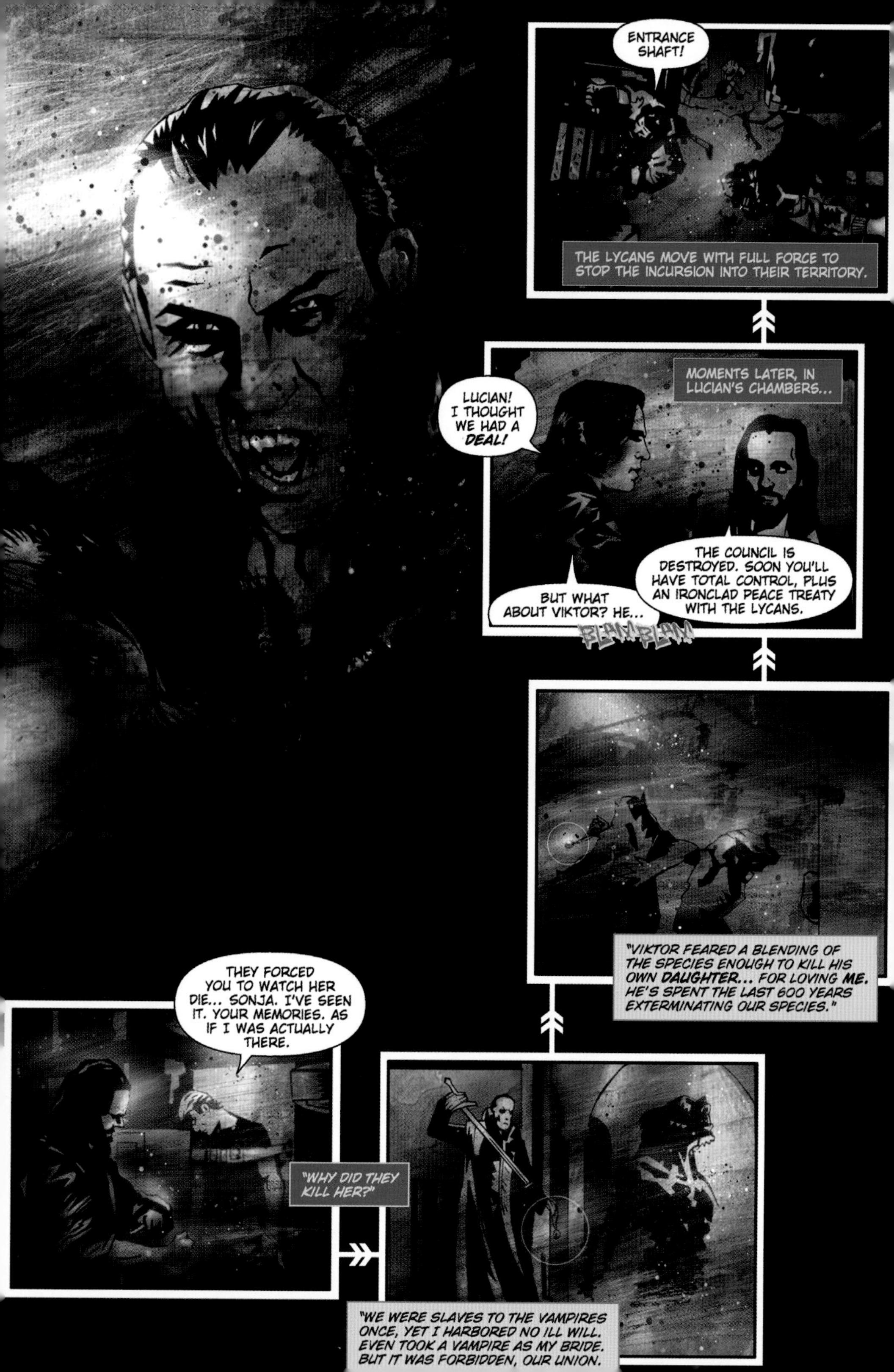
ENTRANCE SHAFT!
THE LYCANS MOVE WITH FULL FORCE TO STOP THE INCURSION INTO THEIR TERRITORY.
MOMENTS LATER, IN LUCIAN'S CHAMBERS...
LUCIAN! I THOUGHT WE HAD A *DEAL!*
THE COUNCIL IS DESTROYED. SOON YOU'LL HAVE TOTAL CONTROL, PLUS AN IRONCLAD PEACE TREATY WITH THE LYCANS.
BUT WHAT ABOUT VIKTOR? HE...
BLAM BLAM
"VIKTOR FEARED A BLENDING OF THE SPECIES ENOUGH TO KILL HIS OWN **DAUGHTER**... FOR LOVING **ME.** HE'S SPENT THE LAST 600 YEARS EXTERMINATING OUR SPECIES."
THEY FORCED YOU TO WATCH HER DIE... SONJA. I'VE SEEN IT. YOUR MEMORIES. AS IF I WAS ACTUALLY THERE.
"WHY DID THEY KILL HER?"
"WE WERE SLAVES TO THE VAMPIRES ONCE, YET I HARBORED NO ILL WILL. EVEN TOOK A VAMPIRE AS MY BRIDE. BUT IT WAS FORBIDDEN, OUR UNION.

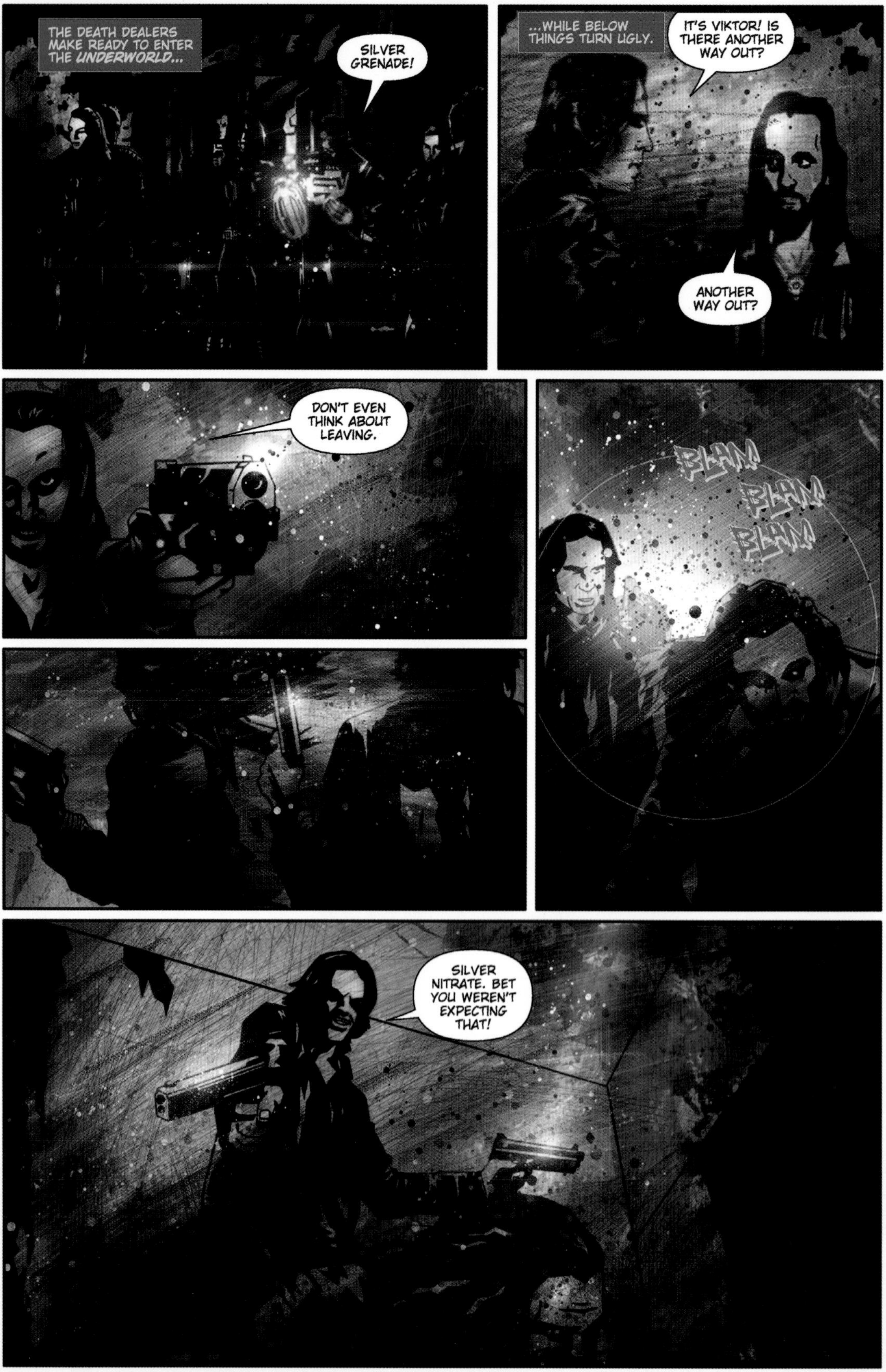
THE DEATH DEALERS MAKE READY TO ENTER THE *UNDERWORLD*...
SILVER GRENADE!
...WHILE BELOW THINGS TURN UGLY.
IT'S VIKTOR! IS THERE ANOTHER WAY OUT?
ANOTHER WAY OUT?
DON'T EVEN THINK ABOUT LEAVING.
BLAM
BLAM
BLAM
SILVER NITRATE. BET YOU WEREN'T EXPECTING THAT!

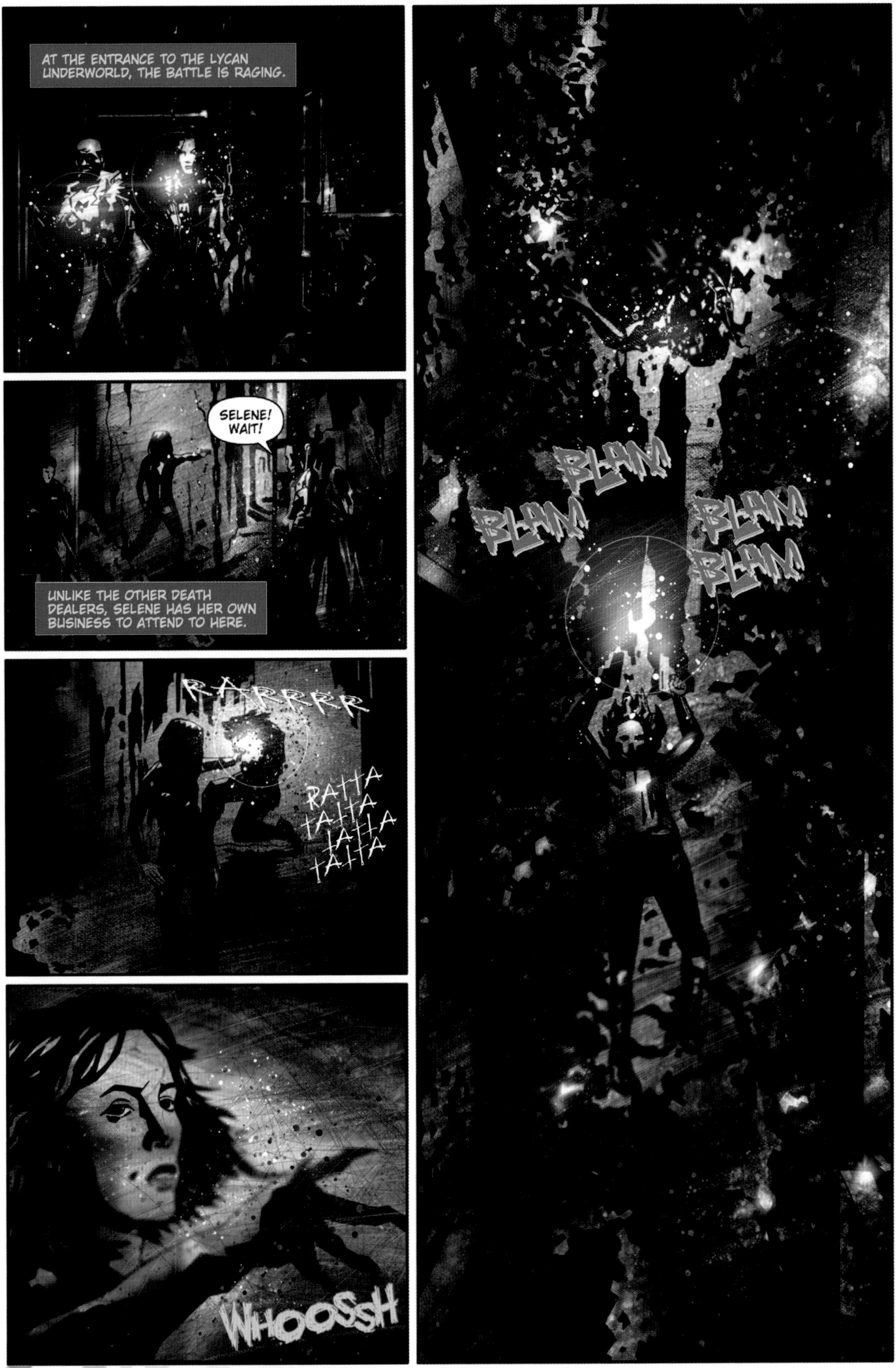
AT THE ENTRANCE TO THE LYCAN UNDERWORLD, THE BATTLE IS RAGING.
SELENE! WAIT!
UNLIKE THE OTHER DEATH DEALERS, SELENE HAS HER OWN BUSINESS TO ATTEND TO HERE.
RARRRRR
RATTA TATTA TATTA TATTA
WHOOSSH
BLAM
BLAM
BLAM
BLAM

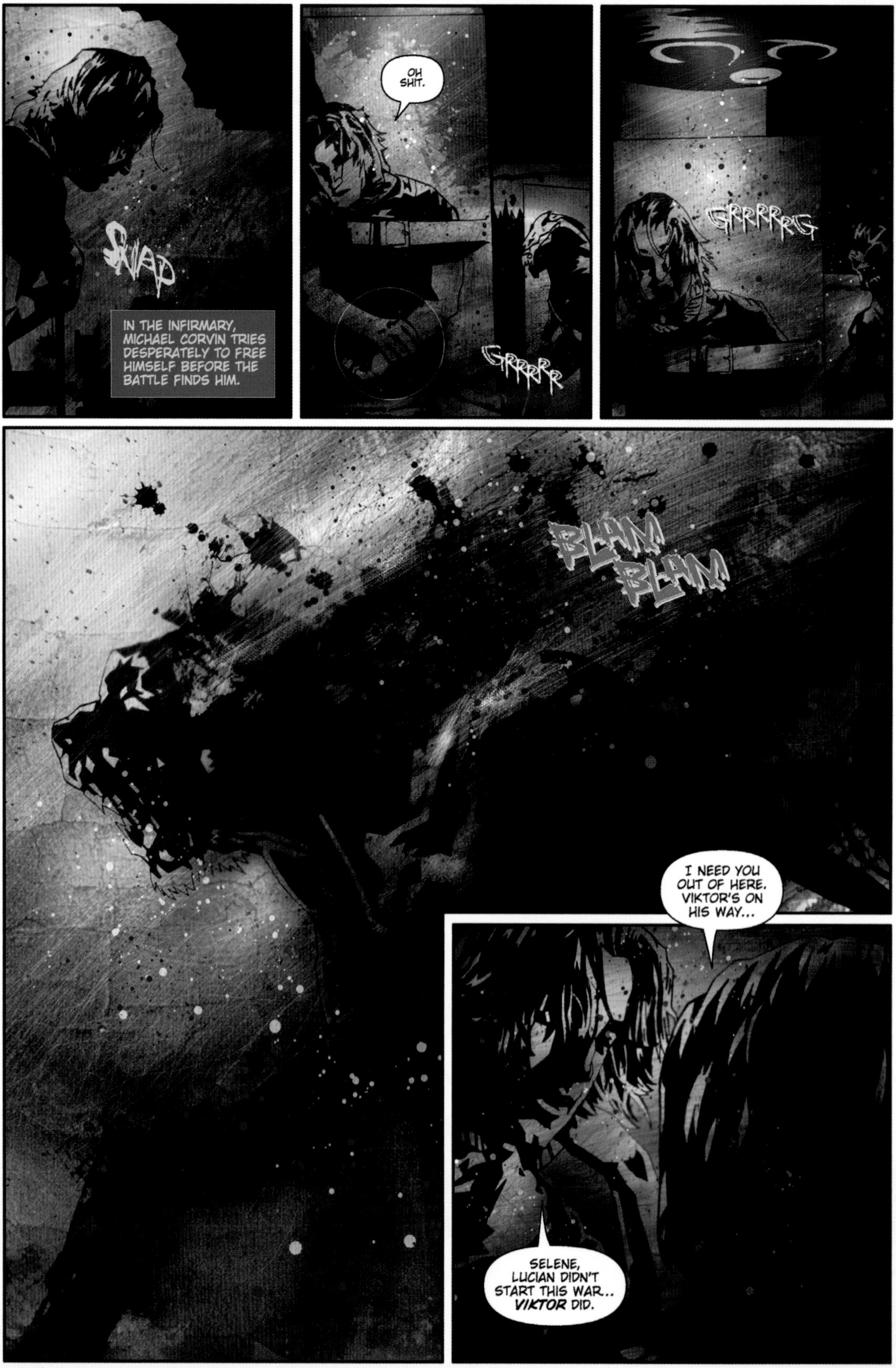
SNAP
IN THE INFIRMARY, MICHAEL CORVIN TRIES DESPERATELY TO FREE HIMSELF BEFORE THE BATTLE FINDS HIM.
OH SHIT.
GRRRRR
GRRRRRG
BLAM BLAM
I NEED YOU OUT OF HERE. VIKTOR'S ON HIS WAY...
SELENE, LUCIAN DIDN'T START THIS WAR... VIKTOR DID.

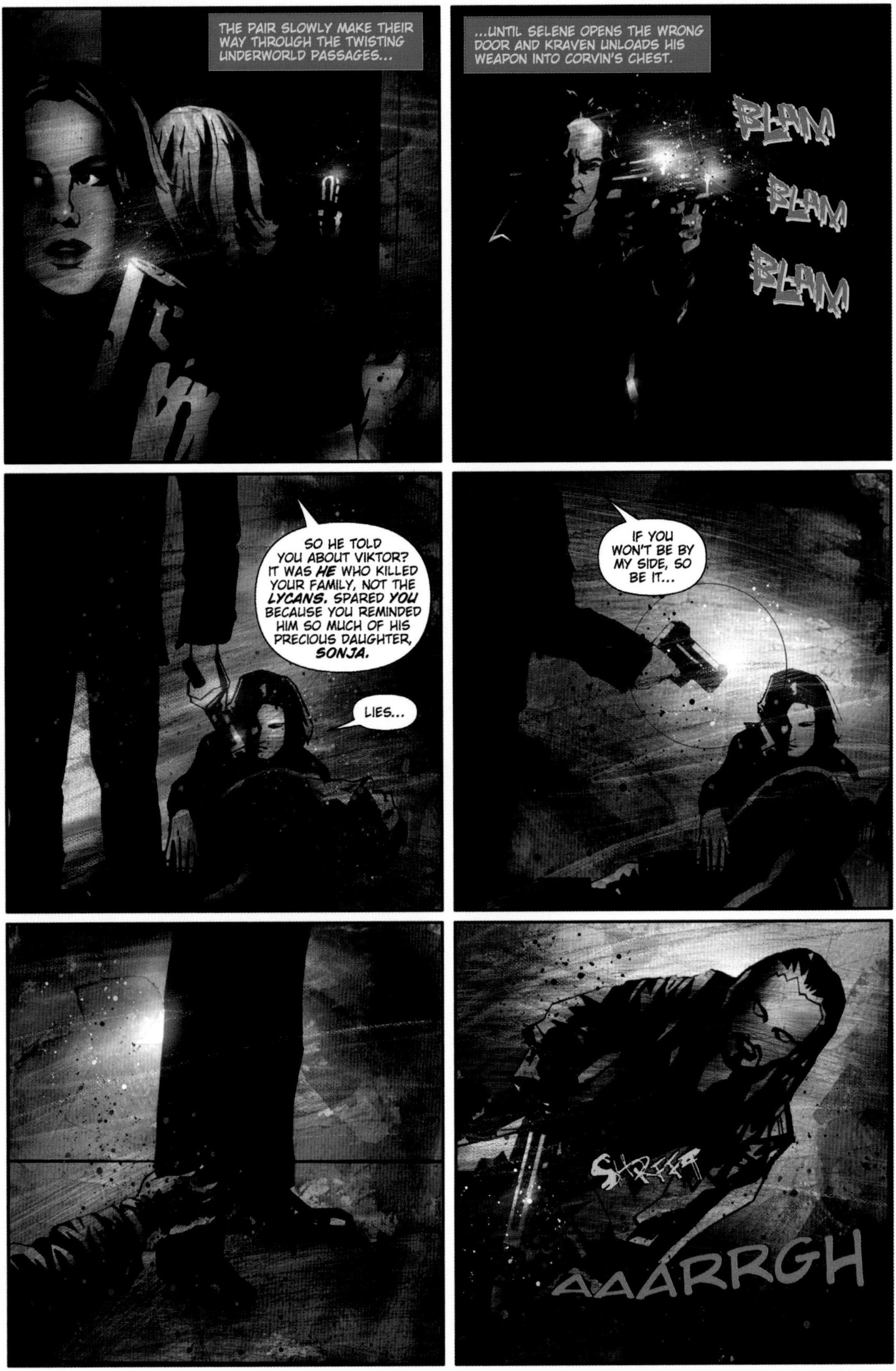
THE PAIR SLOWLY MAKE THEIR WAY THROUGH THE TWISTING UNDERWORLD PASSAGES...
...UNTIL SELENE OPENS THE WRONG DOOR AND KRAVEN UNLOADS HIS WEAPON INTO CORVIN'S CHEST.
BLAM
BLAM
BLAM
SO HE TOLD YOU ABOUT VIKTOR? IT WAS HE WHO KILLED YOUR FAMILY, NOT THE LYCANS. SPARED YOU BECAUSE YOU REMINDED HIM SO MUCH OF HIS PRECIOUS DAUGHTER, SONJA.
LIES...
IF YOU WON'T BE BY MY SIDE, SO BE IT...
AAARRGH

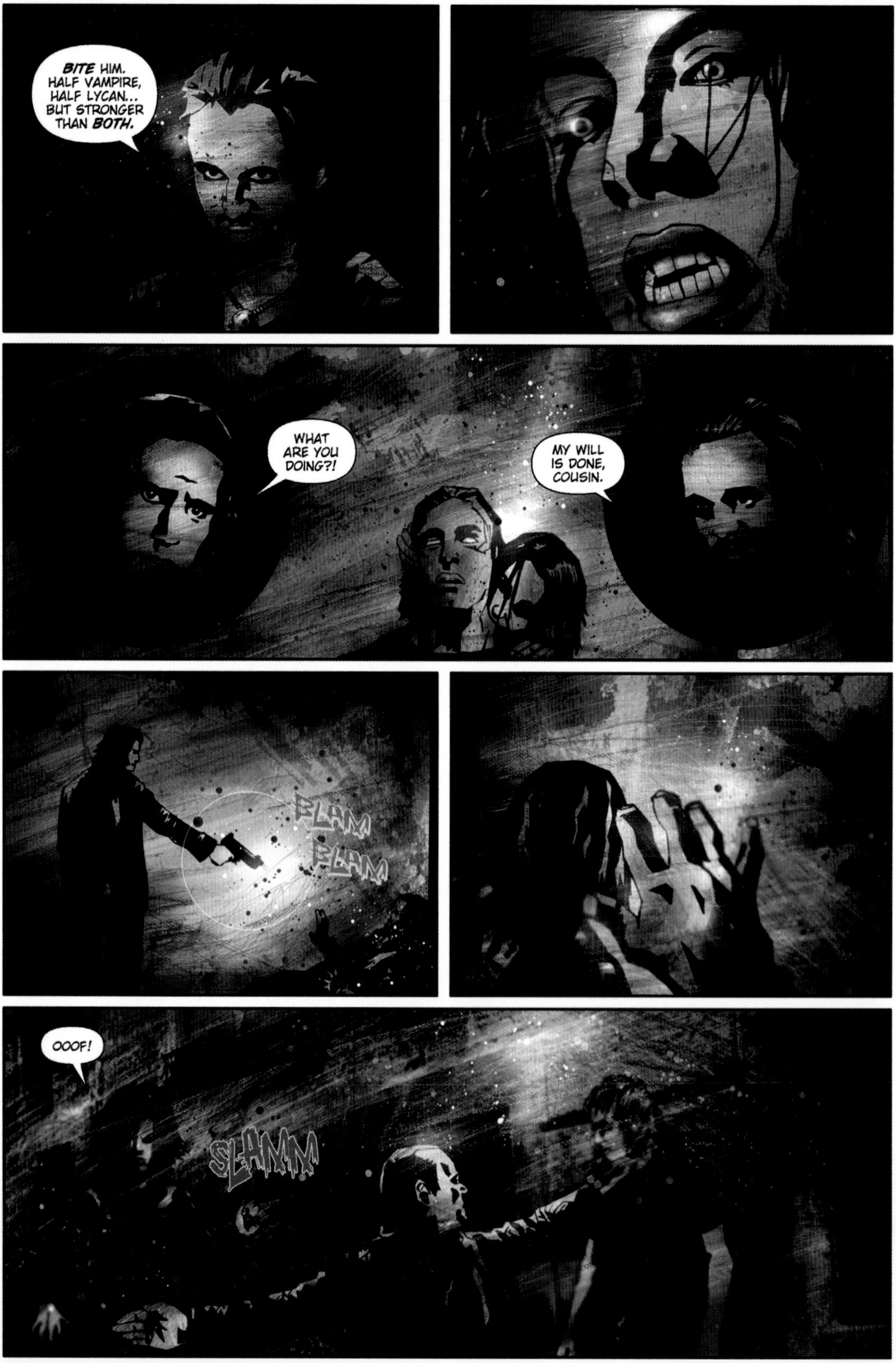
BITE HIM. HALF VAMPIRE, HALF LYCAN... BUT STRONGER THAN BOTH.
WHAT ARE YOU DOING?!
MY WILL IS DONE, COUSIN.
BLAM
BLAM
OOOF!
SLAMM

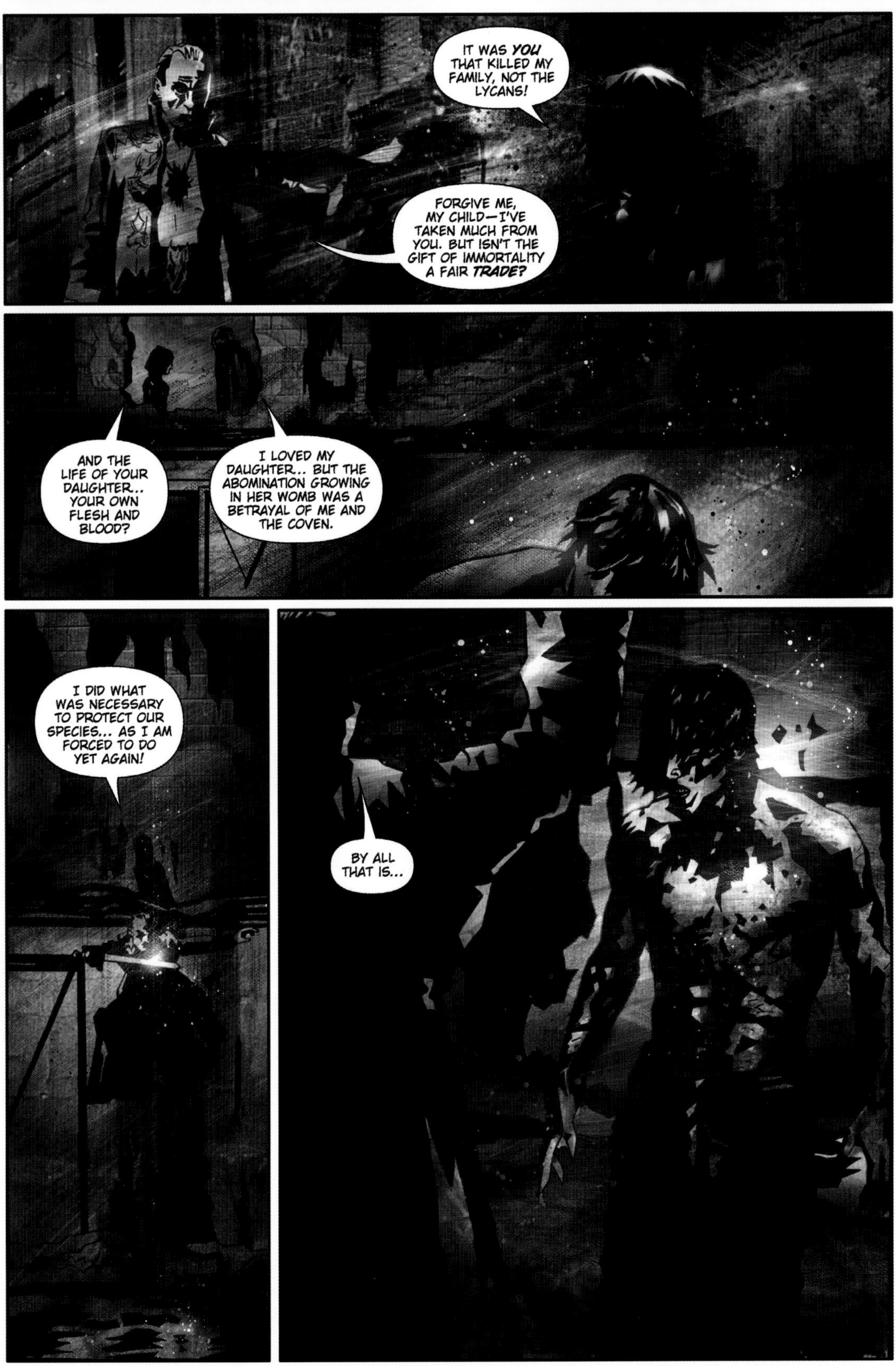
IT WAS *YOU* THAT KILLED MY FAMILY, NOT THE LYCANS!
FORGIVE ME, MY CHILD—I'VE TAKEN MUCH FROM YOU. BUT ISN'T THE GIFT OF IMMORTALITY A FAIR *TRADE?*
AND THE LIFE OF YOUR DAUGHTER.. YOUR OWN FLESH AND BLOOD?
I LOVED MY DAUGHTER... BUT THE ABOMINATION GROWING IN HER WOMB WAS A BETRAYAL OF ME AND THE COVEN.
I DID WHAT WAS NECESSARY TO PROTECT OUR SPECIES... AS I AM FORCED TO DO YET AGAIN!
BY ALL THAT IS...

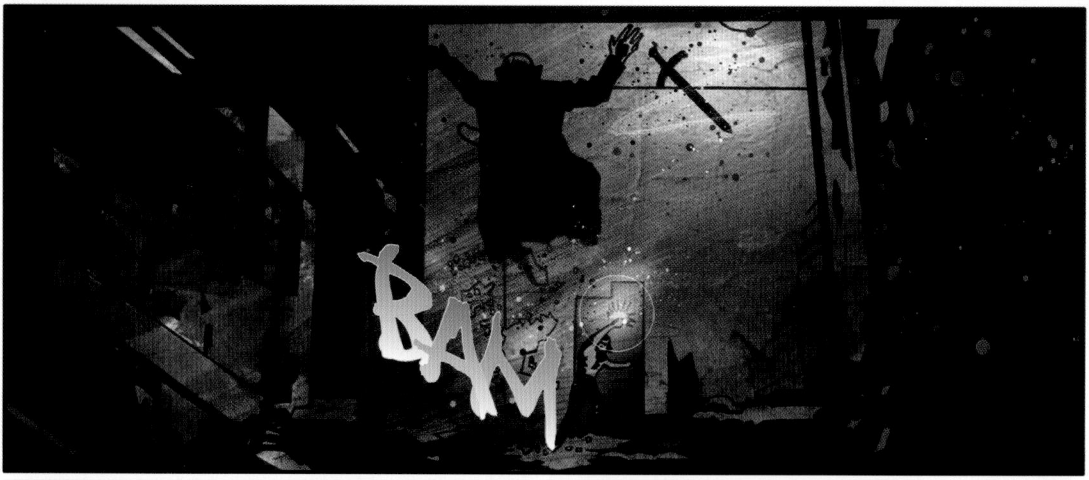
BAM

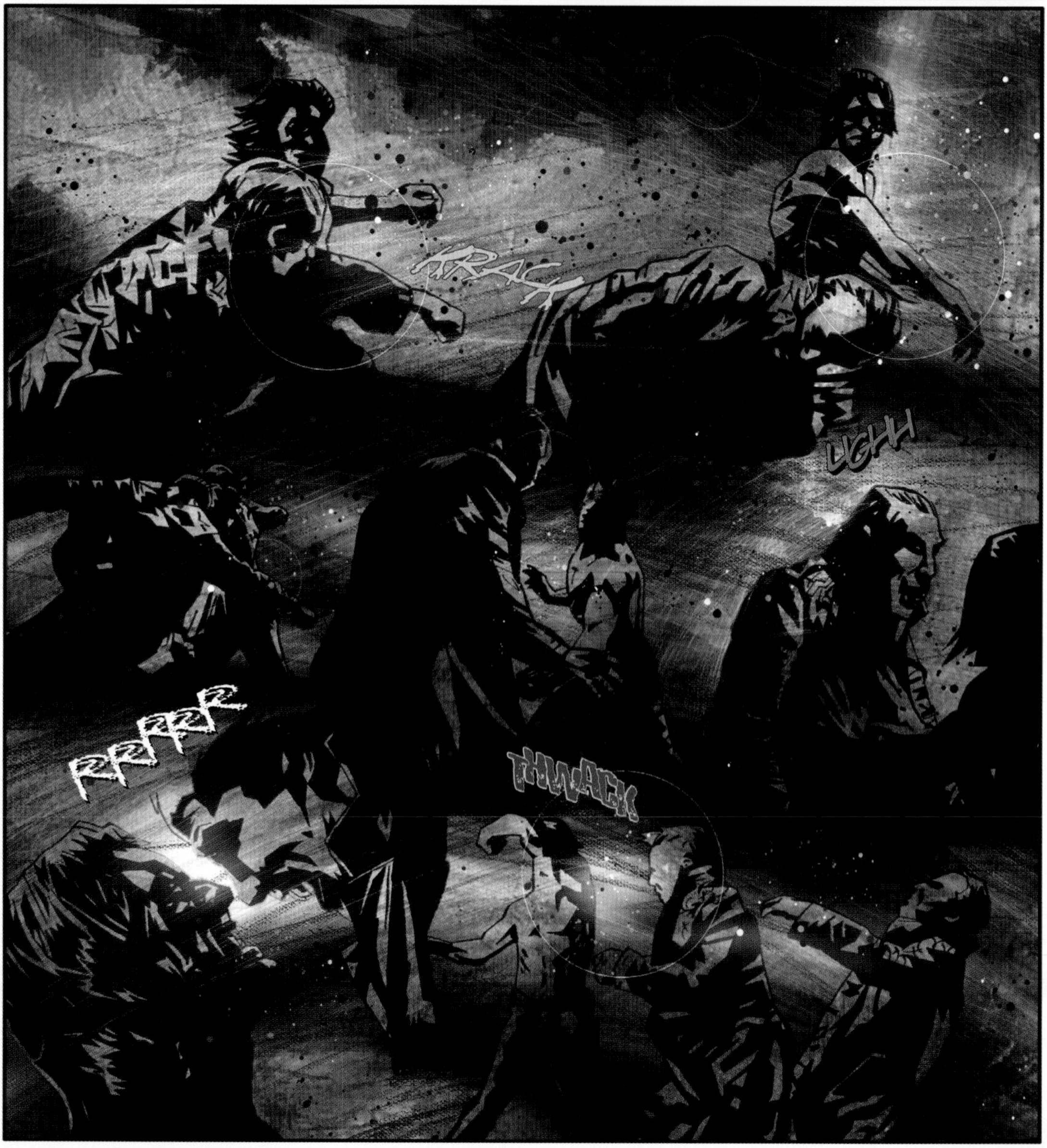
KRACK
UGHH
RRRRR
THWACK

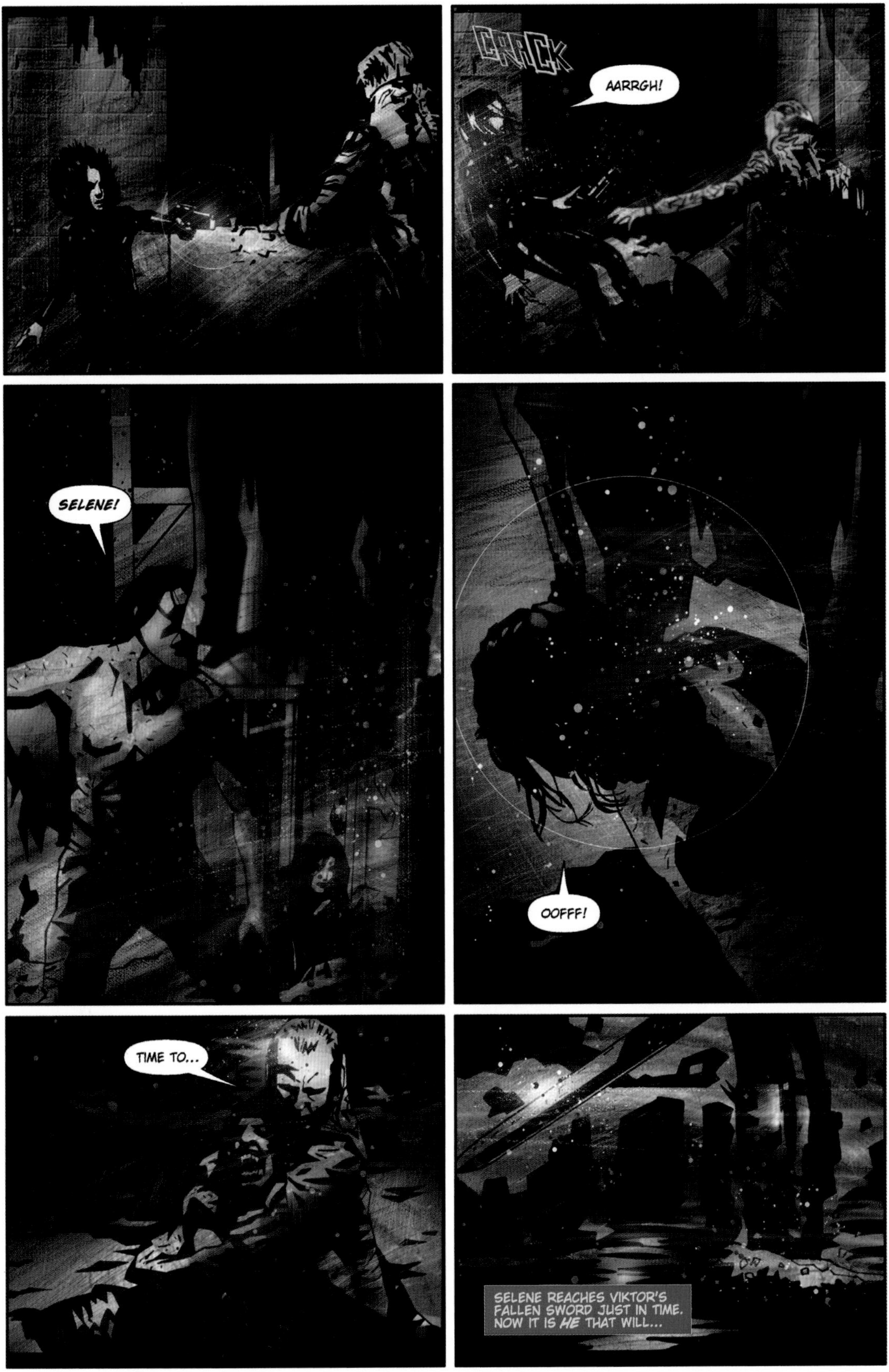
CRACK
AARRGH!
SELENE!
OOFFF!
TIME TO...
SELENE REACHES VIKTOR'S FALLEN SWORD JUST IN TIME. NOW IT IS *HE* THAT WILL...

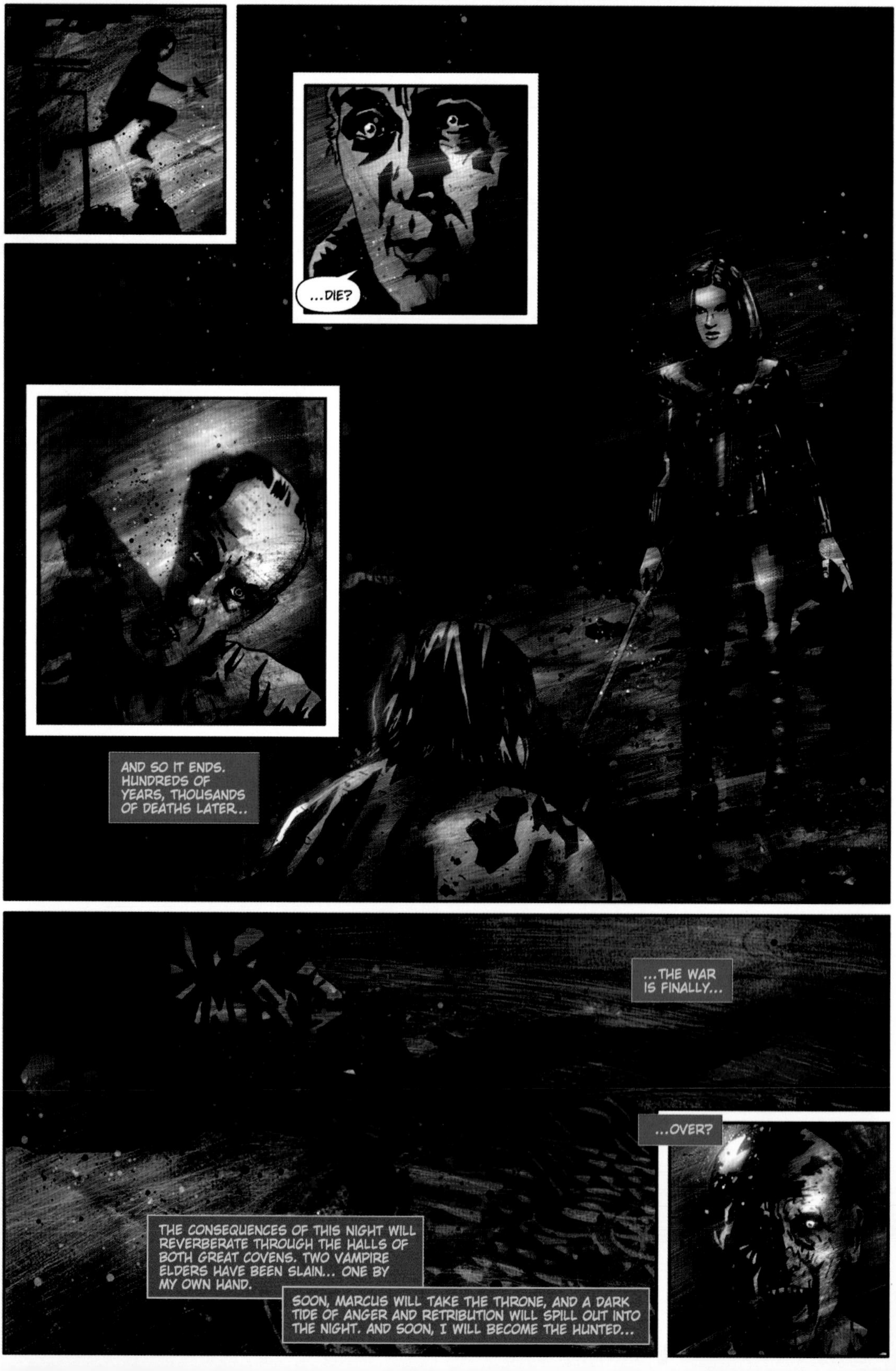
...DIE?
AND SO IT ENDS. HUNDREDS OF YEARS, THOUSANDS OF DEATHS LATER..
...THE WAR IS FINALLY...
...OVER?
THE CONSEQUENCES OF THIS NIGHT WILL REVERBERATE THROUGH THE HALLS OF BOTH GREAT COVENS. TWO VAMPIRE ELDERS HAVE BEEN SLAIN... ONE BY MY OWN HAND.
SOON, MARCUS WILL TAKE THE THRONE, AND A DARK TIDE OF ANGER AND RETRIBUTION WILL SPILL OUT INTO THE NIGHT. AND SOON, I WILL BECOME THE HUNTED...

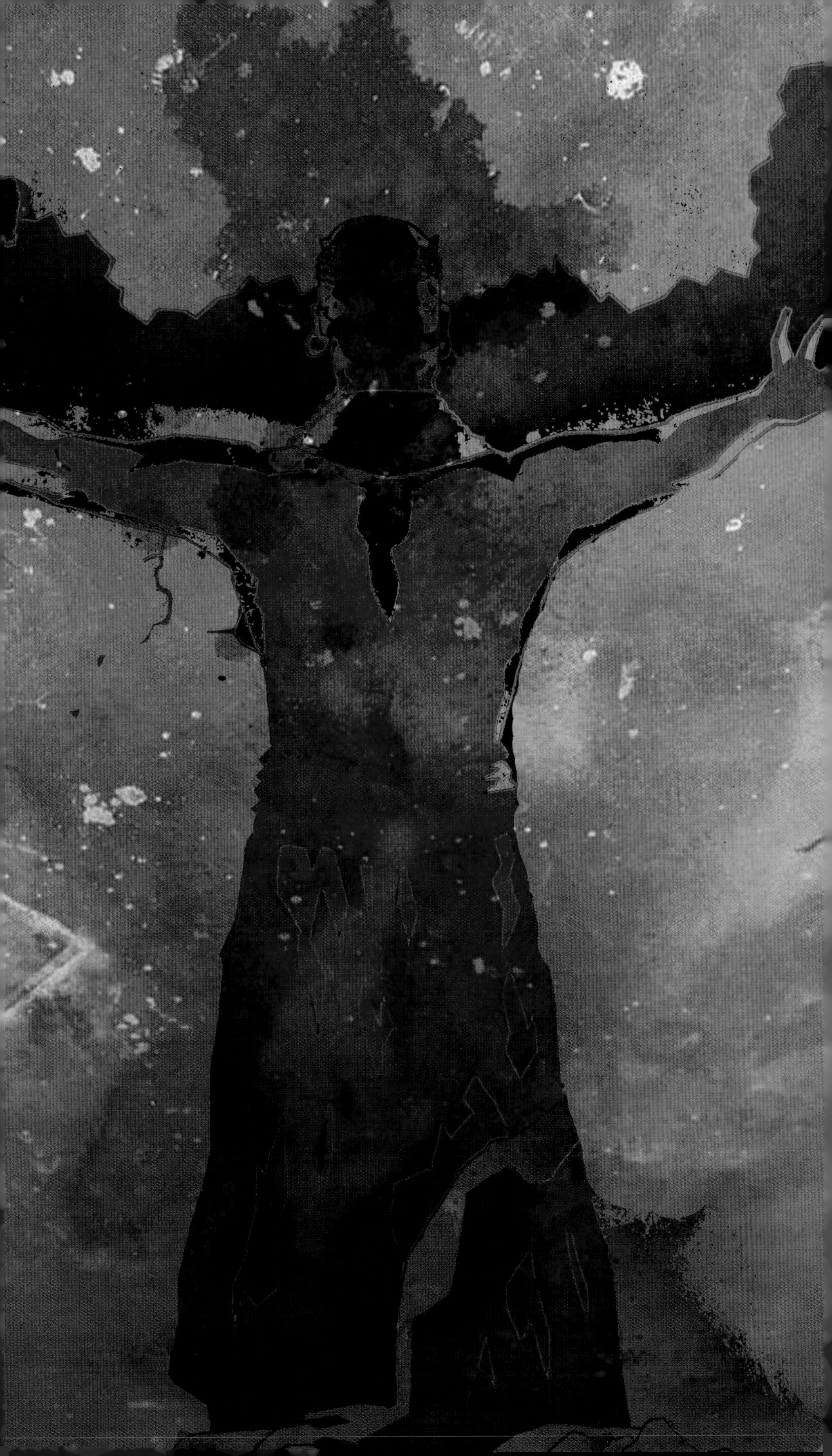

UNDERWORLD
RED IN TOOTH AND CLAW

CHAPTER

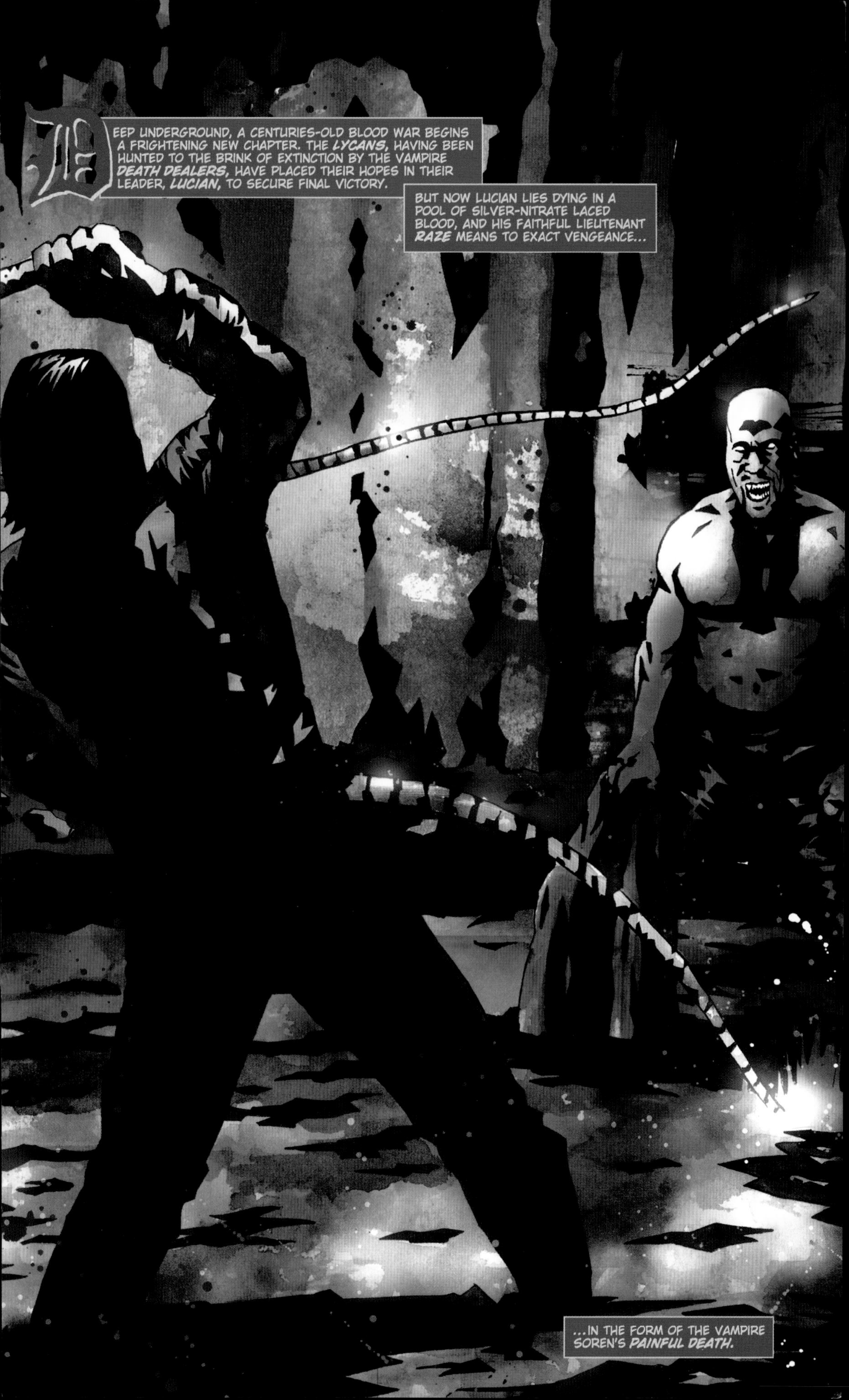
DEEP UNDERGROUND, A CENTURIES-OLD BLOOD WAR BEGINS A FRIGHTENING NEW CHAPTER. THE LYCANS, HAVING BEEN HUNTED TO THE BRINK OF EXTINCTION BY THE VAMPIRE DEATH DEALERS, HAVE PLACED THEIR HOPES IN THEIR LEADER, LUCIAN, TO SECURE FINAL VICTORY.
BUT NOW LUCIAN LIES DYING IN A POOL OF SILVER-NITRATE LACED BLOOD, AND HIS FAITHFUL LIEUTENANT RAZE MEANS TO EXACT VENGEANCE...
...IN THE FORM OF THE VAMPIRE SOREN'S PAINFUL DEATH.

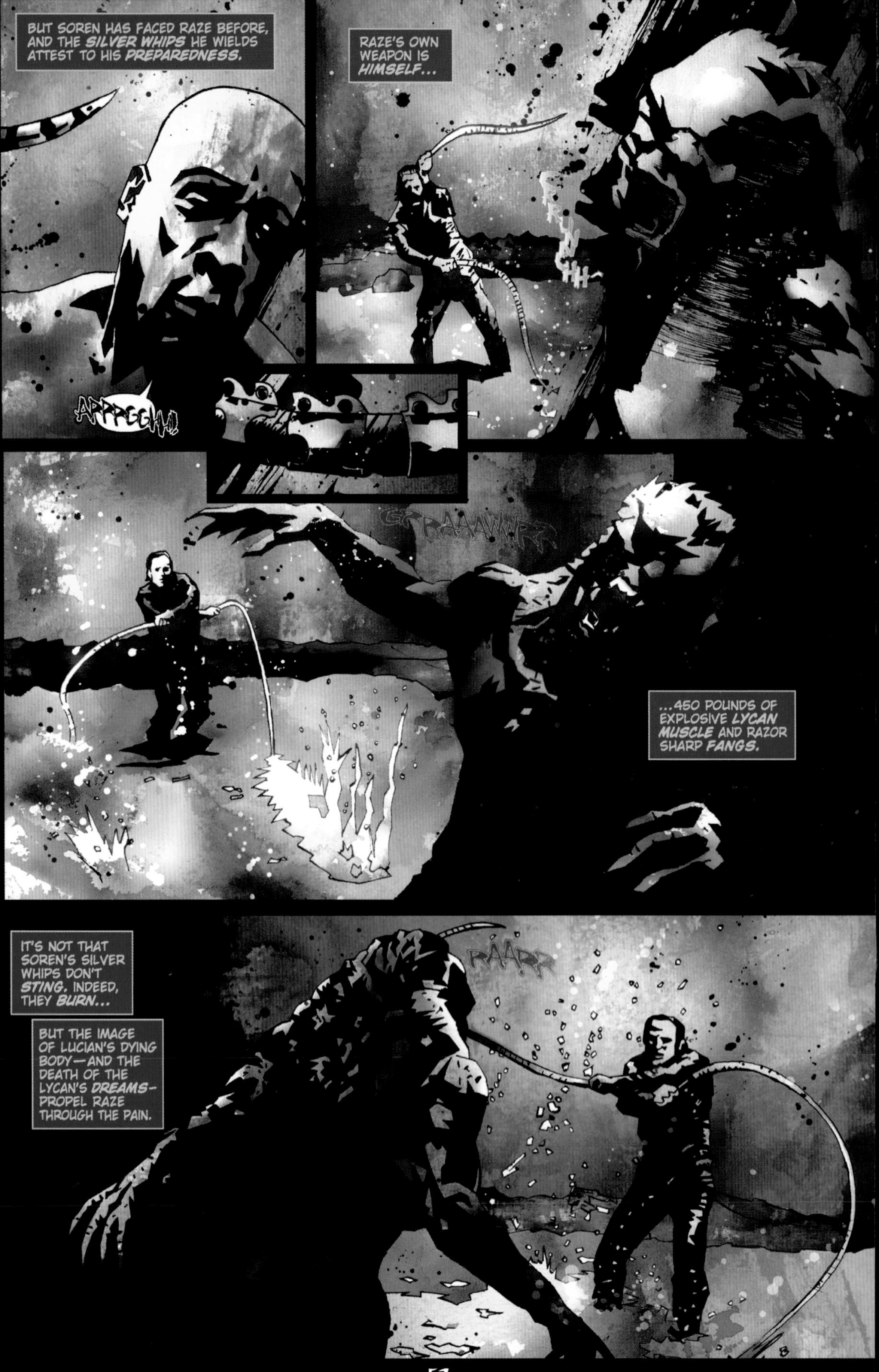
BUT SOREN HAS FACED RAZE BEFORE, AND THE SILVER WHIPS HE WIELDS ATTEST TO HIS PREPAREDNESS.
RAZE'S OWN WEAPON IS HIMSELF...
FRUNCHH
ARRRGGHH!
GRRAAAWWRR
...450 POUNDS OF EXPLOSIVE LYCAN MUSCLE AND RAZOR SHARP FANGS.
IT'S NOT THAT SOREN'S SILVER WHIPS DON'T STING. INDEED, THEY BURN...
BUT THE IMAGE OF LUCIAN'S DYING BODY—AND THE DEATH OF THE LYCAN'S DREAMS—PROPEL RAZE THROUGH THE PAIN.
RAARR

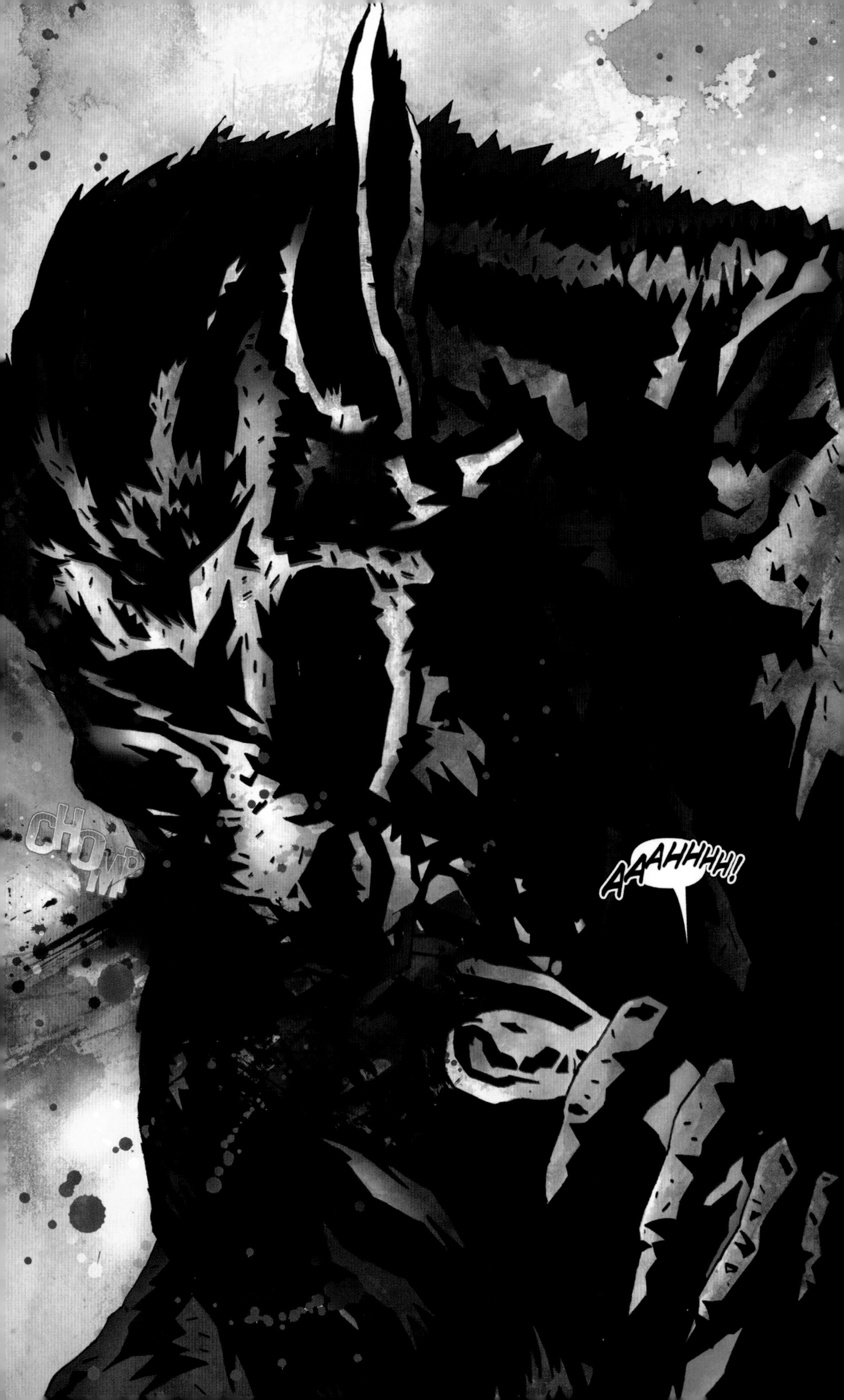
CHOMP
AAAHHHH!

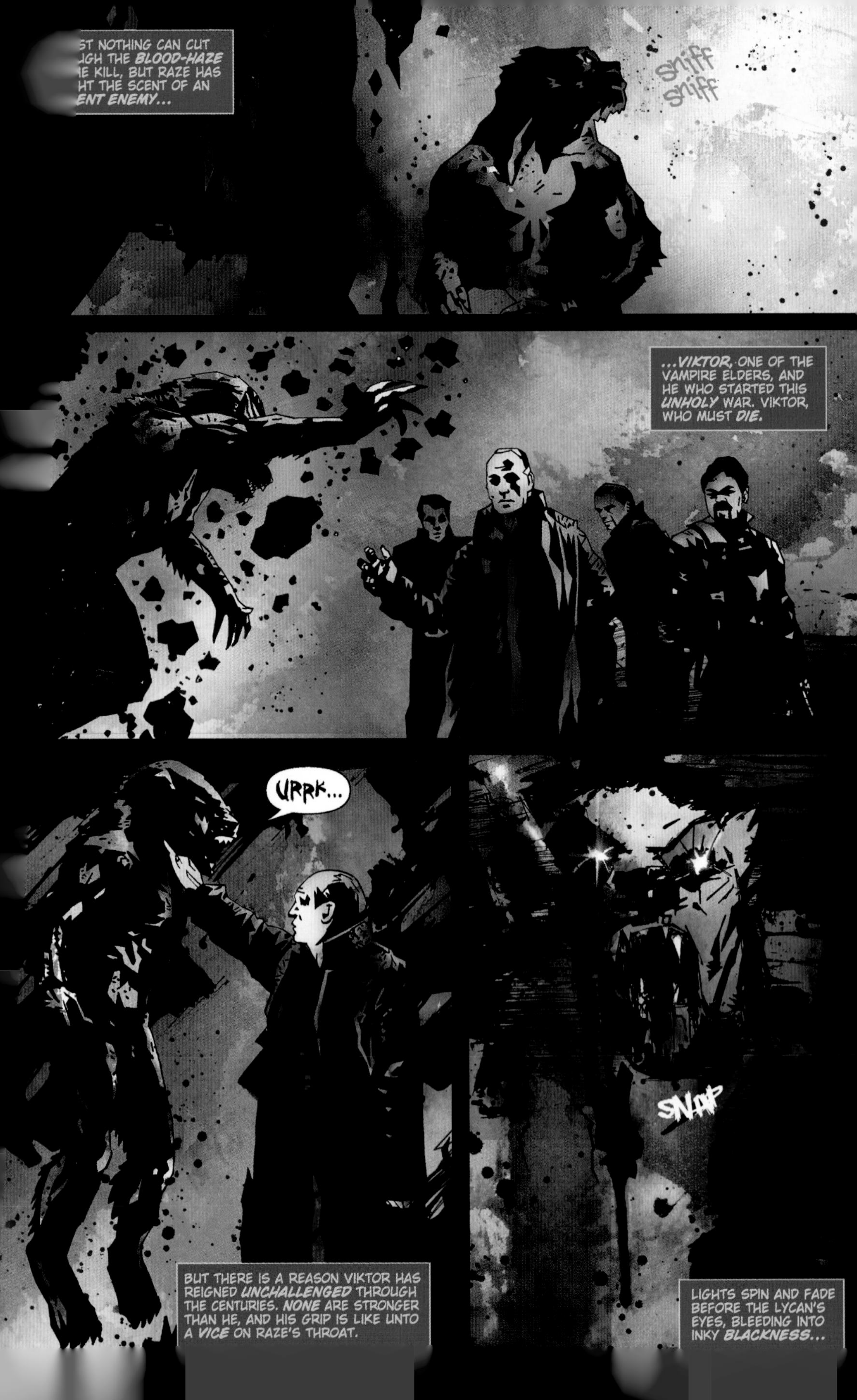

ST NOTHING CAN CUT UGH THE BLOOD-HAZE E KILL, BUT RAZE HAS HT THE SCENT OF AN ENT ENEMY...
sniff sniff
...VIKTOR, ONE OF THE VAMPIRE ELDERS, AND HE WHO STARTED THIS UNHOLY WAR. VIKTOR, WHO MUST DIE.
URRK...
BUT THERE IS A REASON VIKTOR HAS REIGNED UNCHALLENGED THROUGH THE CENTURIES. NONE ARE STRONGER THAN HE, AND HIS GRIP IS LIKE UNTO A VICE ON RAZE'S THROAT.
SNAP
LIGHTS SPIN AND FADE BEFORE THE LYCAN'S EYES, BLEEDING INTO INKY BLACKNESS...

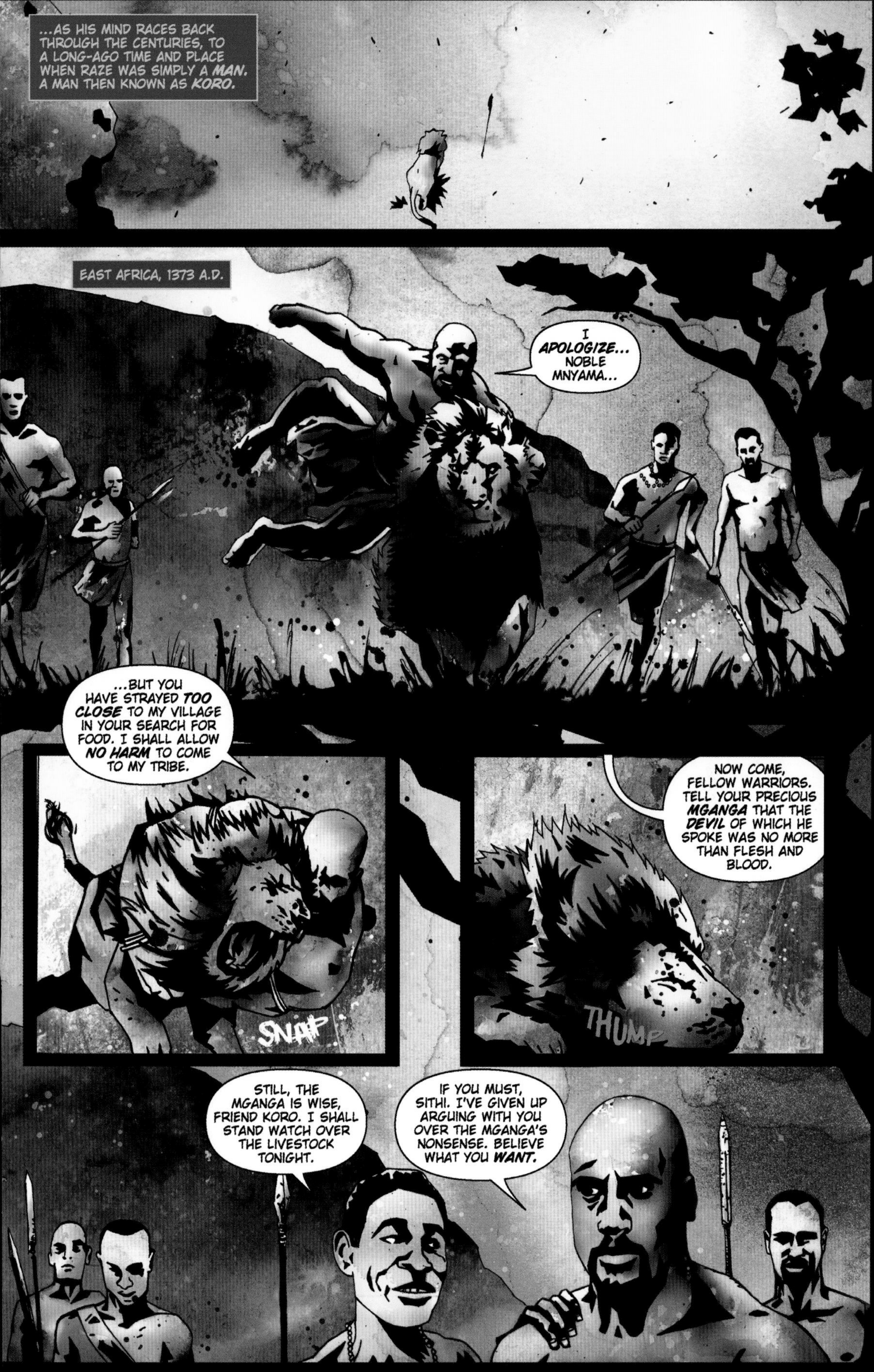
...AS HIS MIND RACES BACK THROUGH THE CENTURIES, TO A LONG-AGO TIME AND PLACE WHEN RAZE WAS SIMPLY A MAN. A MAN THEN KNOWN AS KORO.
EAST AFRICA, 1373 A.D.
I APOLOGIZE... NOBLE MNYAMA...
...BUT YOU HAVE STRAYED TOO CLOSE TO MY VILLAGE IN YOUR SEARCH FOR FOOD. I SHALL ALLOW NO HARM TO COME TO MY TRIBE.
SNAP
NOW COME, FELLOW WARRIORS. TELL YOUR PRECIOUS MGANGA THAT THE DEVIL OF WHICH HE SPOKE WAS NO MORE THAN FLESH AND BLOOD.
THUMP
STILL, THE MGANGA IS WISE, FRIEND KORO. I SHALL STAND WATCH OVER THE LIVESTOCK TONIGHT.
IF YOU MUST, SITHI. I'VE GIVEN UP ARGUING WITH YOU OVER THE MGANGA'S NONSENSE. BELIEVE WHAT YOU WANT.

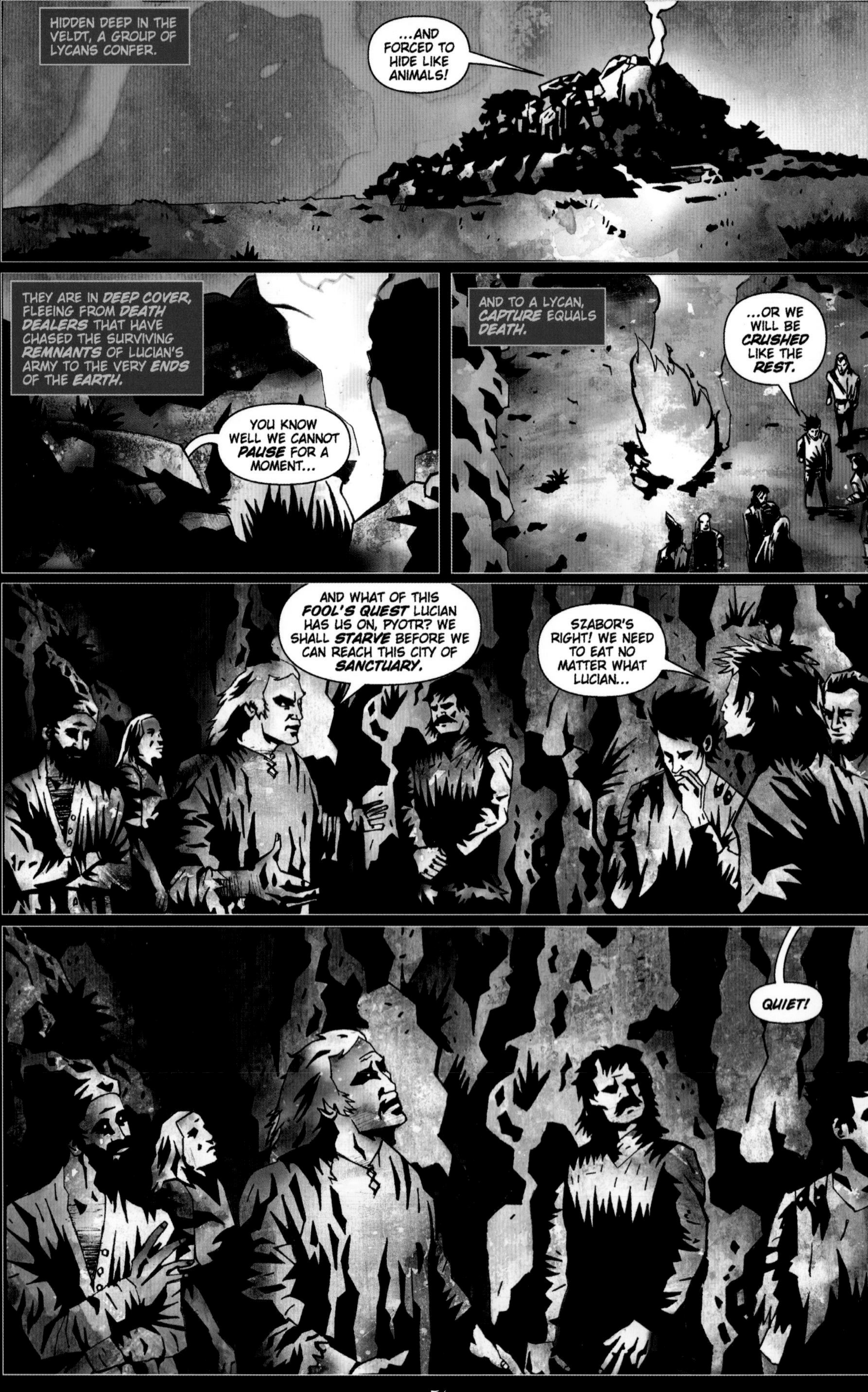
HIDDEN DEEP IN THE VELDT, A GROUP OF LYCANS CONFER.
...AND FORCED TO HIDE LIKE ANIMALS!
THEY ARE IN DEEP COVER, FLEEING FROM DEATH DEALERS THAT HAVE CHASED THE SURVIVING REMNANTS OF LUCIAN'S ARMY TO THE VERY ENDS OF THE EARTH.
YOU KNOW WELL WE CANNOT PAUSE FOR A MOMENT...
AND TO A LYCAN, CAPTURE EQUALS DEATH.
...OR WE WILL BE CRUSHED LIKE THE REST.
AND WHAT OF THIS FOOL'S QUEST LUCIAN HAS US ON, PYOTR? WE SHALL STARVE BEFORE WE CAN REACH THIS CITY OF SANCTUARY.
SZABOR'S RIGHT! WE NEED TO EAT NO MATTER WHAT LUCIAN...
QUIET!

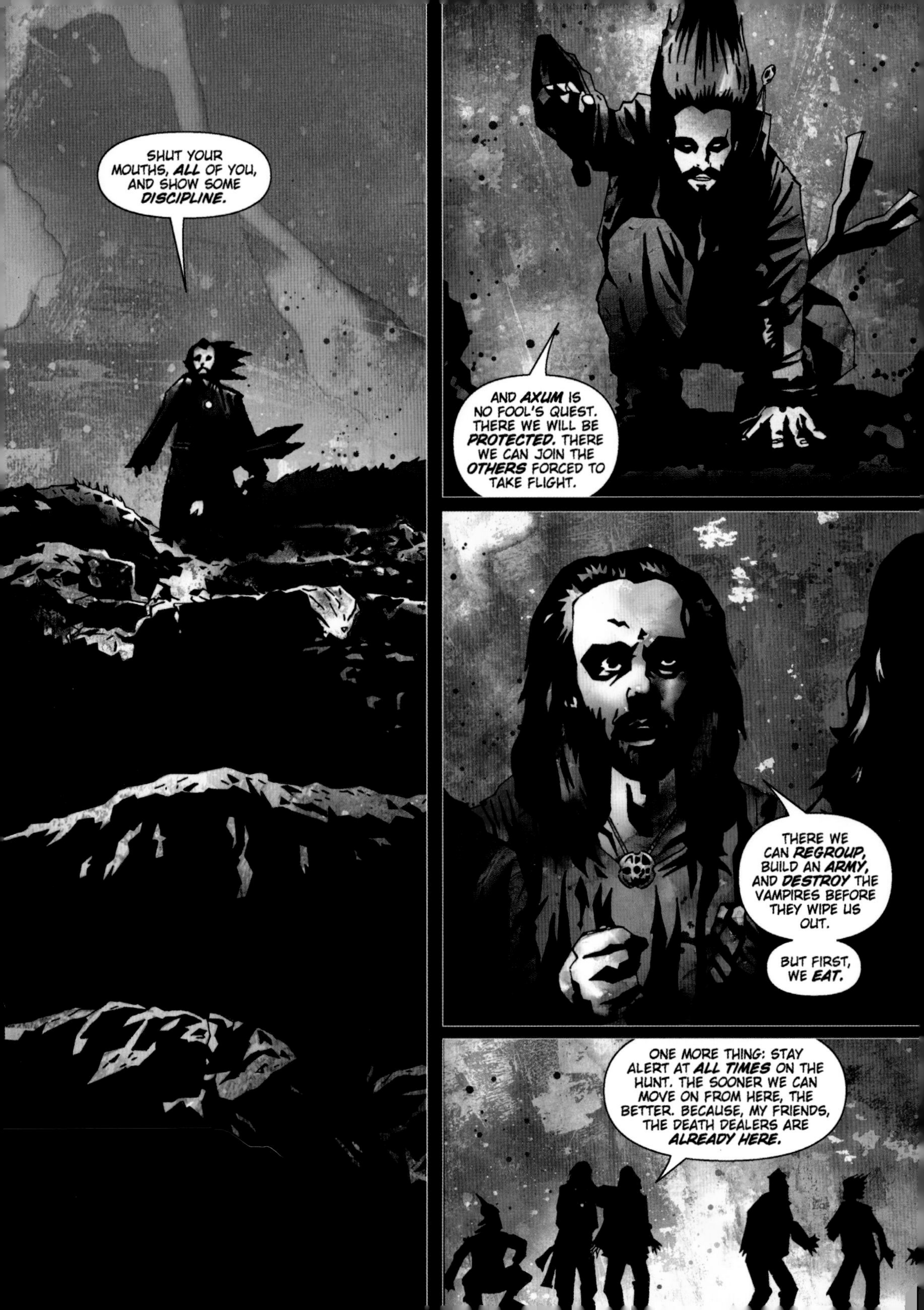
SHUT YOUR MOUTHS, ALL OF YOU, AND SHOW SOME DISCIPLINE.
AND AXUM IS NO FOOL'S QUEST. THERE WE WILL BE PROTECTED. THERE WE CAN JOIN THE OTHERS FORCED TO TAKE FLIGHT.
THERE WE CAN REGROUP, BUILD AN ARMY, AND DESTROY THE VAMPIRES BEFORE THEY WIPE US OUT.
BUT FIRST, WE EAT.
ONE MORE THING: STAY ALERT AT ALL TIMES ON THE HUNT. THE SOONER WE CAN MOVE ON FROM HERE, THE BETTER. BECAUSE, MY FRIENDS, THE DEATH DEALERS ARE ALREADY HERE.

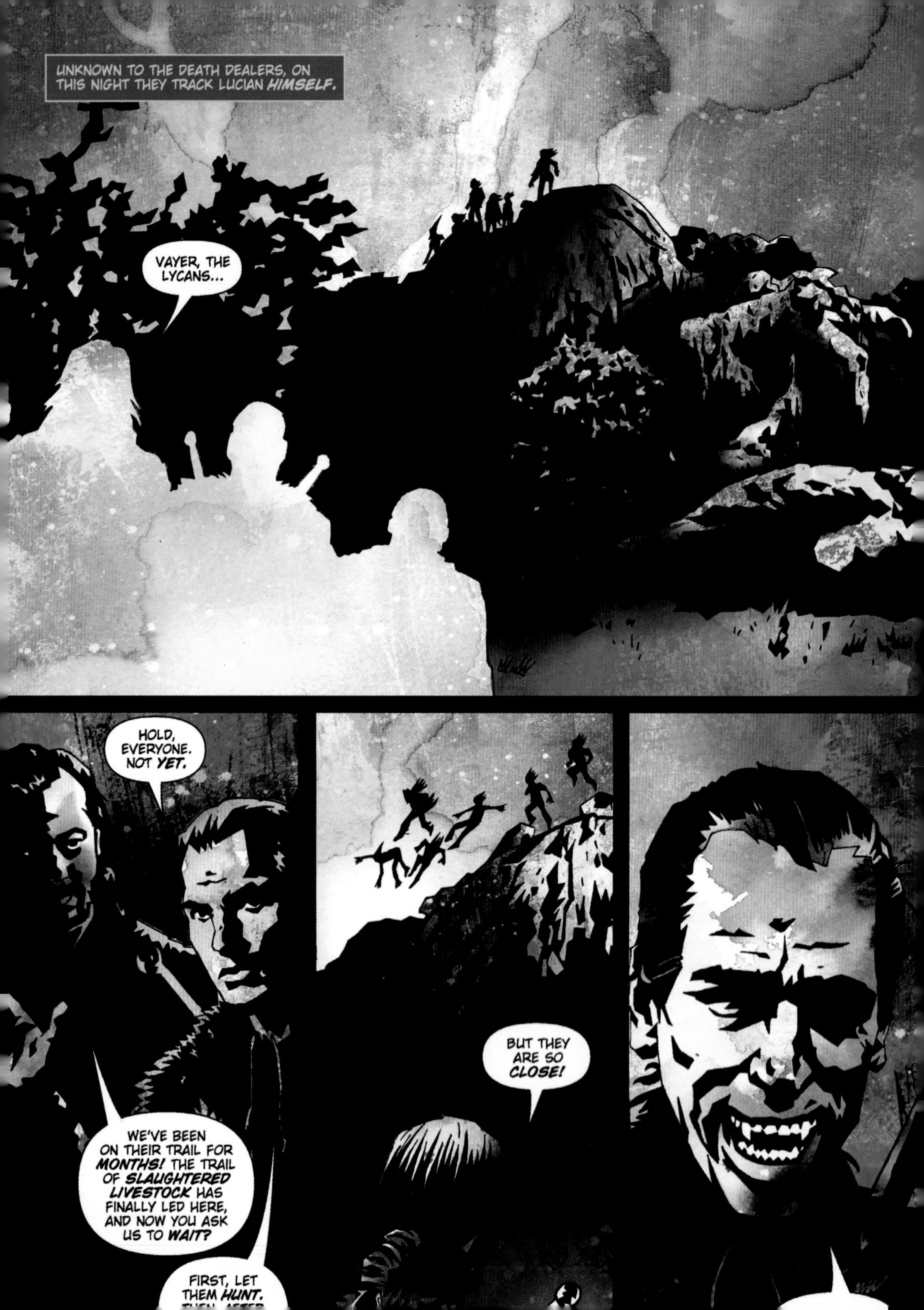
UNKNOWN TO THE DEATH DEALERS, ON THIS NIGHT THEY TRACK LUCIAN HIMSELF.
VAYER, THE LYCANS...
HOLD, EVERYONE. NOT YET.
WE'VE BEEN ON THEIR TRAIL FOR MONTHS! THE TRAIL OF SLAUGHTERED LIVESTOCK HAS FINALLY LED HERE, AND NOW YOU ASK US TO WAIT?
FIRST, LET THEM HUNT.
BUT THEY ARE SO CLOSE!

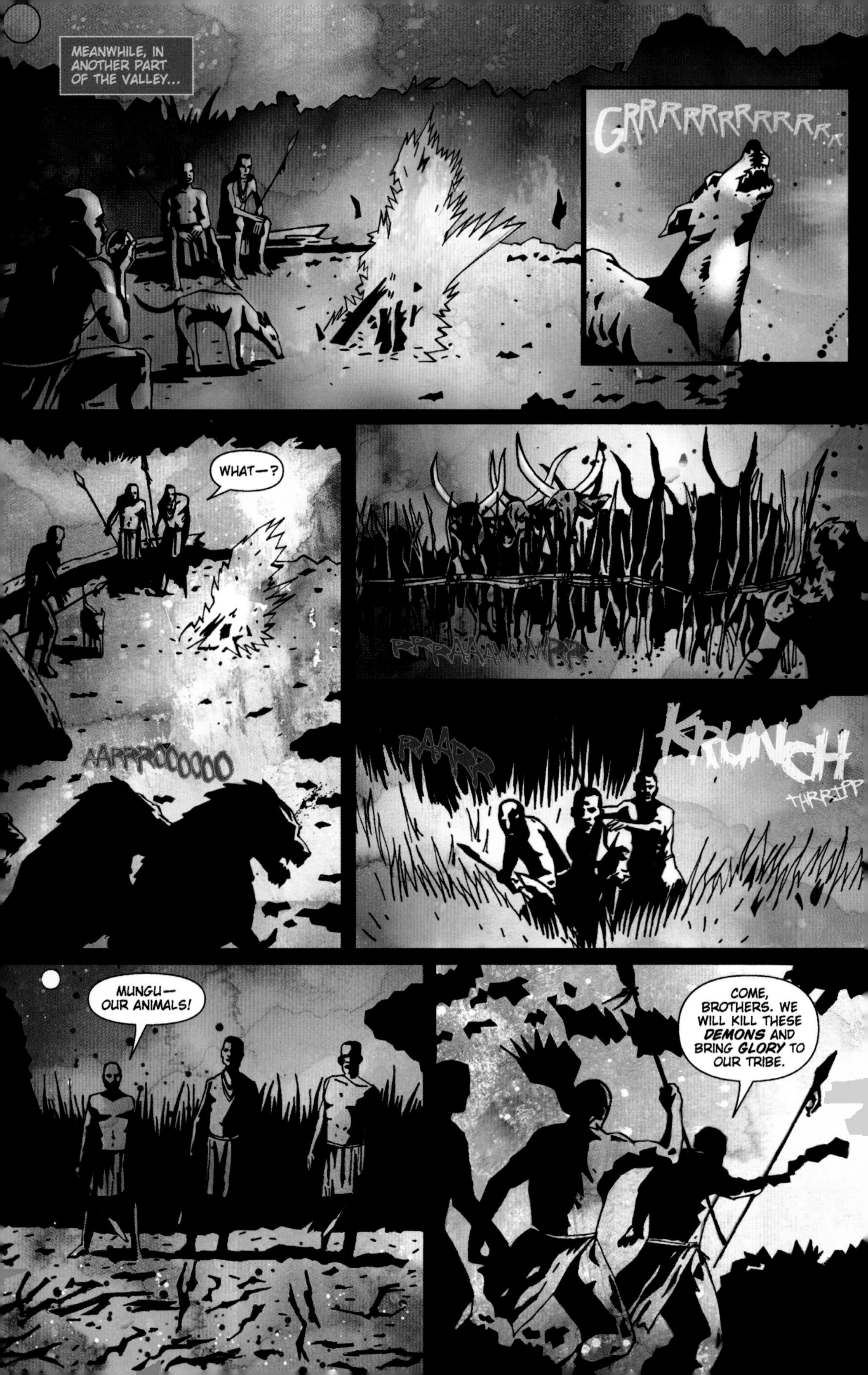
MEANWHILE, IN ANOTHER PART OF THE VALLEY...
GRRRRRRRRRRRR
WHAT—?
AARRRROOOOOO
RRRAAAWWRR
RAARR
KRUNCH
THRIPP
MUNGU— OUR ANIMALS!
COME, BROTHERS. WE WILL KILL THESE *DEMONS* AND BRING *GLORY* TO OUR TRIBE.

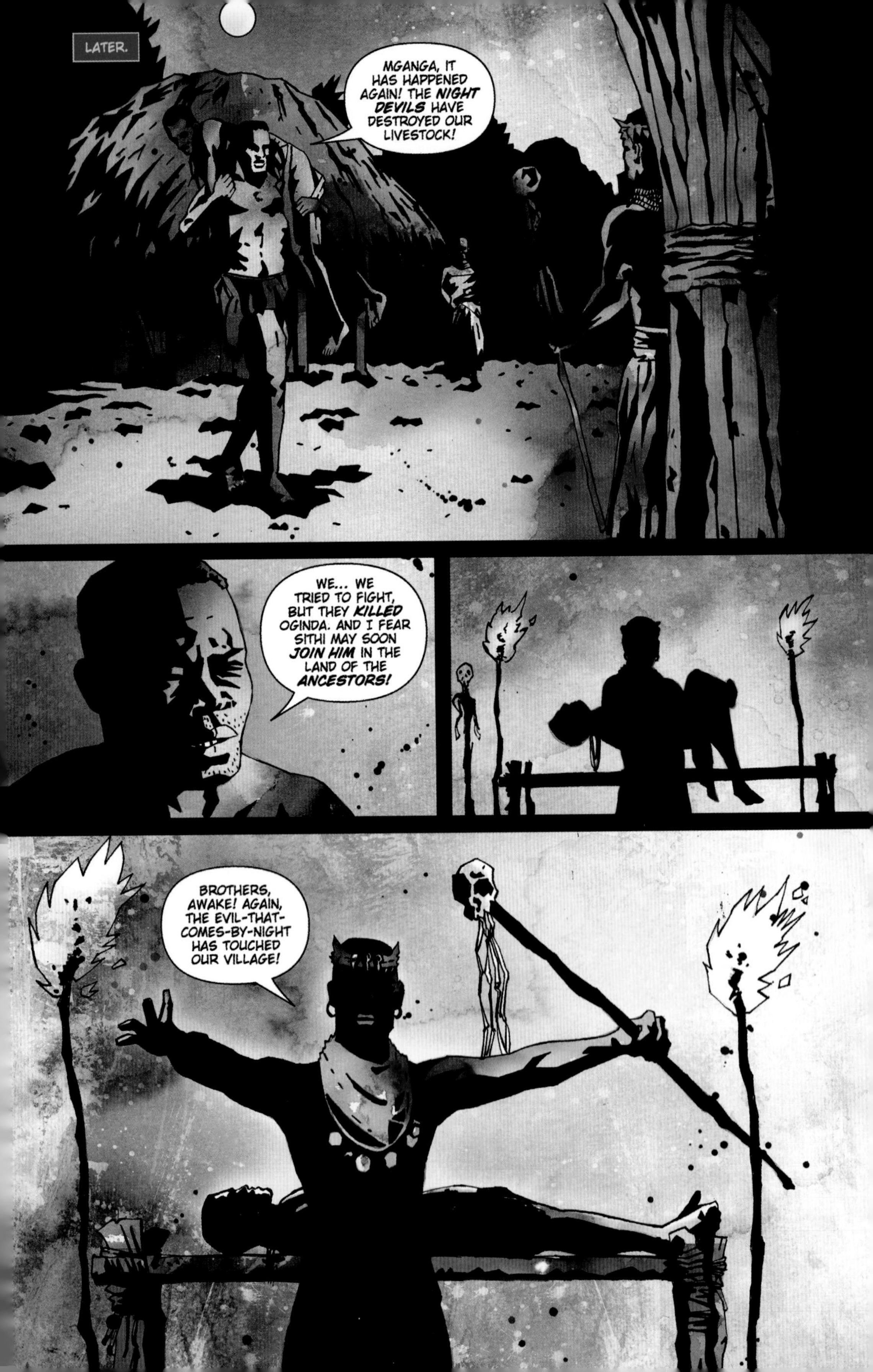
LATER.
MGANGA, IT HAS HAPPENED AGAIN! THE NIGHT DEVILS HAVE DESTROYED OUR LIVESTOCK!
WE... WE TRIED TO FIGHT, BUT THEY KILLED OGINDA. AND I FEAR SITHI MAY SOON JOIN HIM IN THE LAND OF THE ANCESTORS!
BROTHERS, AWAKE! AGAIN, THE EVIL-THAT-COMES-BY-NIGHT HAS TOUCHED OUR VILLAGE!

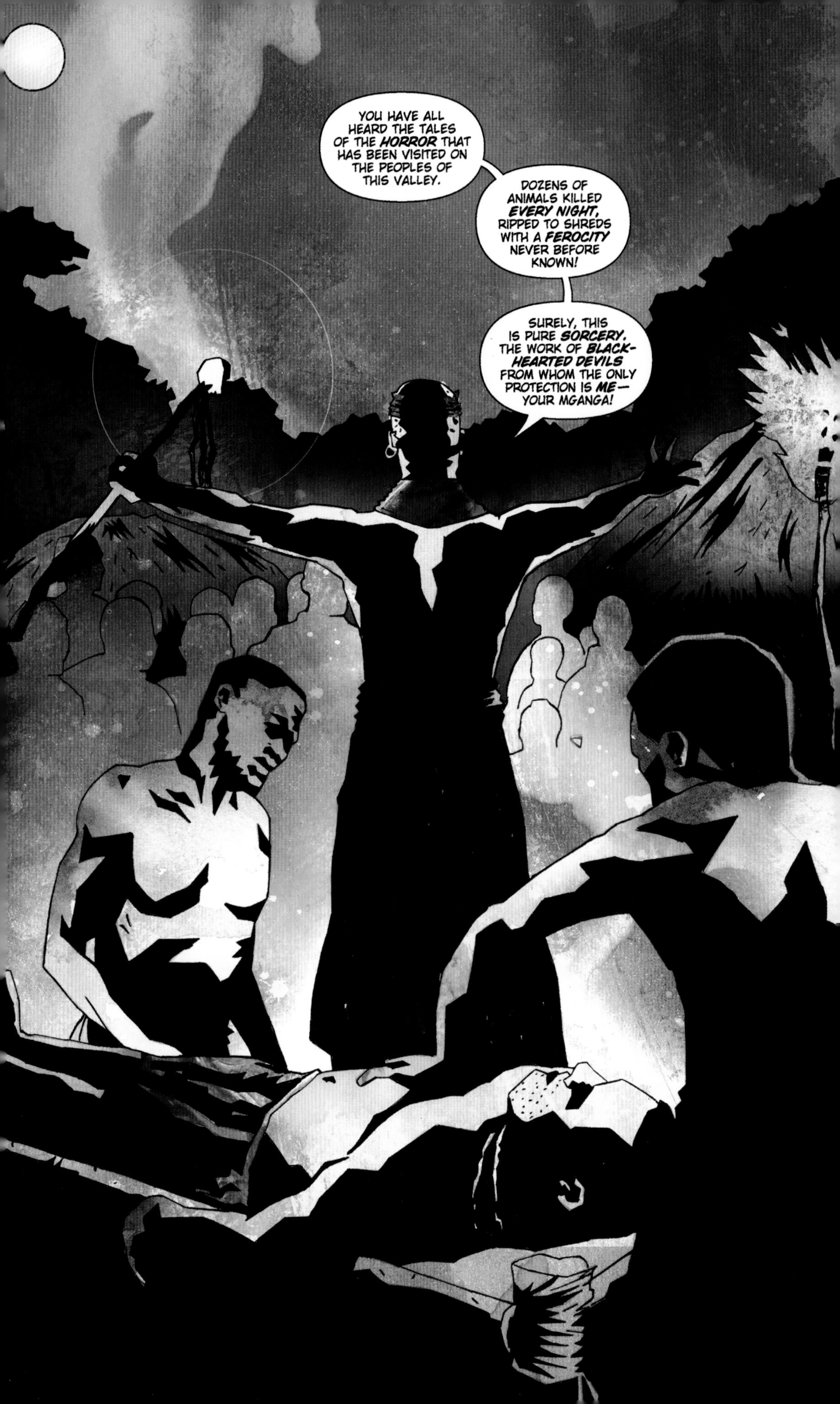
YOU HAVE ALL HEARD THE TALES OF THE *HORROR* THAT HAS BEEN VISITED ON THE PEOPLES OF THIS VALLEY.
DOZENS OF ANIMALS KILLED *EVERY NIGHT*, RIPPED TO SHREDS WITH A *FEROCITY* NEVER BEFORE KNOWN!
SURELY, THIS IS PURE *SORCERY*. THE WORK OF *BLACK-HEARTED DEVILS* FROM WHOM THE ONLY PROTECTION IS *ME*—YOUR MGANGA!

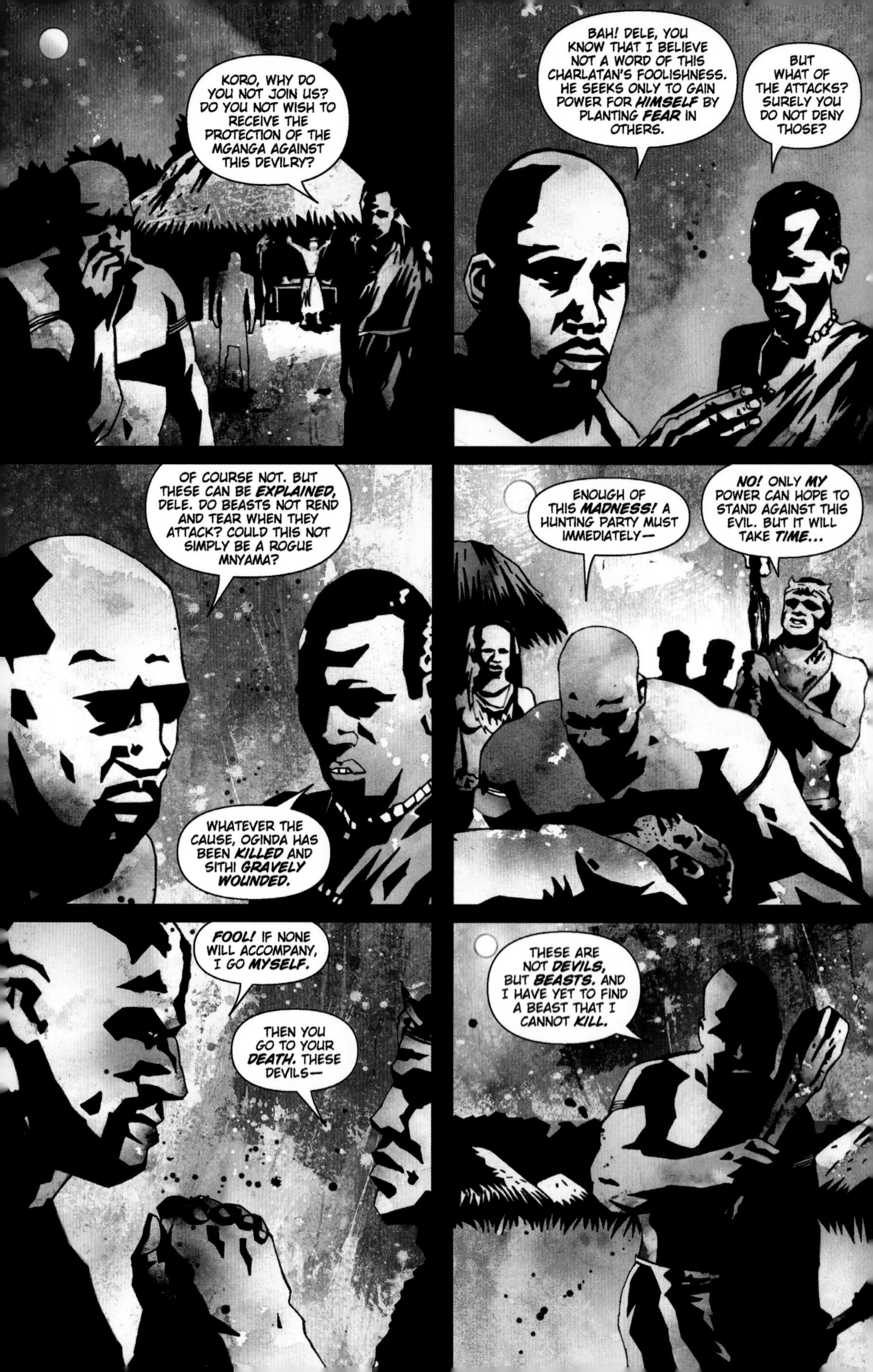
KORO, WHY DO YOU NOT JOIN US? DO YOU NOT WISH TO RECEIVE THE PROTECTION OF THE MGANGA AGAINST THIS DEVILRY?
BAH! DELE, YOU KNOW THAT I BELIEVE NOT A WORD OF THIS CHARLATAN'S FOOLISHNESS. HE SEEKS ONLY TO GAIN POWER FOR *HIMSELF* BY PLANTING *FEAR* IN OTHERS.
BUT WHAT OF THE ATTACKS? SURELY YOU DO NOT DENY THOSE?
OF COURSE NOT. BUT THESE CAN BE *EXPLAINED,* DELE. DO BEASTS NOT REND AND TEAR WHEN THEY ATTACK? COULD THIS NOT SIMPLY BE A ROGUE MNYAMA?
WHATEVER THE CAUSE, OGINDA HAS BEEN *KILLED* AND SITHI *GRAVELY WOUNDED.*
ENOUGH OF THIS *MADNESS!* A HUNTING PARTY MUST IMMEDIATELY—
NO! ONLY *MY* POWER CAN HOPE TO STAND AGAINST THIS EVIL. BUT IT WILL TAKE *TIME...*
FOOL! IF NONE WILL ACCOMPANY, I GO *MYSELF.*
THEN YOU GO TO YOUR *DEATH.* THESE DEVILS—
THESE ARE NOT *DEVILS,* BUT *BEASTS.* AND I HAVE YET TO FIND A BEAST THAT I CANNOT *KILL.*

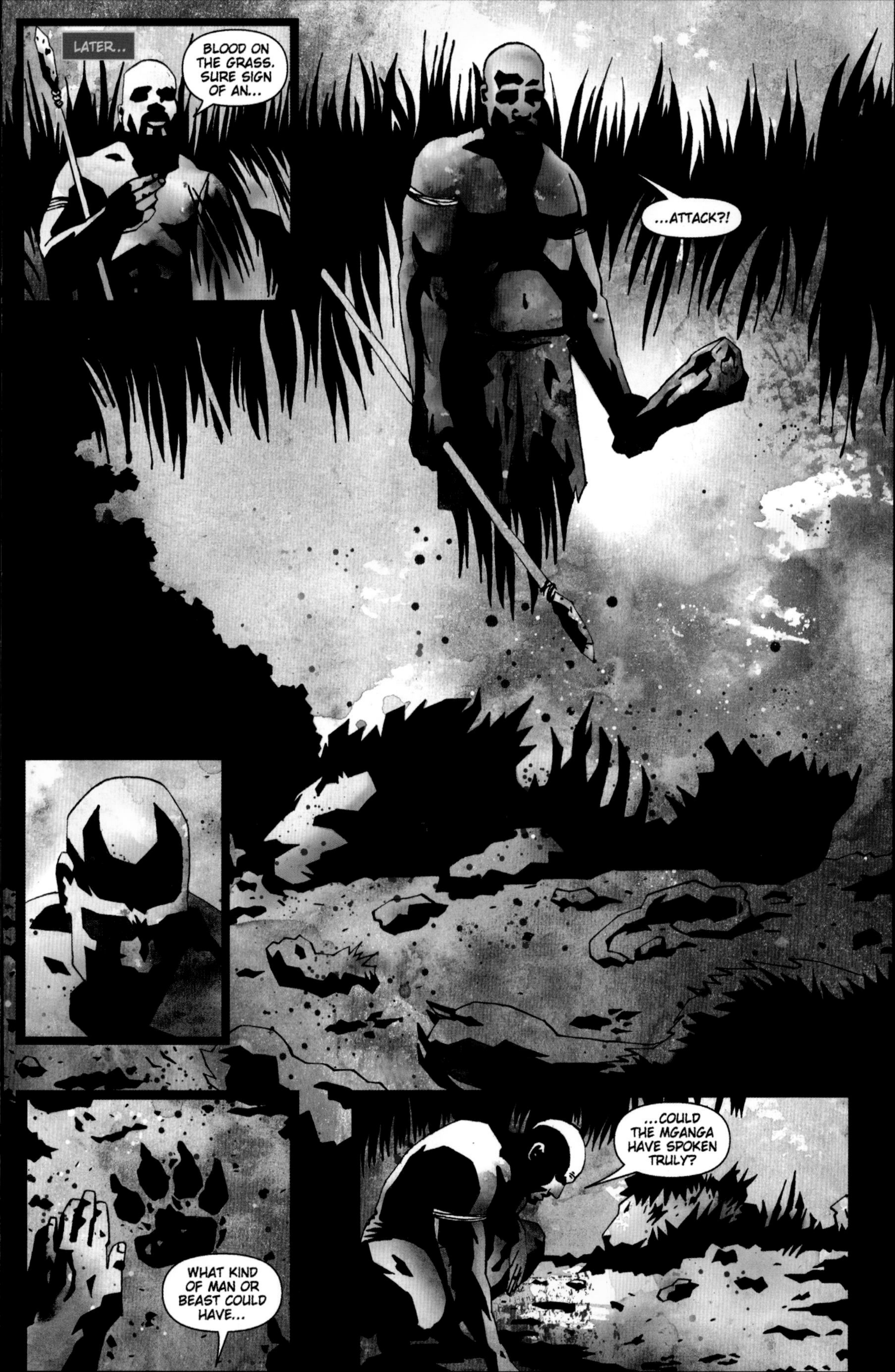
LATER...
BLOOD ON THE GRASS. SURE SIGN OF AN...
...ATTACK?!
WHAT KIND OF MAN OR BEAST COULD HAVE...
...COULD THE MGANGA HAVE SPOKEN TRULY?

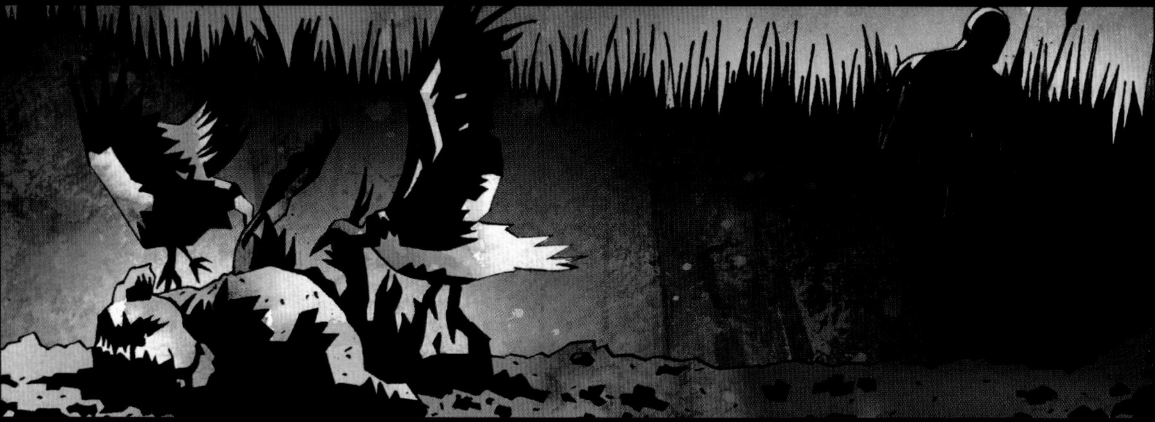

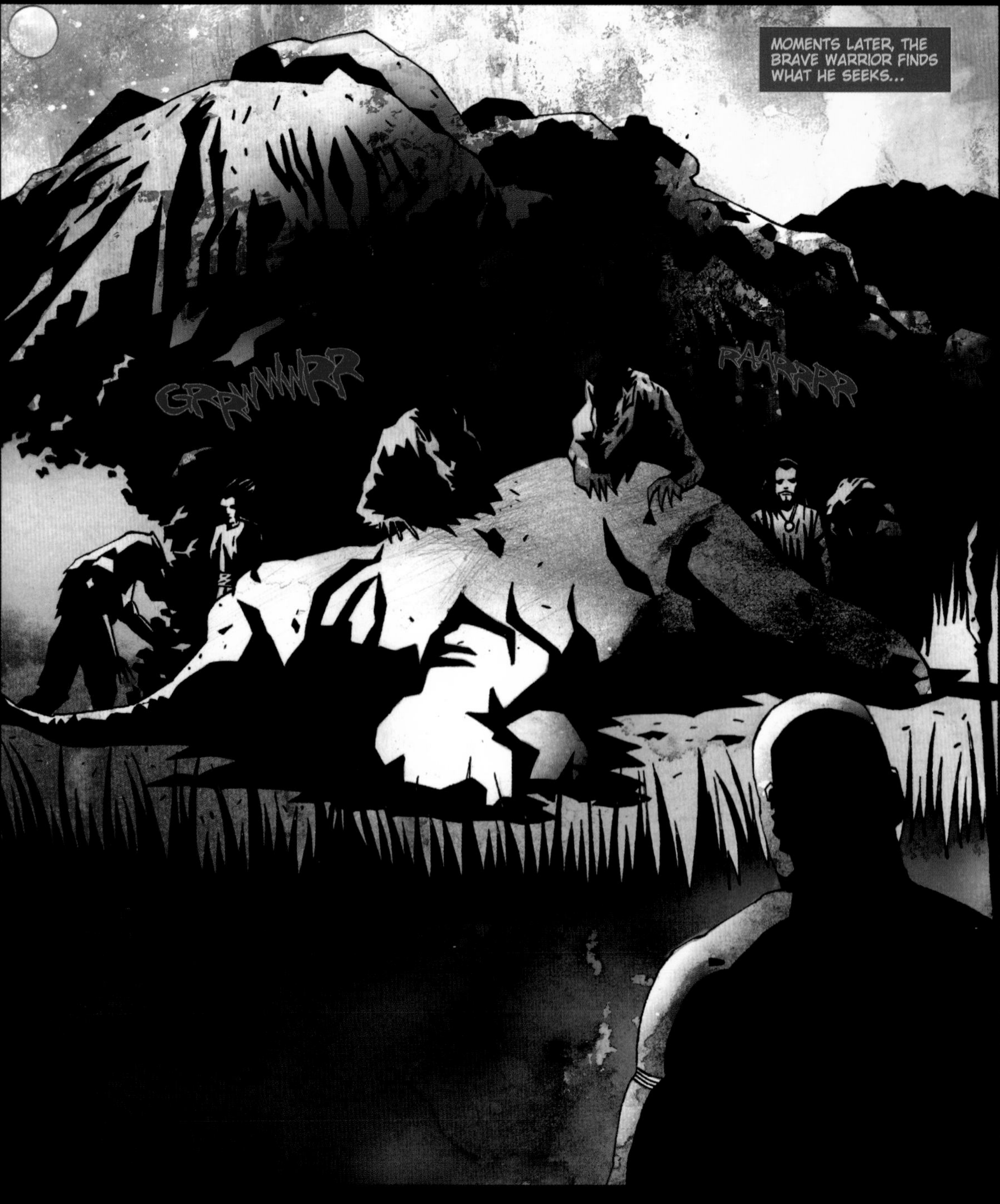
MOMENTS LATER, THE BRAVE WARRIOR FINDS WHAT HE SEEKS...
GRRWWWRR
RAARRRR

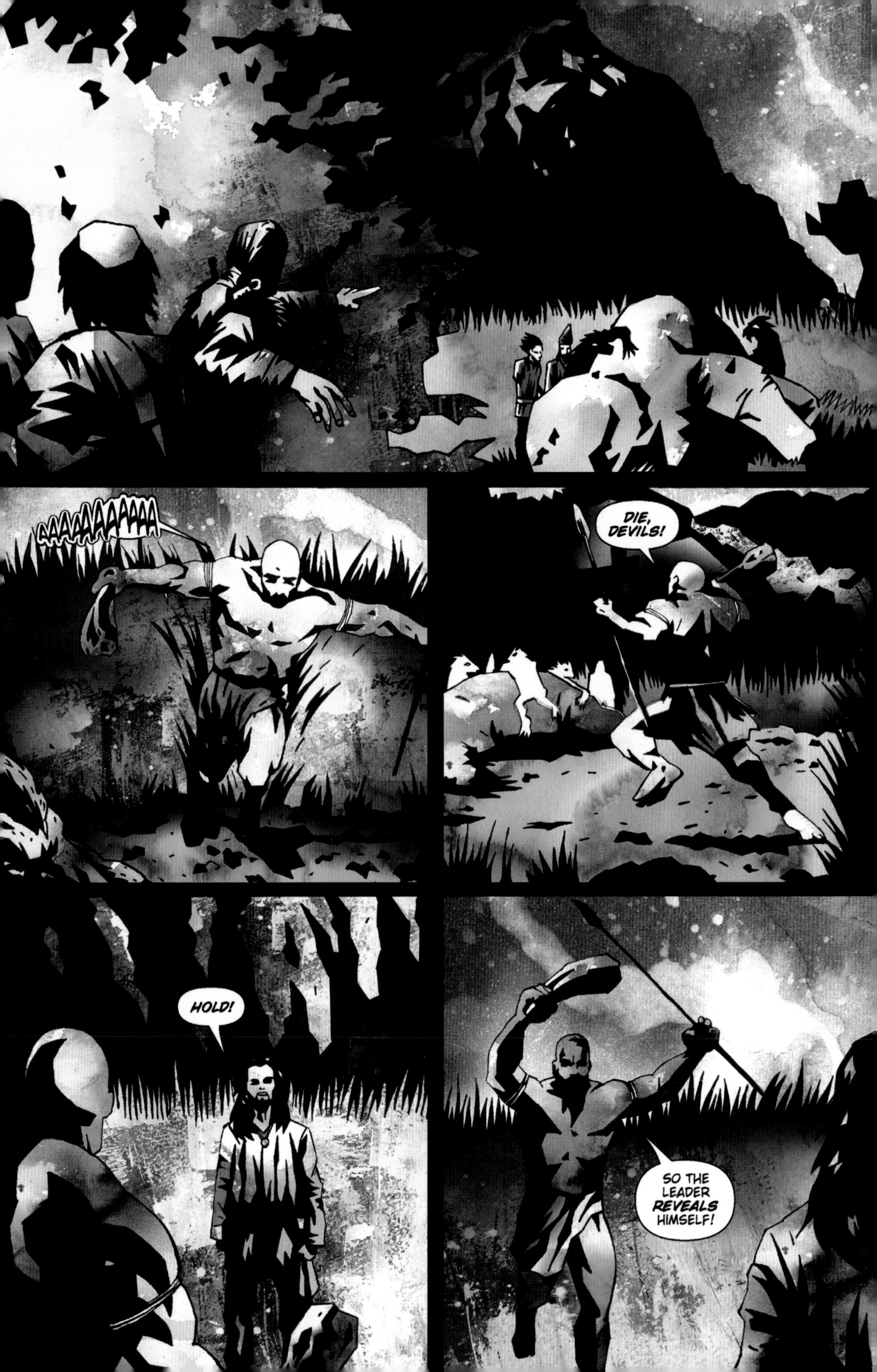
AAAAAAAAAAAA
DIE, DEVILS!
HOLD!
SO THE LEADER REVEALS HIMSELF!

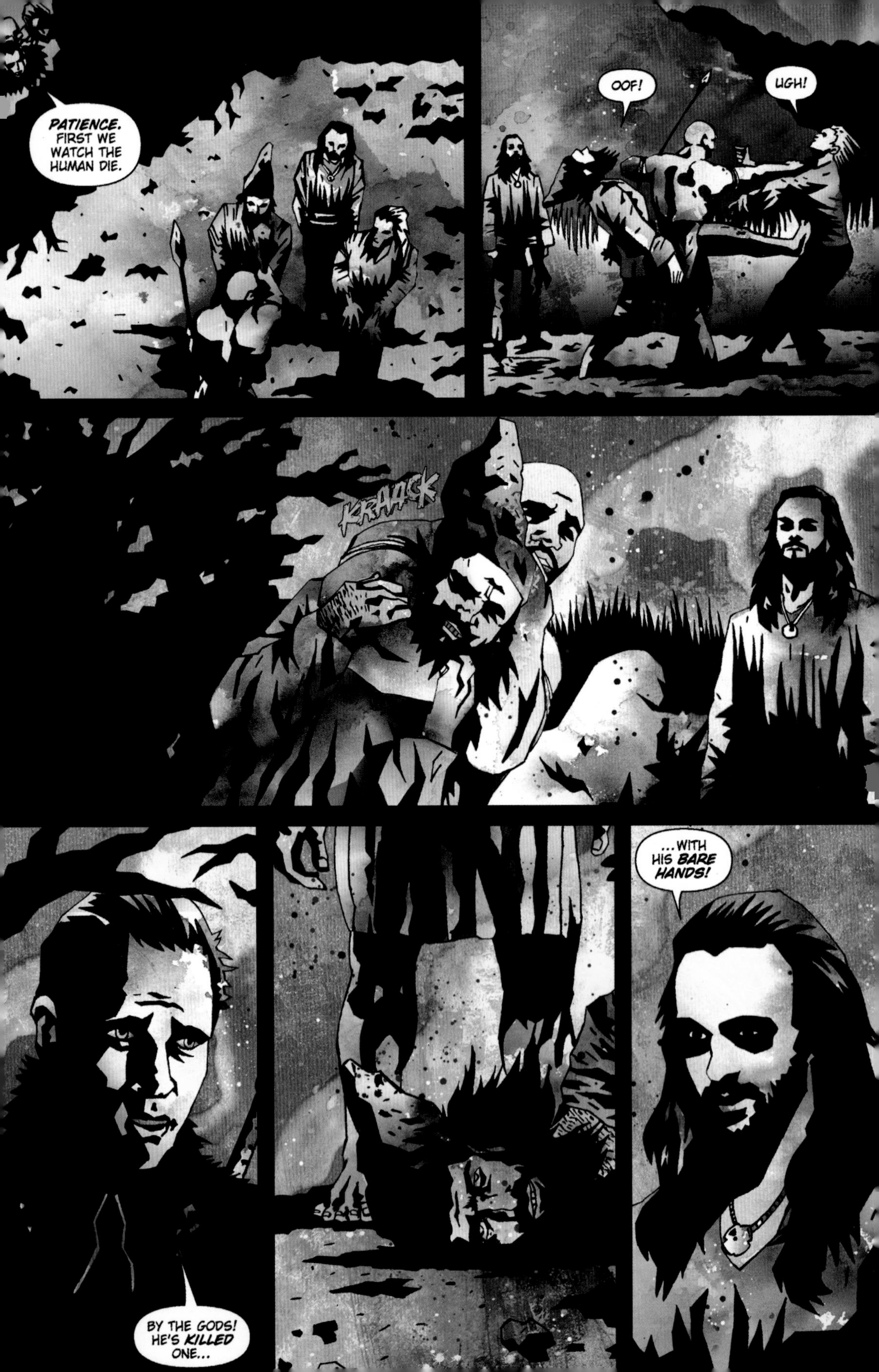
PATIENCE. FIRST WE WATCH THE HUMAN DIE.
OOF!
UGH!
KRAACK
BY THE GODS! HE'S KILLED ONE...
...WITH HIS BARE HANDS!

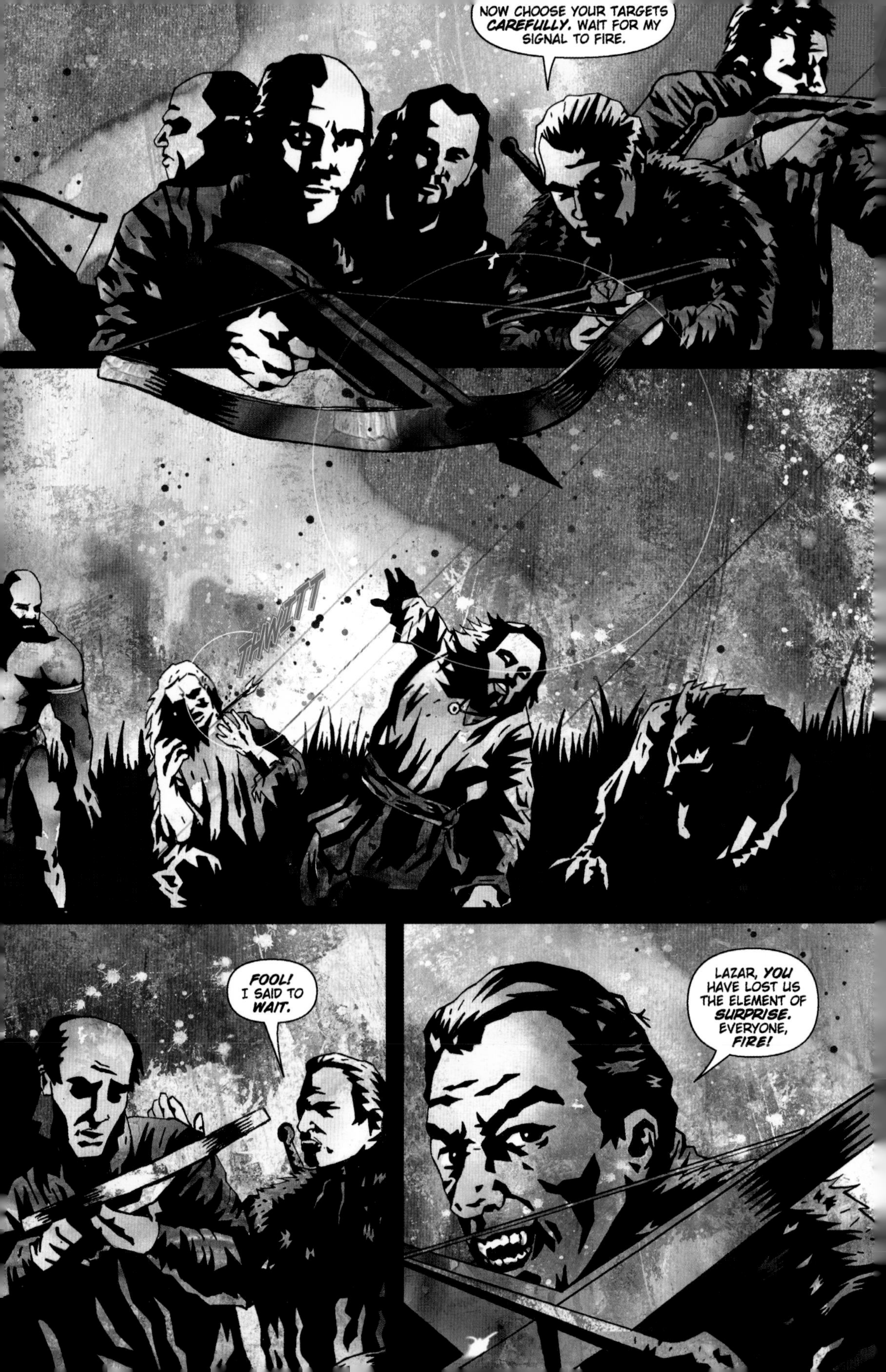
NOW CHOOSE YOUR TARGETS CAREFULLY. WAIT FOR MY SIGNAL TO FIRE.
THWITT
FOOL! I SAID TO WAIT.
LAZAR, YOU HAVE LOST US THE ELEMENT OF SURPRISE. EVERYONE, FIRE!

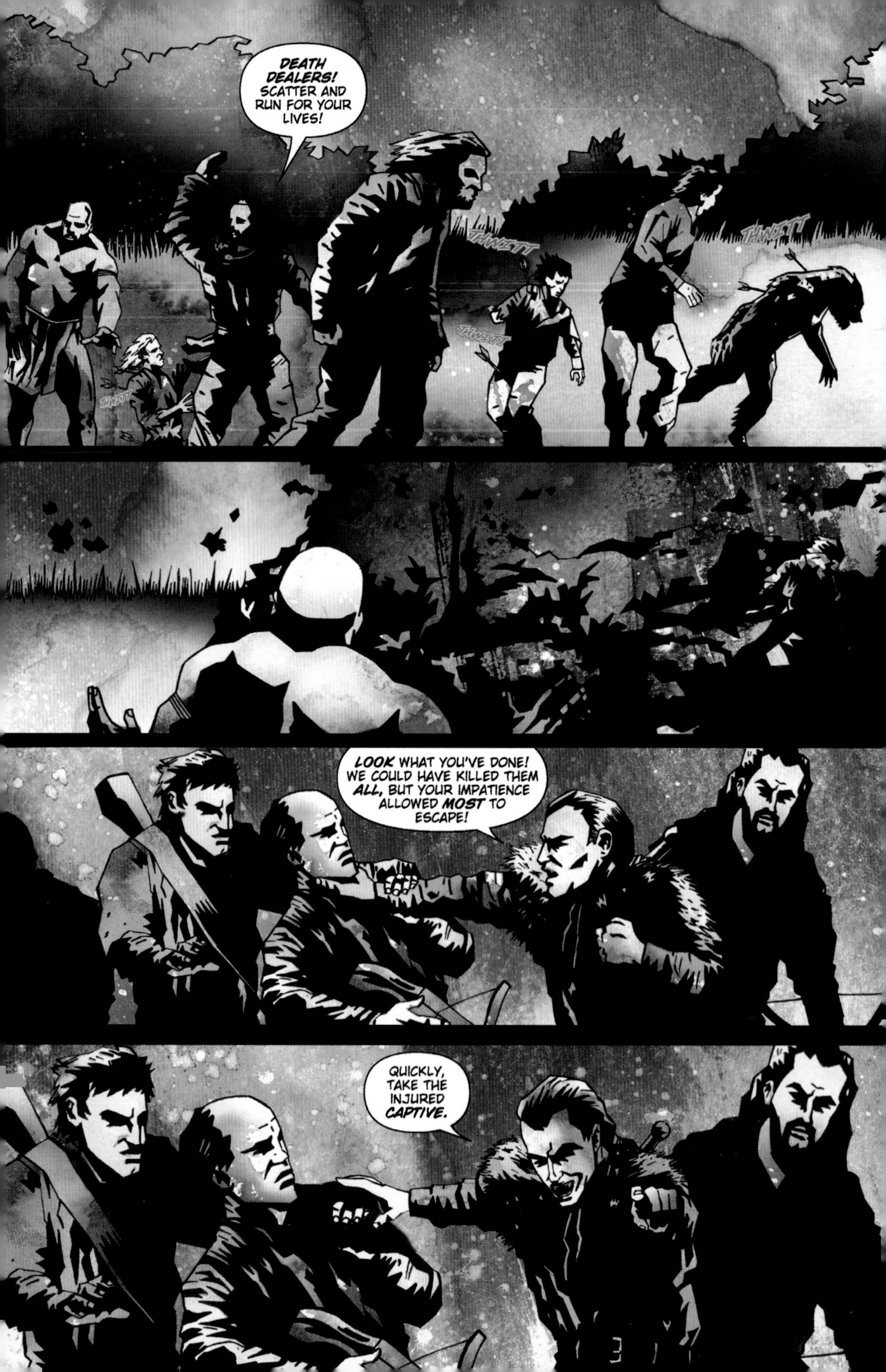
DEATH DEALERS! SCATTER AND RUN FOR YOUR LIVES!
LOOK WHAT YOU'VE DONE! WE COULD HAVE KILLED THEM ALL, BUT YOUR IMPATIENCE ALLOWED MOST TO ESCAPE!
QUICKLY, TAKE THE INJURED CAPTIVE.

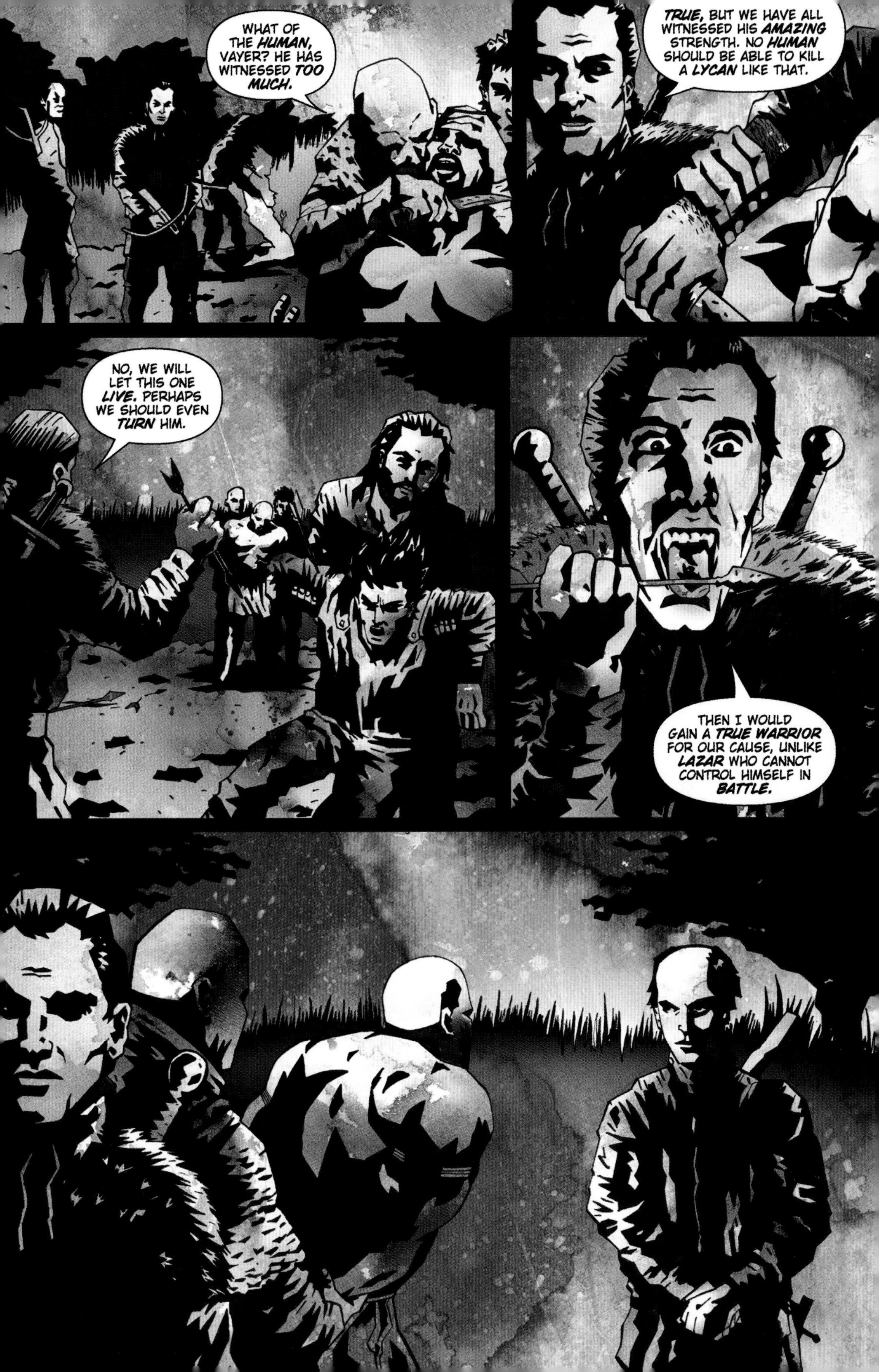
WHAT OF THE HUMAN, VAYER? HE HAS WITNESSED TOO MUCH.
TRUE, BUT WE HAVE ALL WITNESSED HIS AMAZING STRENGTH. NO HUMAN SHOULD BE ABLE TO KILL A LYCAN LIKE THAT.
NO, WE WILL LET THIS ONE LIVE. PERHAPS WE SHOULD EVEN TURN HIM.
THEN I WOULD GAIN A TRUE WARRIOR FOR OUR CAUSE, UNLIKE LAZAR WHO CANNOT CONTROL HIMSELF IN BATTLE.

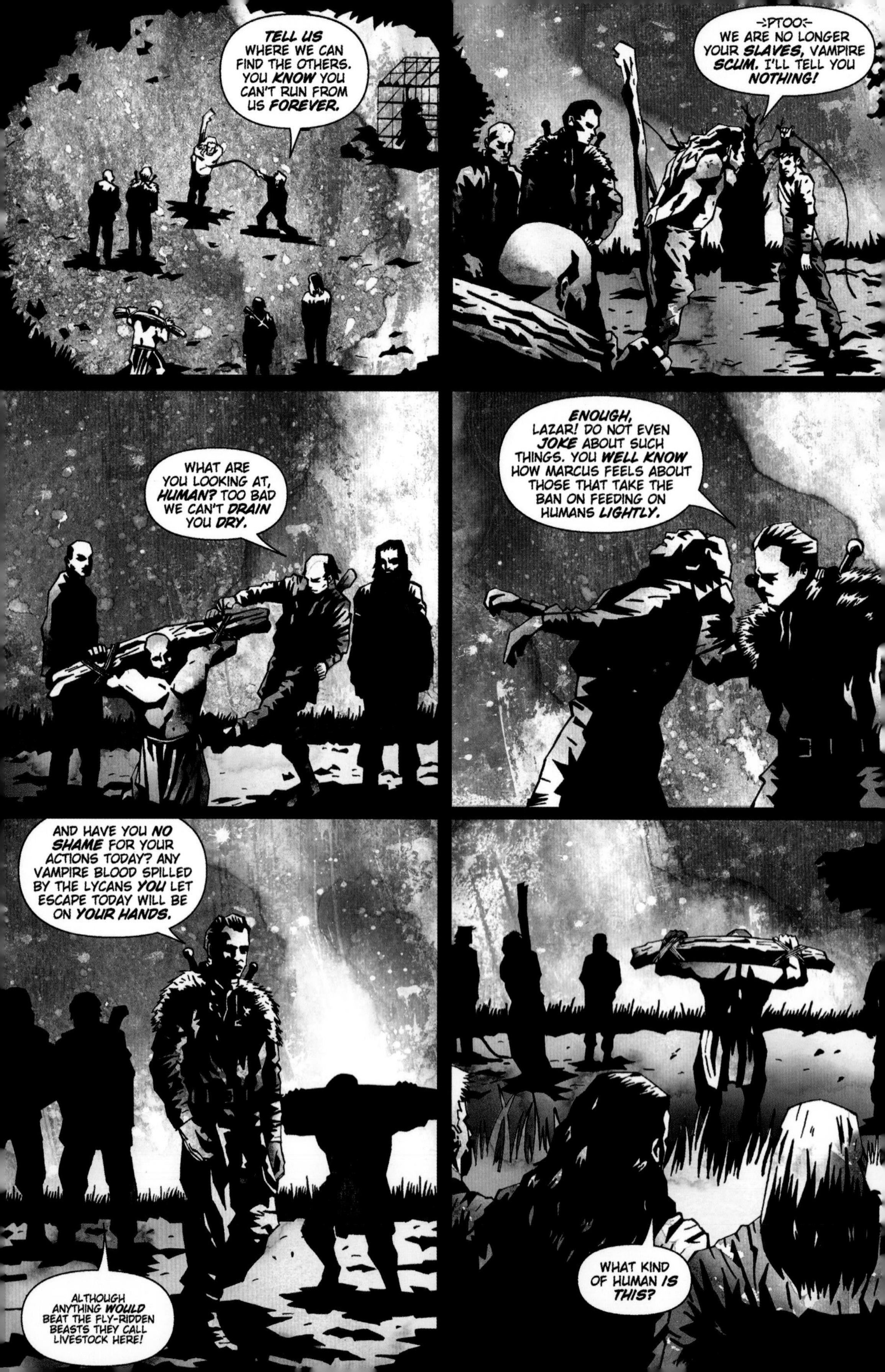
TELL US WHERE WE CAN FIND THE OTHERS. YOU KNOW YOU CAN'T RUN FROM US FOREVER.
-PTOO-
WE ARE NO LONGER YOUR SLAVES, VAMPIRE SCUM. I'LL TELL YOU NOTHING!
WHAT ARE YOU LOOKING AT, HUMAN? TOO BAD WE CAN'T DRAIN YOU DRY.
ENOUGH, LAZAR! DO NOT EVEN JOKE ABOUT SUCH THINGS. YOU WELL KNOW HOW MARCUS FEELS ABOUT THOSE THAT TAKE THE BAN ON FEEDING ON HUMANS LIGHTLY.
AND HAVE YOU NO SHAME FOR YOUR ACTIONS TODAY? ANY VAMPIRE BLOOD SPILLED BY THE LYCANS YOU LET ESCAPE TODAY WILL BE ON YOUR HANDS.
ALTHOUGH ANYTHING WOULD BEAT THE FLY-RIDDEN BEASTS THEY CALL LIVESTOCK HERE!
WHAT KIND OF HUMAN IS THIS?

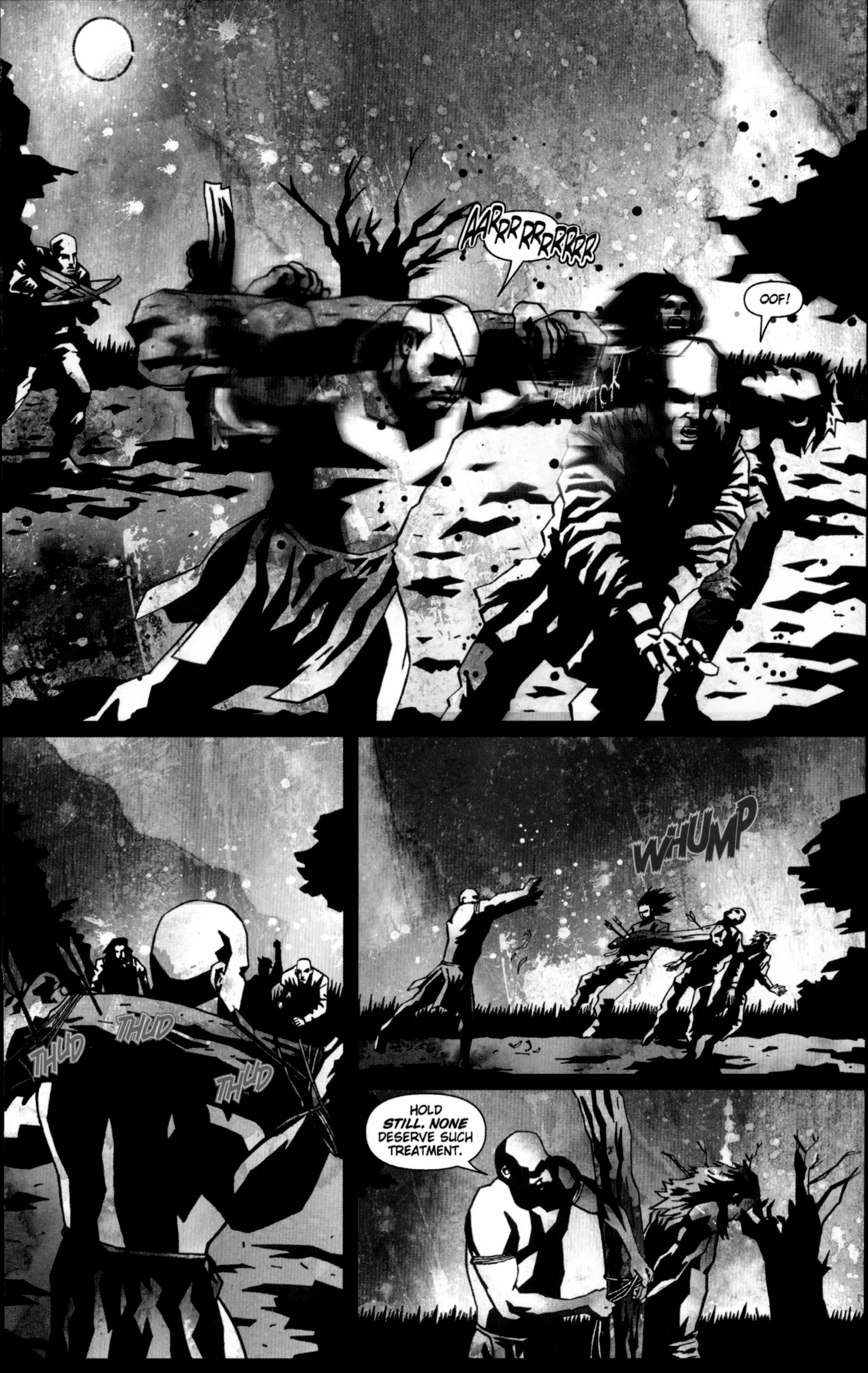
AARRRRRRRRRR
OOF!
THWACK
THUD
THUD
THUD
WHUMP
HOLD STILL. NONE DESERVE SUCH TREATMENT.

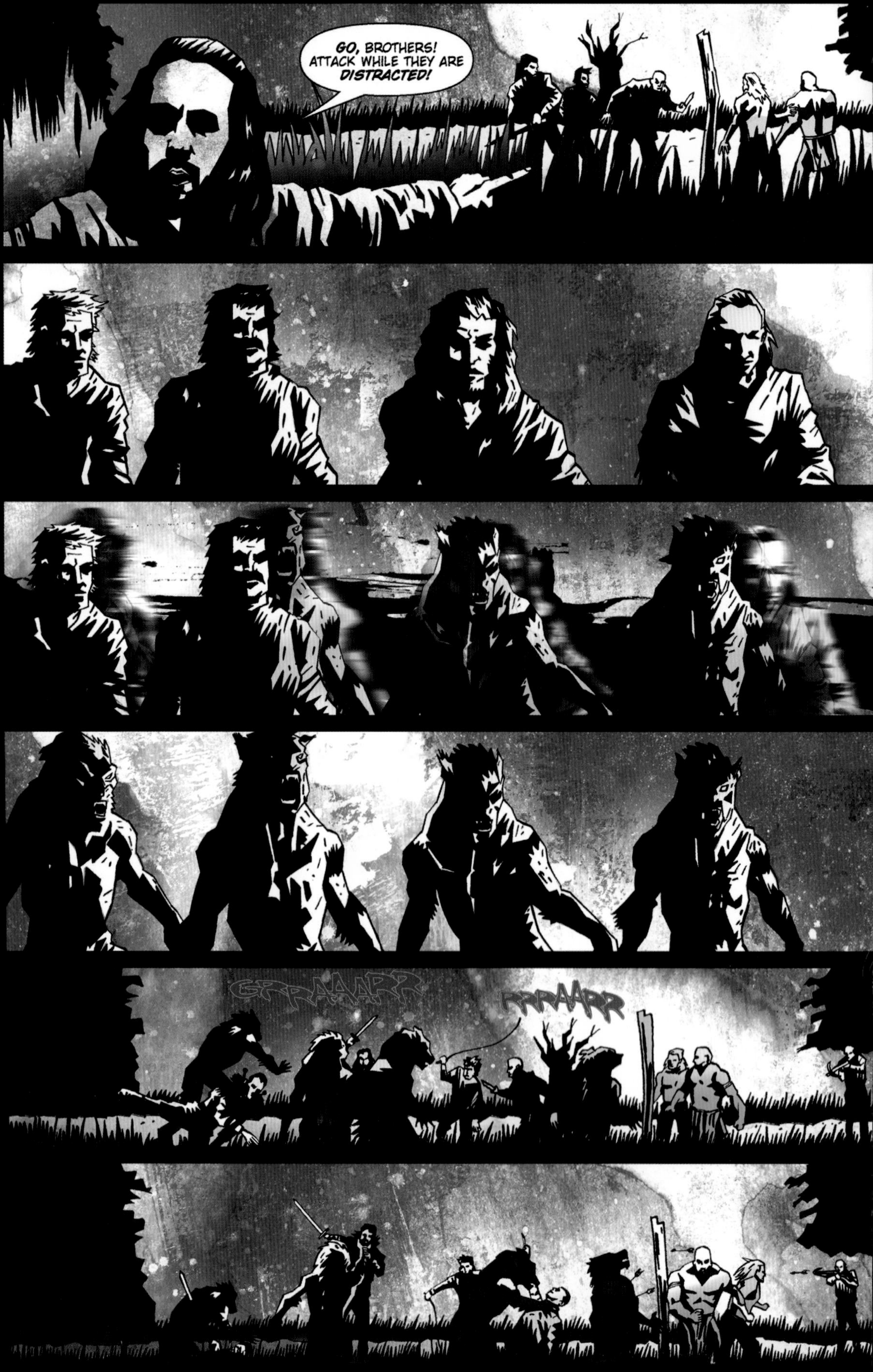
GO, BROTHERS! ATTACK WHILE THEY ARE DISTRACTED!
GRRAAARR
RRRAARR

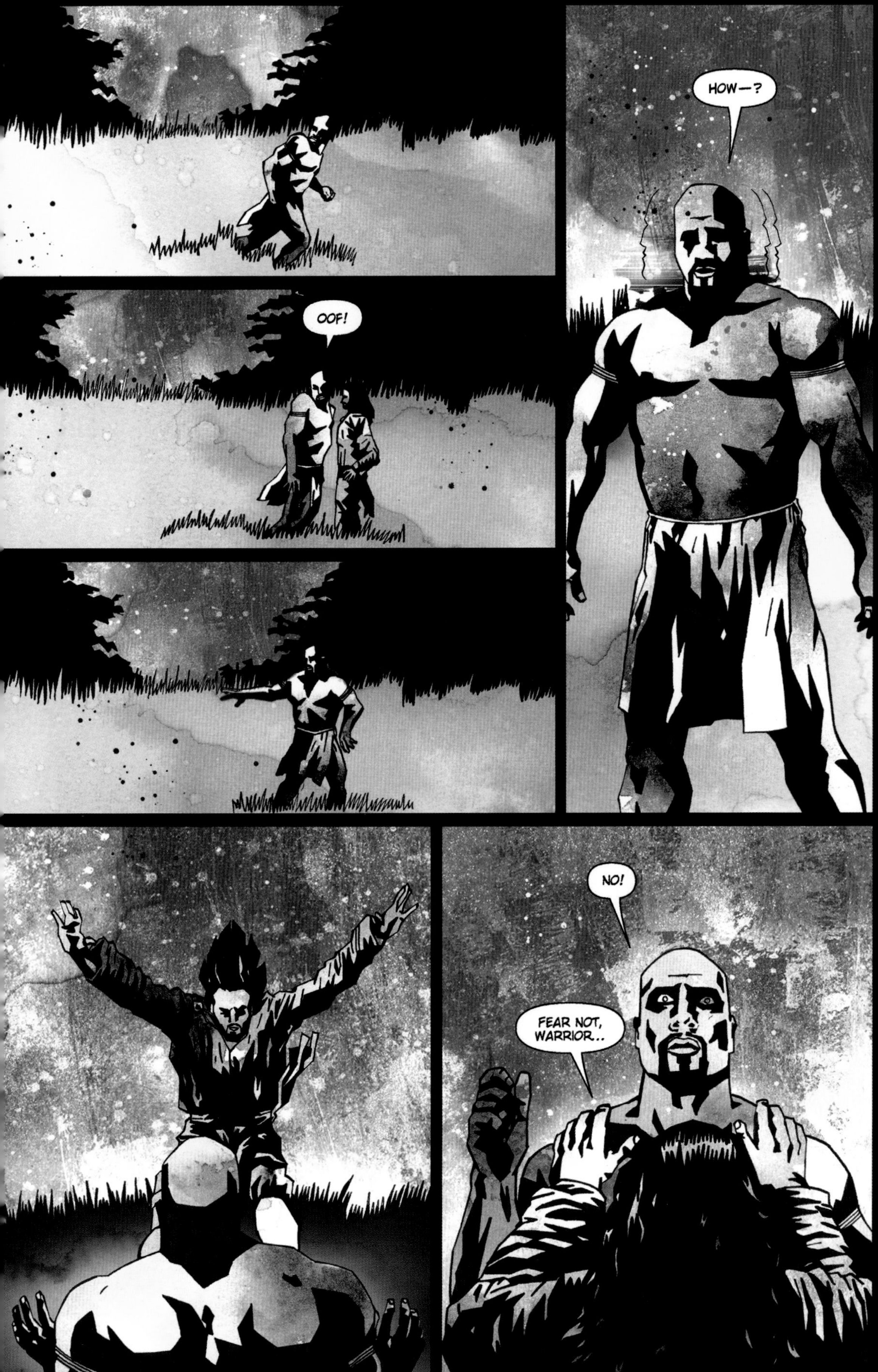
OOF!
HOW—?
NO!
FEAR NOT, WARRIOR...

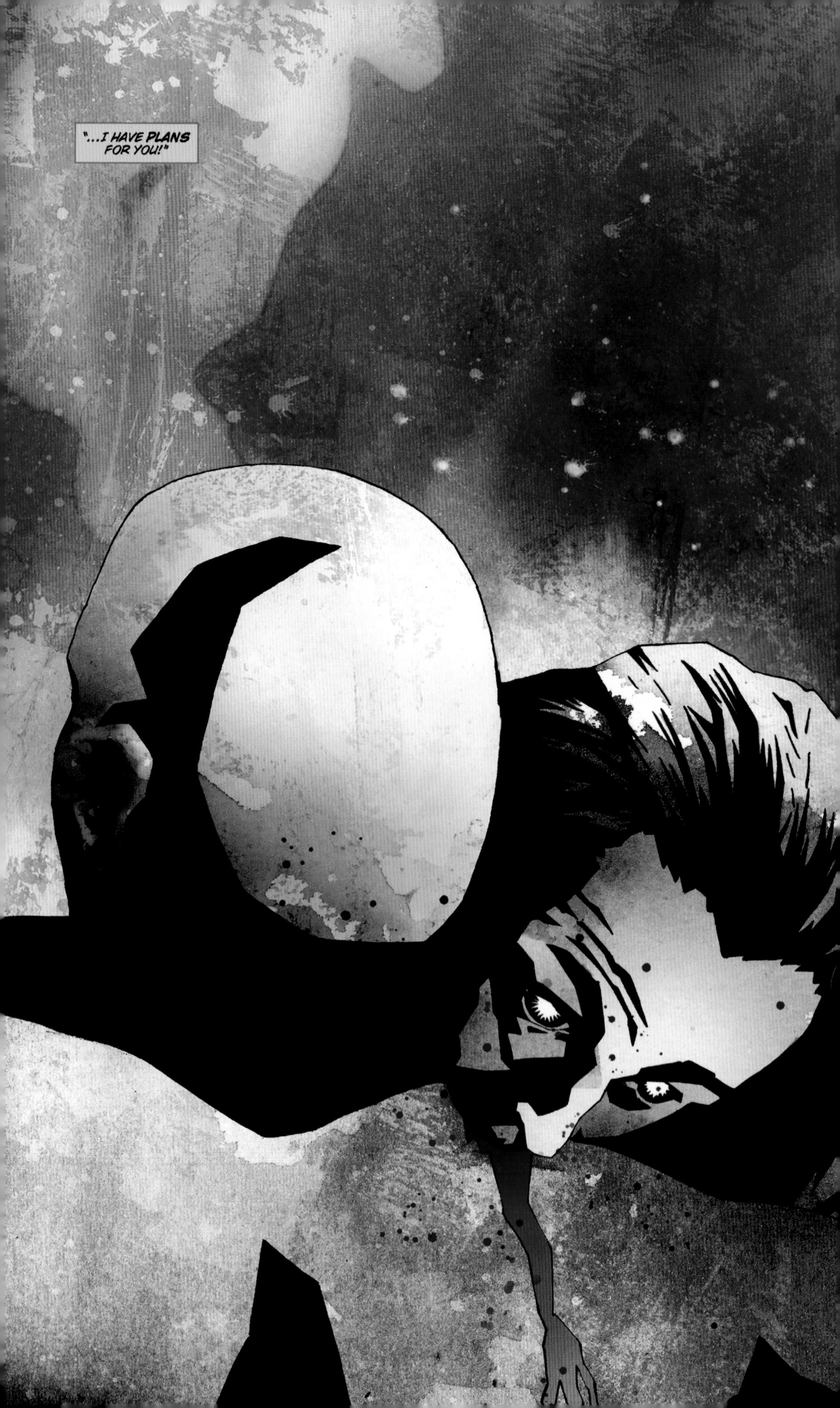
"...I HAVE PLANS FOR YOU!"

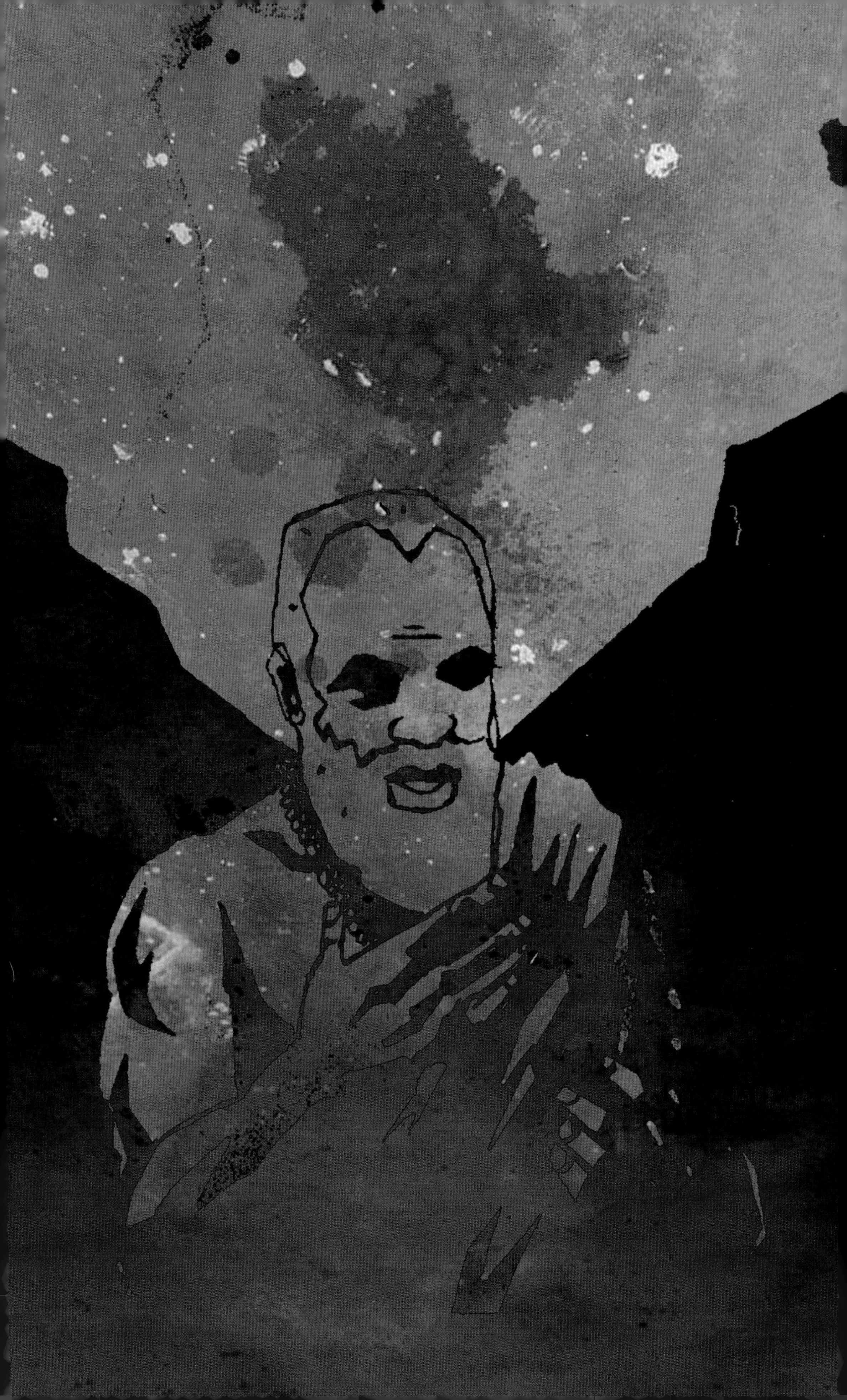

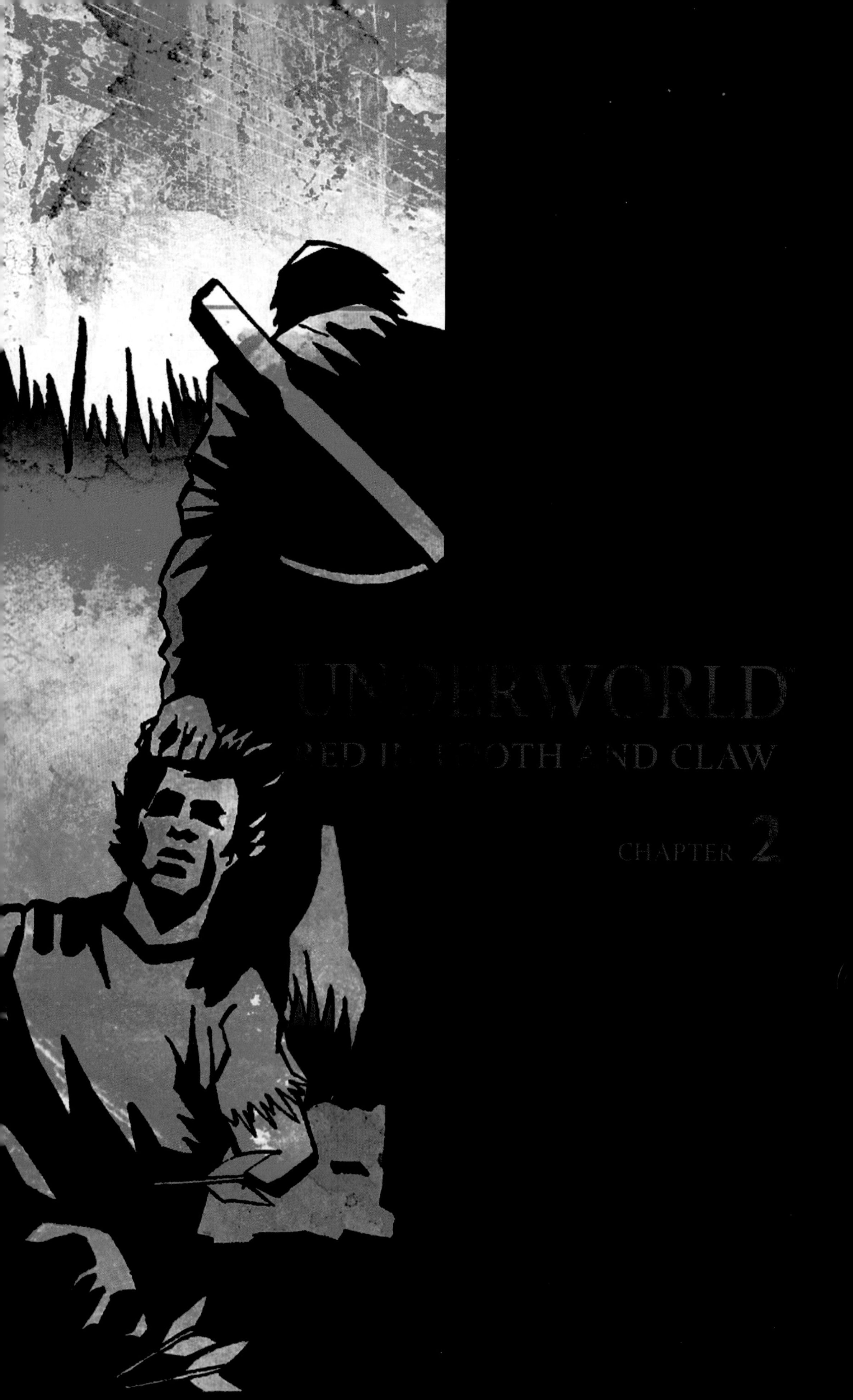

UNDERWORLD

RED IN TOOTH AND CLAW

CHAPTER 2

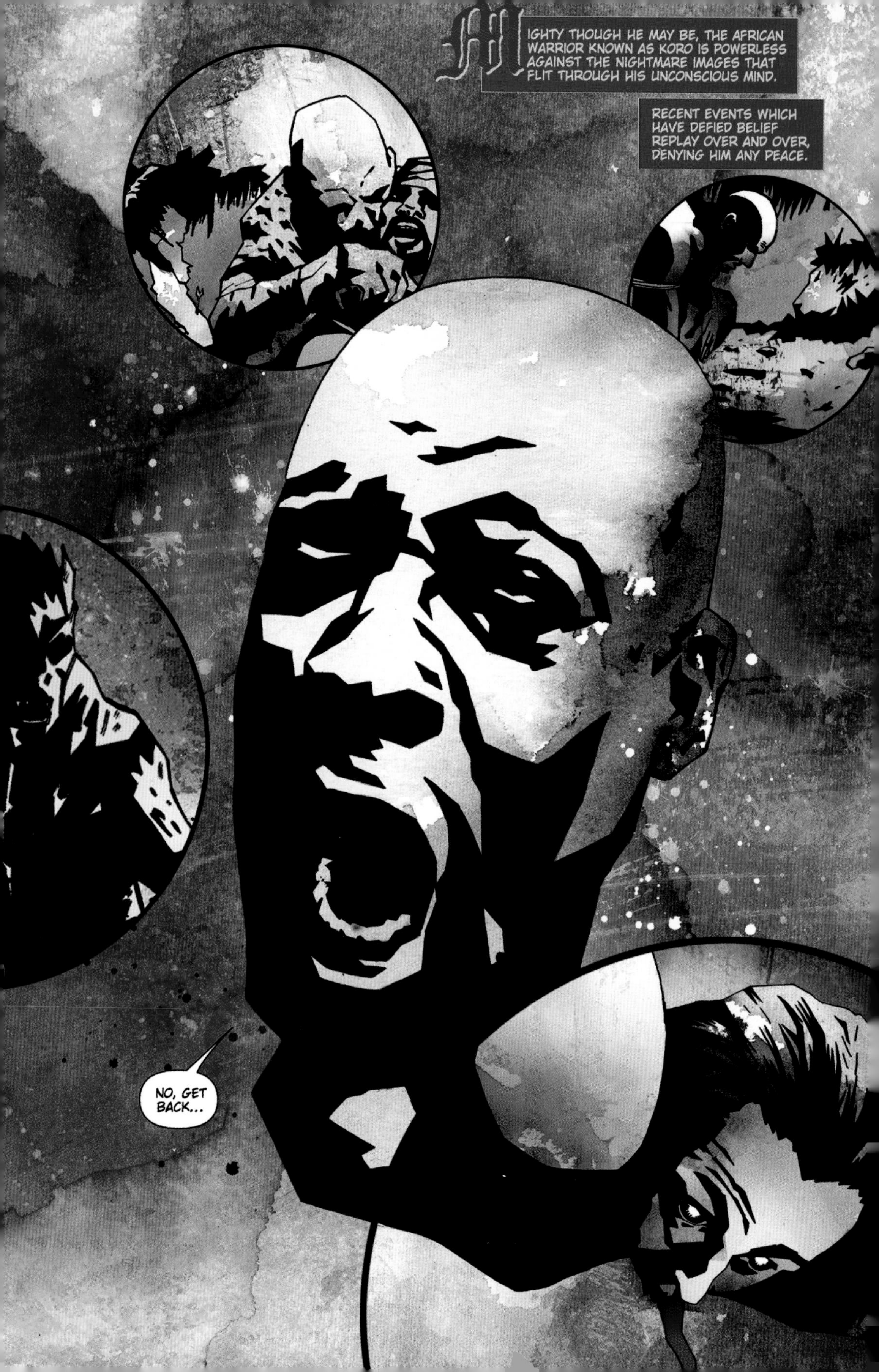
MIGHTY THOUGH HE MAY BE, THE AFRICAN WARRIOR KNOWN AS KORO IS POWERLESS AGAINST THE NIGHTMARE IMAGES THAT FLIT THROUGH HIS UNCONSCIOUS MIND.
RECENT EVENTS WHICH HAVE DEFIED BELIEF REPLAY OVER AND OVER, DENYING HIM ANY PEACE.
NO, GET BACK...

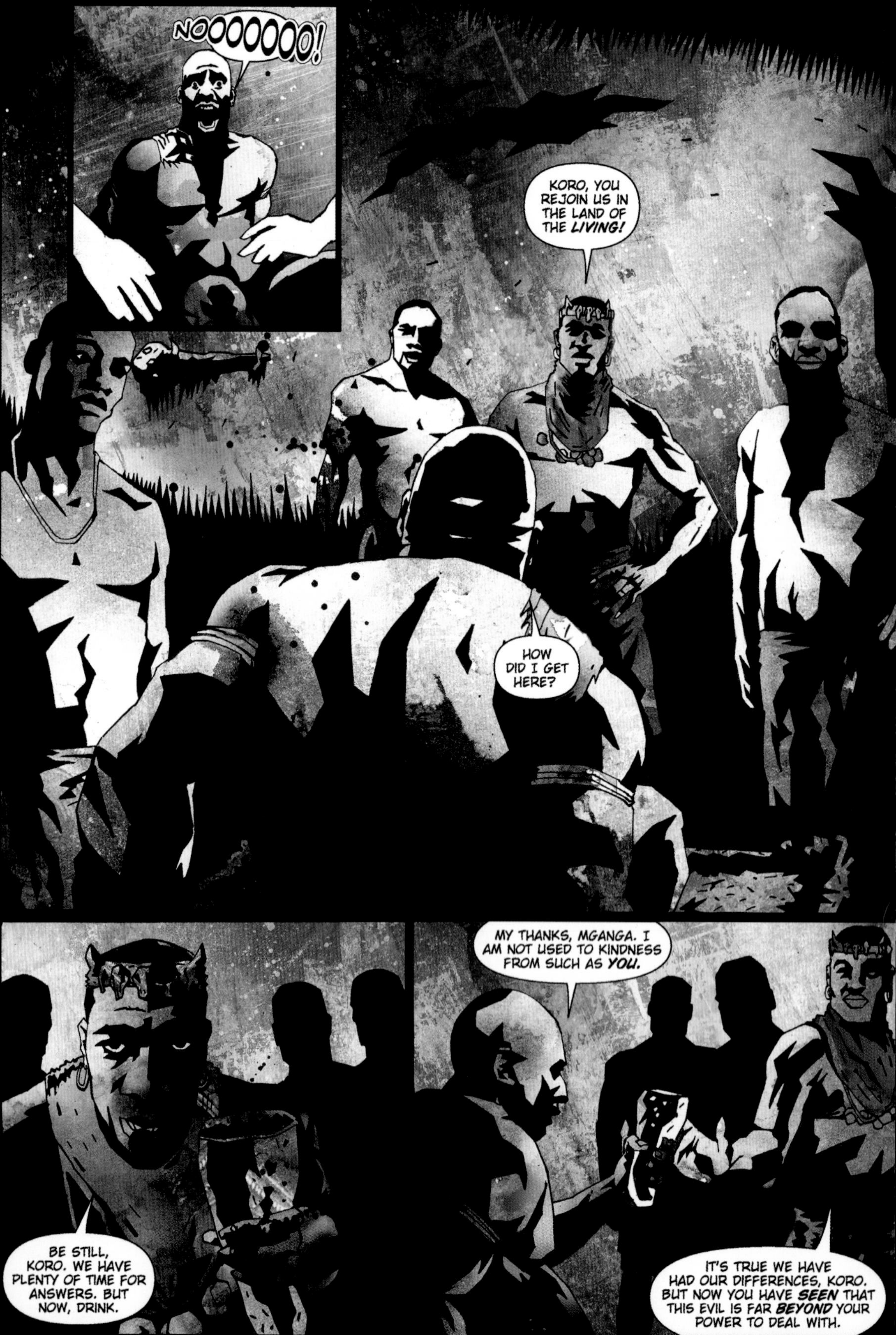
NOOOOOOO!
KORO, YOU REJOIN US IN THE LAND OF THE *LIVING!*
HOW DID I GET HERE?
BE STILL, KORO. WE HAVE PLENTY OF TIME FOR ANSWERS. BUT NOW, DRINK.
MY THANKS, MGANGA. I AM NOT USED TO KINDNESS FROM SUCH AS *YOU.*
IT'S TRUE WE HAVE HAD OUR DIFFERENCES, KORO. BUT NOW YOU HAVE *SEEN* THAT THIS EVIL IS FAR *BEYOND* YOUR POWER TO DEAL WITH.

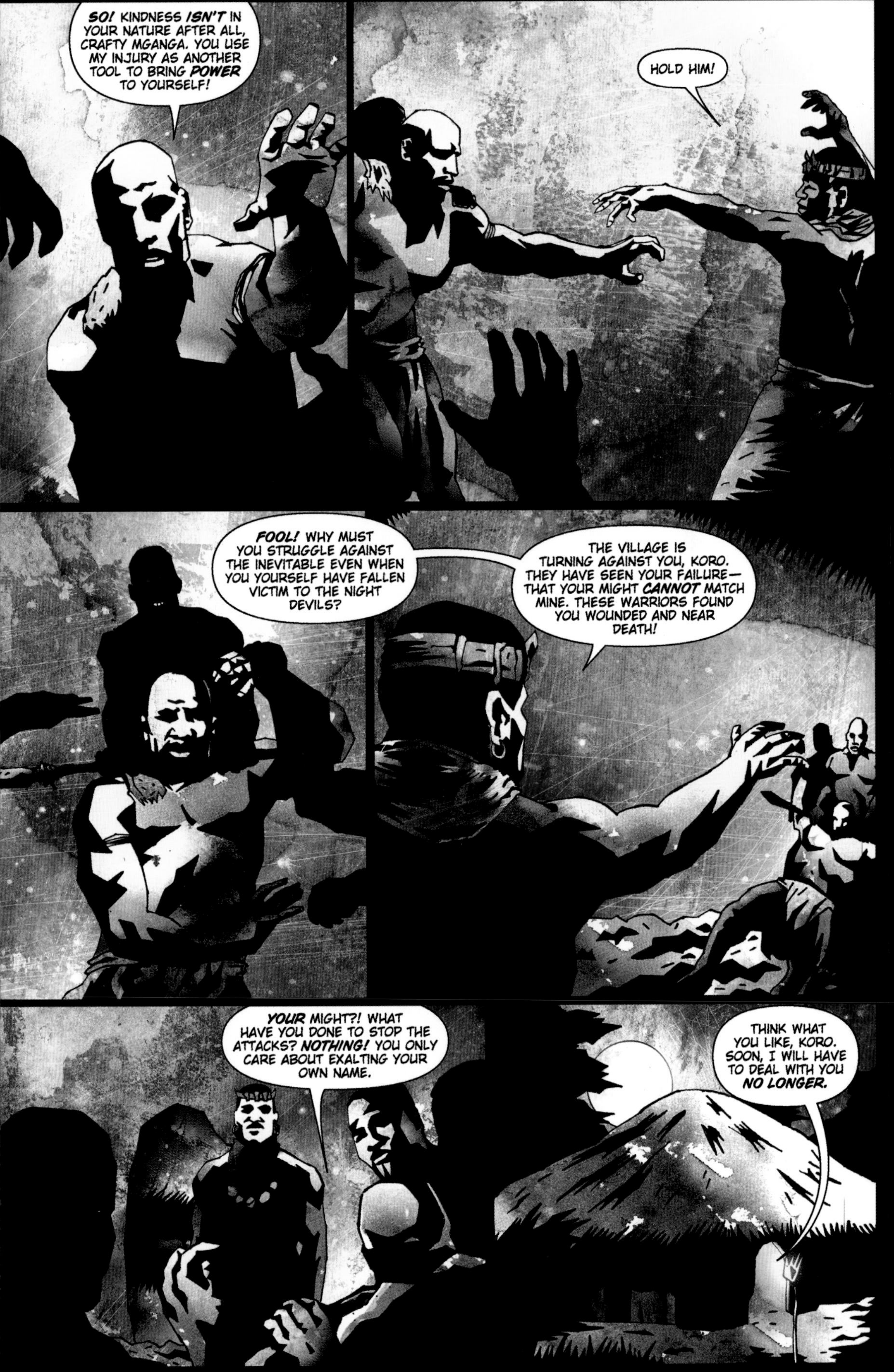
SO! KINDNESS ISN'T IN YOUR NATURE AFTER ALL, CRAFTY MGANGA. YOU USE MY INJURY AS ANOTHER TOOL TO BRING POWER TO YOURSELF!
HOLD HIM!
FOOL! WHY MUST YOU STRUGGLE AGAINST THE INEVITABLE EVEN WHEN YOU YOURSELF HAVE FALLEN VICTIM TO THE NIGHT DEVILS?
THE VILLAGE IS TURNING AGAINST YOU, KORO. THEY HAVE SEEN YOUR FAILURE— THAT YOUR MIGHT CANNOT MATCH MINE. THESE WARRIORS FOUND YOU WOUNDED AND NEAR DEATH!
YOUR MIGHT?! WHAT HAVE YOU DONE TO STOP THE ATTACKS? NOTHING! YOU ONLY CARE ABOUT EXALTING YOUR OWN NAME.
THINK WHAT YOU LIKE, KORO. SOON, I WILL HAVE TO DEAL WITH YOU NO LONGER.

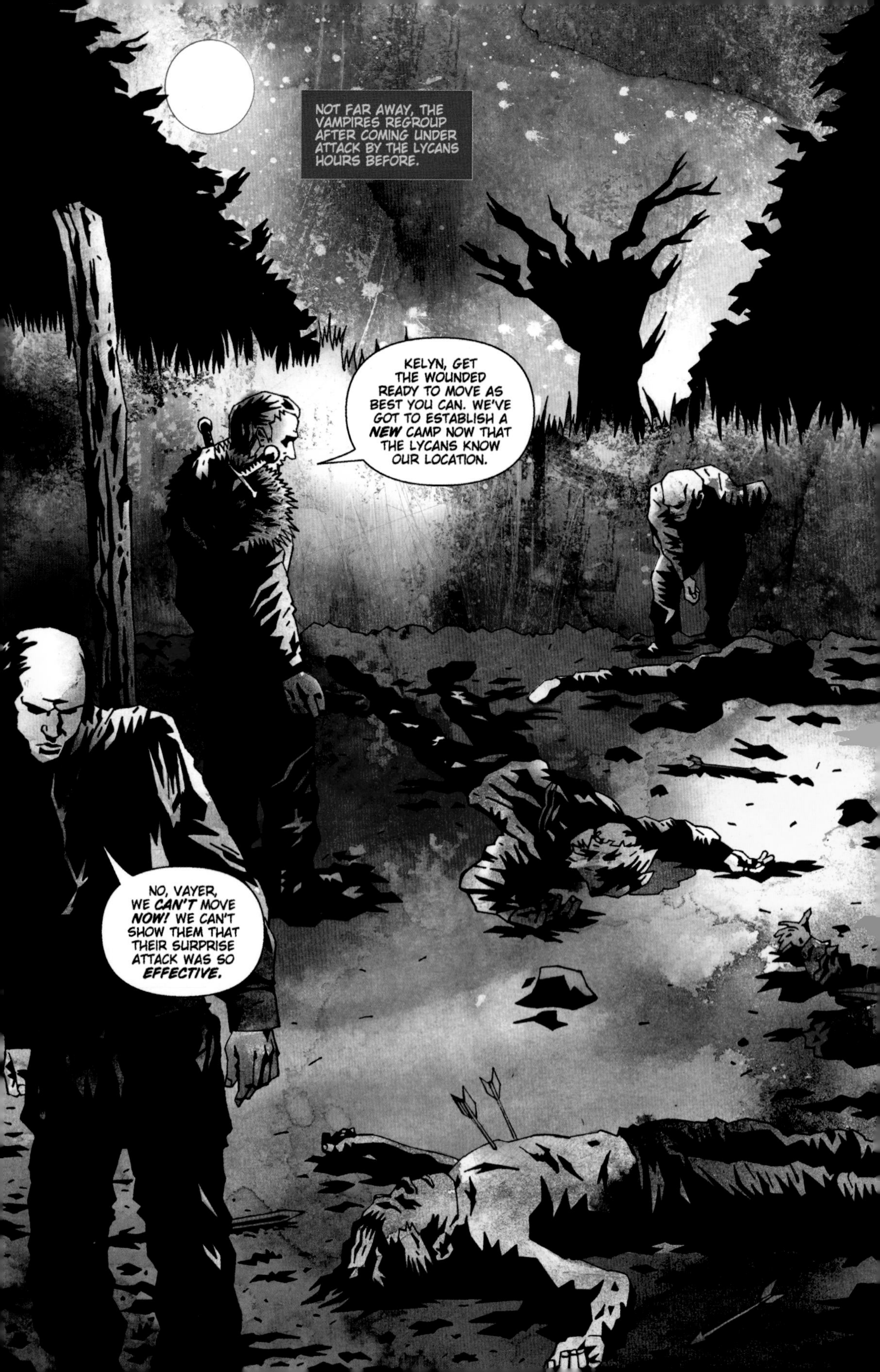
NOT FAR AWAY, THE VAMPIRES REGROUP AFTER COMING UNDER ATTACK BY THE LYCANS HOURS BEFORE.
KELYN, GET THE WOUNDED READY TO MOVE AS BEST YOU CAN. WE'VE GOT TO ESTABLISH A NEW CAMP NOW THAT THE LYCANS KNOW OUR LOCATION.
NO, VAYER, WE CAN'T MOVE NOW! WE CAN'T SHOW THEM THAT THEIR SURPRISE ATTACK WAS SO EFFECTIVE.

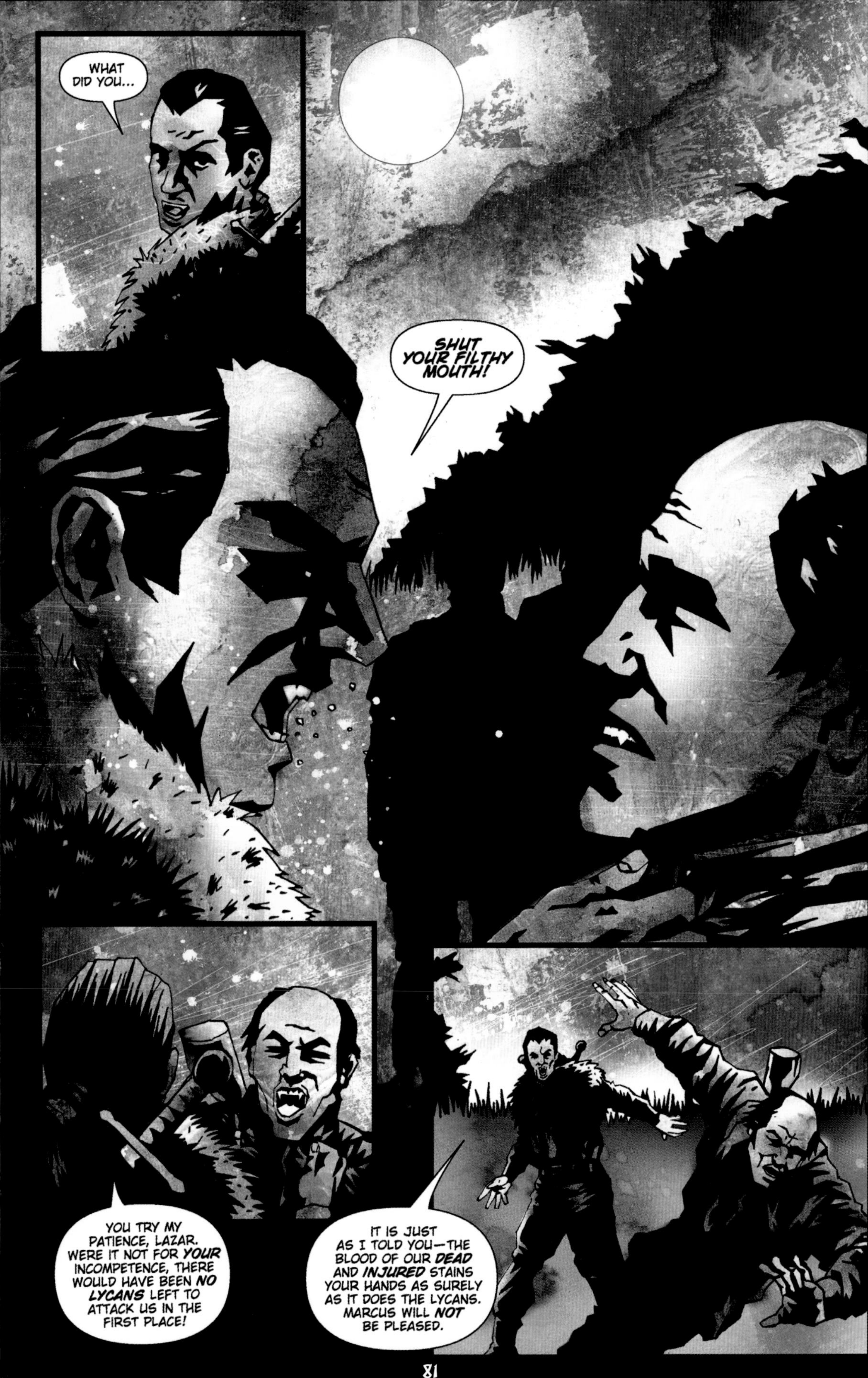

WHAT DID YOU...
SHUT YOUR FILTHY MOUTH!
YOU TRY MY PATIENCE, LAZAR. WERE IT NOT FOR YOUR INCOMPETENCE, THERE WOULD HAVE BEEN NO LYCANS LEFT TO ATTACK US IN THE FIRST PLACE!
IT IS JUST AS I TOLD YOU—THE BLOOD OF OUR DEAD AND INJURED STAINS YOUR HANDS AS SURELY AS IT DOES THE LYCANS. MARCUS WILL NOT BE PLEASED.

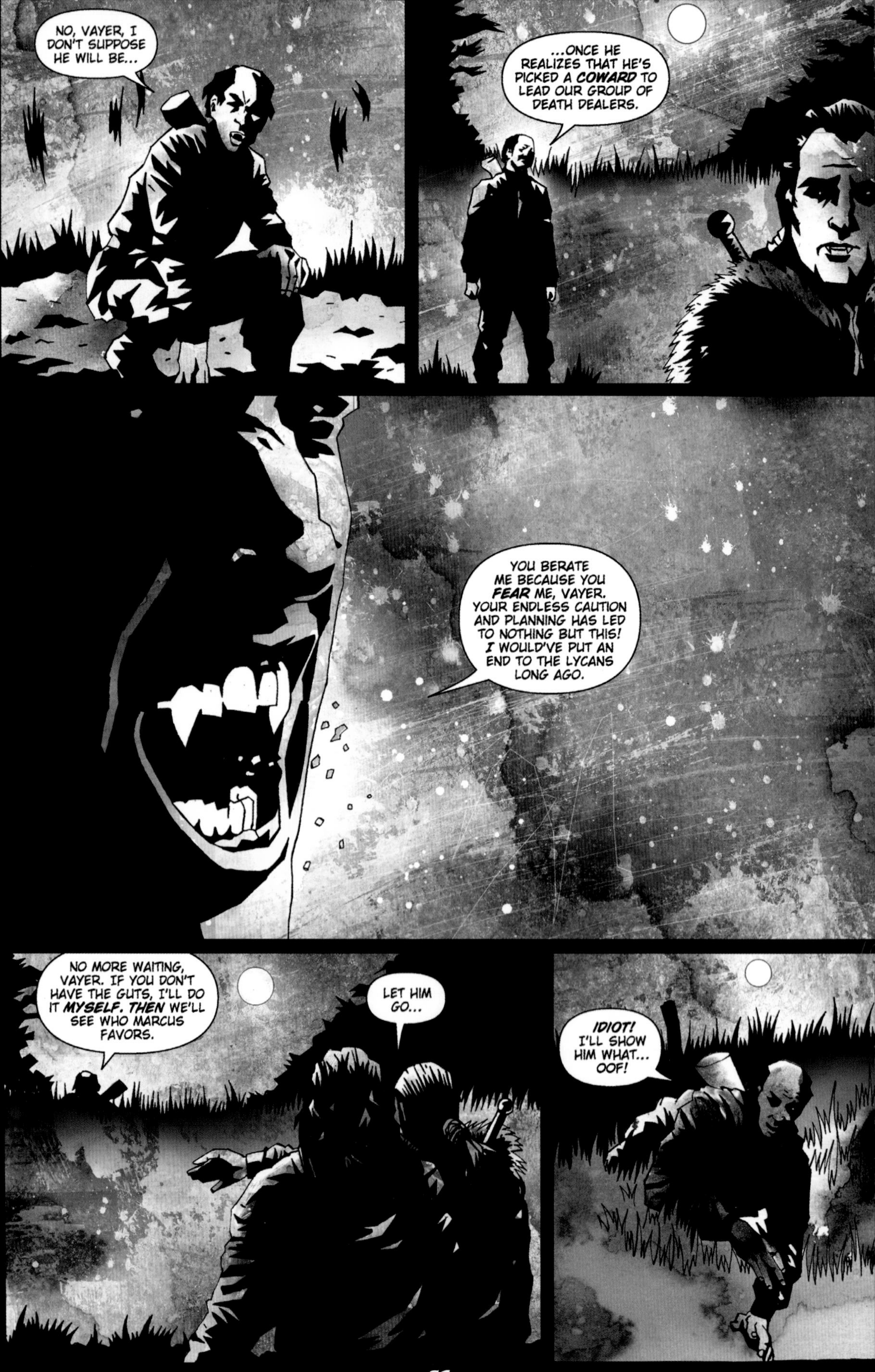

NO, VAYER, I DON'T SUPPOSE HE WILL BE...
...ONCE HE REALIZES THAT HE'S PICKED A COWARD TO LEAD OUR GROUP OF DEATH DEALERS.
YOU BERATE ME BECAUSE YOU FEAR ME, VAYER. YOUR ENDLESS CAUTION AND PLANNING HAS LED TO NOTHING BUT THIS! I WOULD'VE PUT AN END TO THE LYCANS LONG AGO.
NO MORE WAITING, VAYER. IF YOU DON'T HAVE THE GUTS, I'LL DO IT MYSELF. THEN WE'LL SEE WHO MARCUS FAVORS.
LET HIM GO...
IDIOT! I'LL SHOW HIM WHAT... OOF!

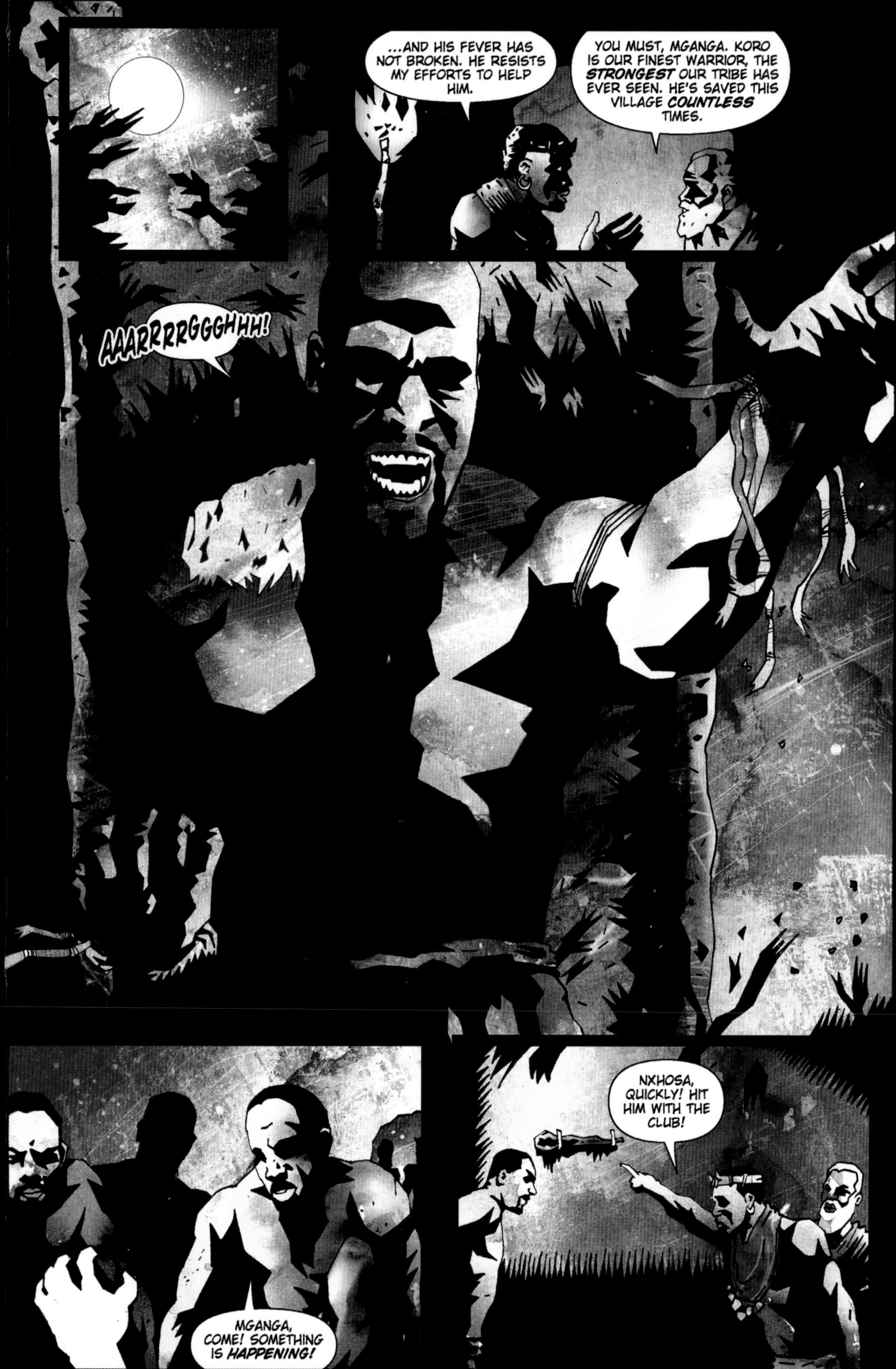
...AND HIS FEVER HAS NOT BROKEN. HE RESISTS MY EFFORTS TO HELP HIM.
YOU MUST, MGANGA. KORO IS OUR FINEST WARRIOR, THE STRONGEST OUR TRIBE HAS EVER SEEN. HE'S SAVED THIS VILLAGE COUNTLESS TIMES.
AAARRRRGGGHHH!
MGANGA, COME! SOMETHING IS HAPPENING!
NXHOSA, QUICKLY! HIT HIM WITH THE CLUB!

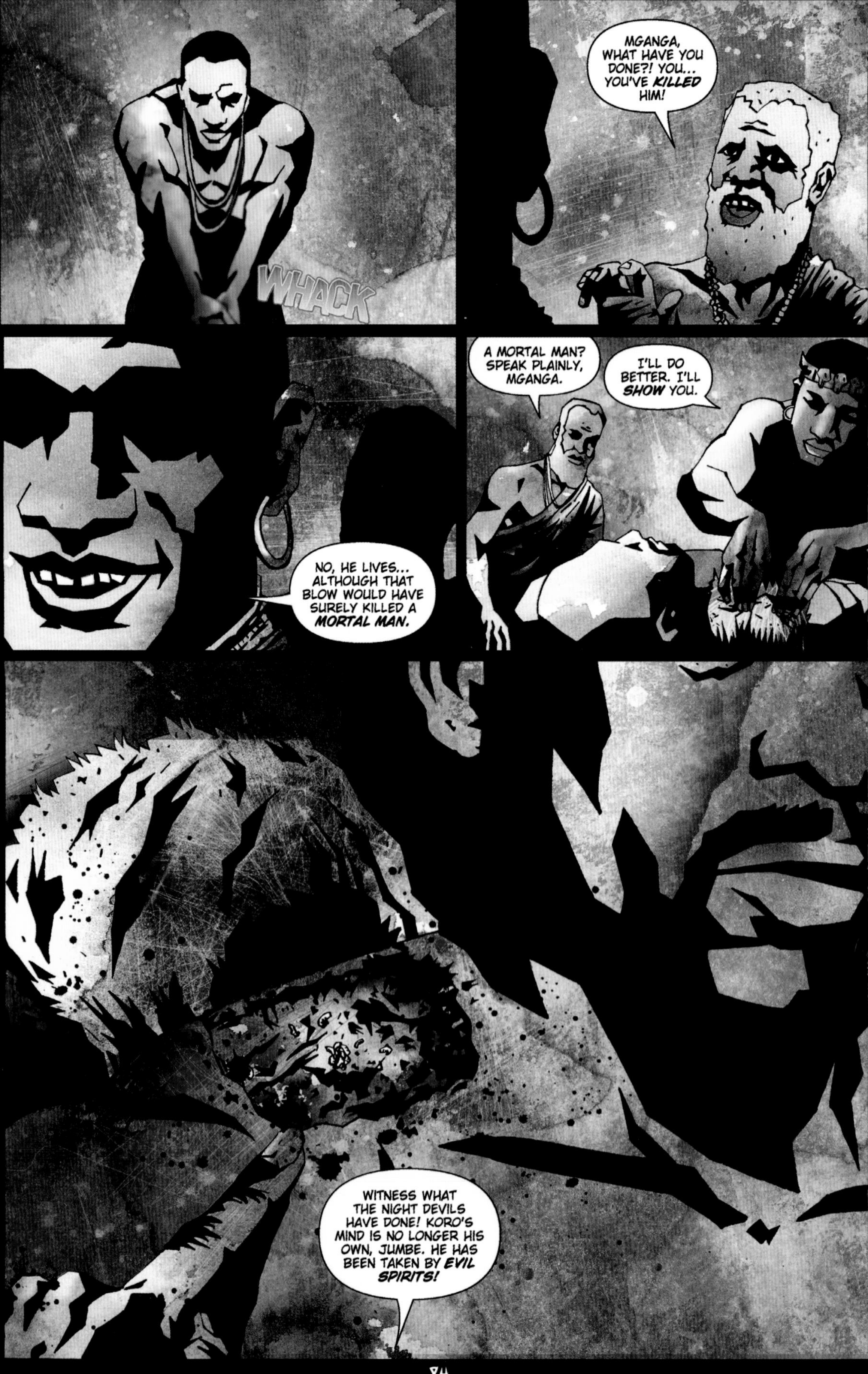
WHACK
MGANGA, WHAT HAVE YOU DONE?! YOU... YOU'VE KILLED HIM!
NO, HE LIVES... ALTHOUGH THAT BLOW WOULD HAVE SURELY KILLED A MORTAL MAN.
A MORTAL MAN? SPEAK PLAINLY, MGANGA.
I'LL DO BETTER. I'LL SHOW YOU.
WITNESS WHAT THE NIGHT DEVILS HAVE DONE! KORO'S MIND IS NO LONGER HIS OWN, JUMBE. HE HAS BEEN TAKEN BY EVIL SPIRITS!

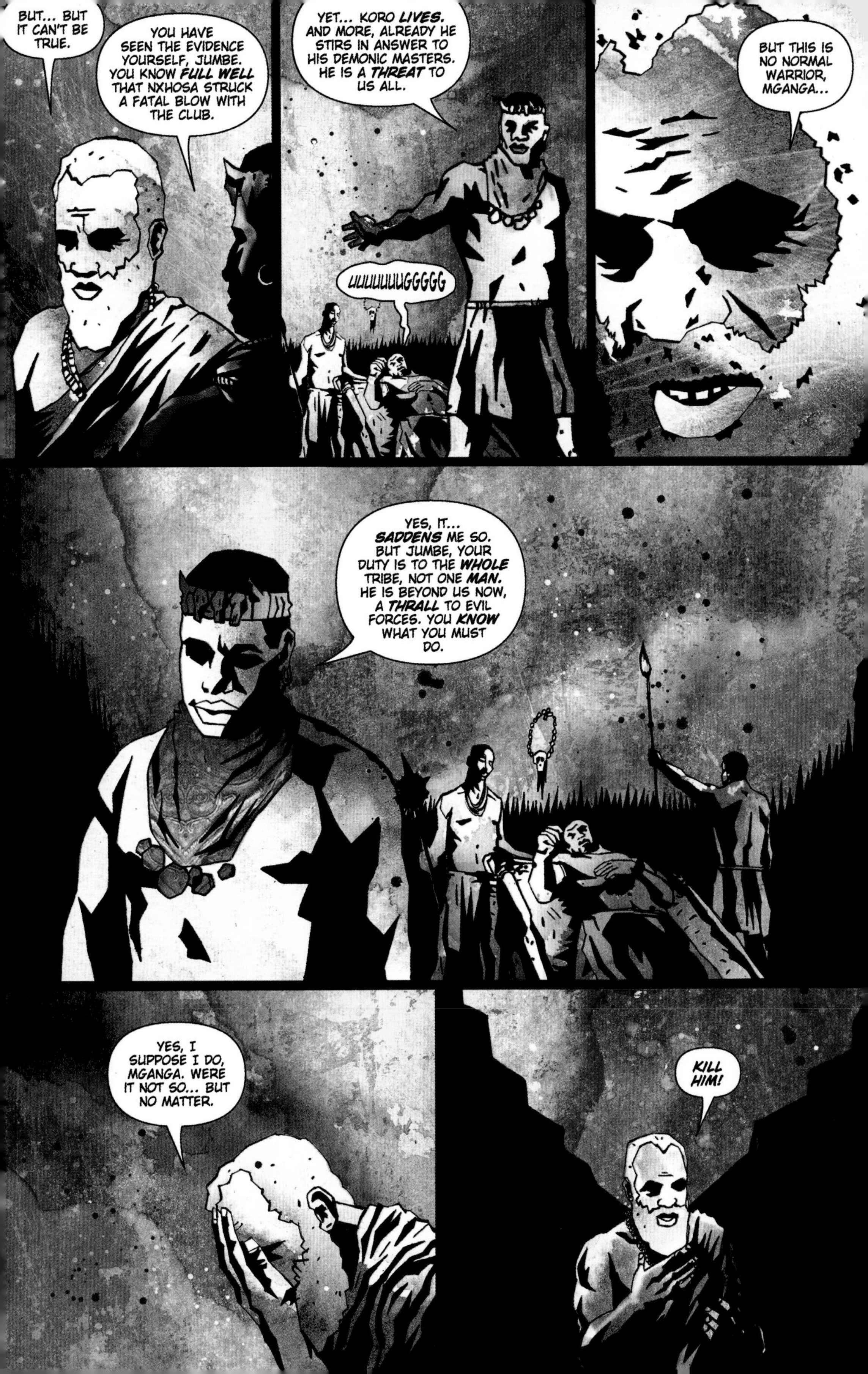
BUT... BUT IT CAN'T BE TRUE.
YOU HAVE SEEN THE EVIDENCE YOURSELF, JUMBE. YOU KNOW FULL WELL THAT NXHOSA STRUCK A FATAL BLOW WITH THE CLUB.
YET... KORO LIVES. AND MORE, ALREADY HE STIRS IN ANSWER TO HIS DEMONIC MASTERS. HE IS A THREAT TO US ALL.
UUUUUUUGGGGG
BUT THIS IS NO NORMAL WARRIOR, MGANGA...
YES, IT... SADDENS ME SO. BUT JUMBE, YOUR DUTY IS TO THE WHOLE TRIBE, NOT ONE MAN. HE IS BEYOND US NOW, A THRALL TO EVIL FORCES. YOU KNOW WHAT YOU MUST DO.
YES, I SUPPOSE I DO, MGANGA. WERE IT NOT SO... BUT NO MATTER.
KILL HIM!

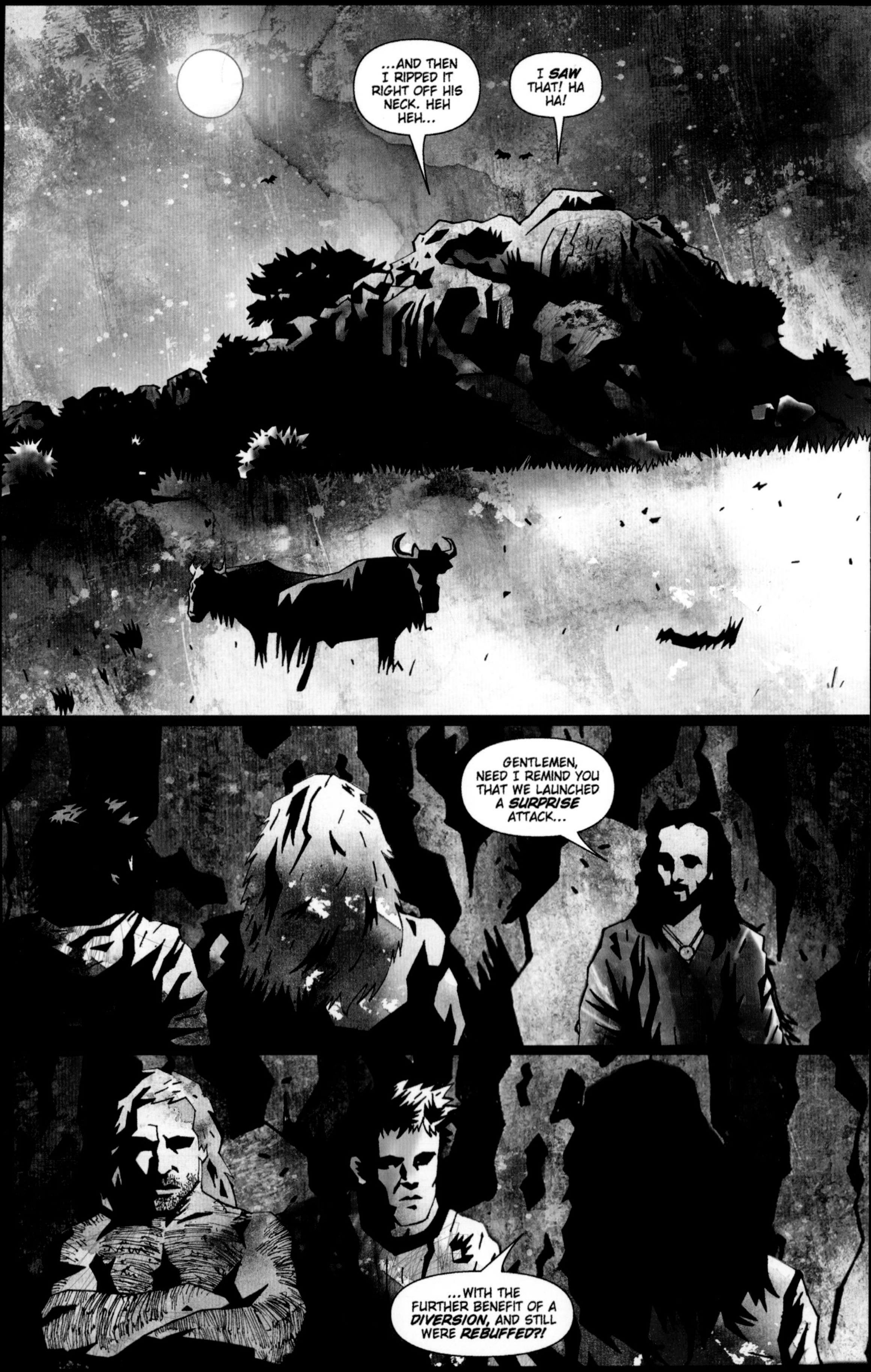
...AND THEN I RIPPED IT RIGHT OFF HIS NECK. HEH HEH...
I SAW THAT! HA HA!
GENTLEMEN, NEED I REMIND YOU THAT WE LAUNCHED A SURPRISE ATTACK...
...WITH THE FURTHER BENEFIT OF A DIVERSION, AND STILL WERE REBUFFED?!

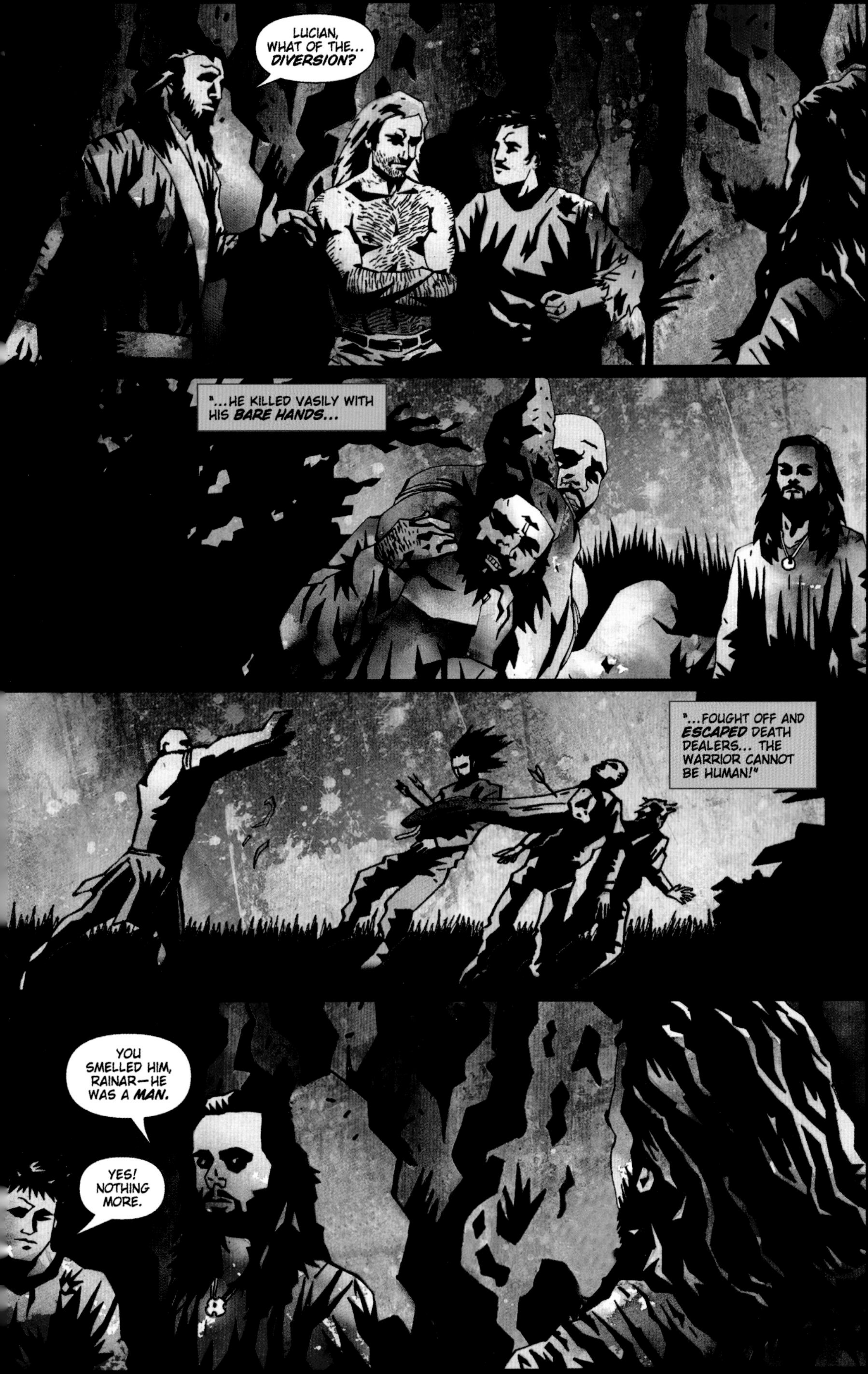
LUCIAN, WHAT OF THE... DIVERSION?
"...HE KILLED VASILY WITH HIS BARE HANDS...
"...FOUGHT OFF AND ESCAPED DEATH DEALERS... THE WARRIOR CANNOT BE HUMAN!"
YOU SMELLED HIM, RAINAR—HE WAS A MAN.
YES! NOTHING MORE.

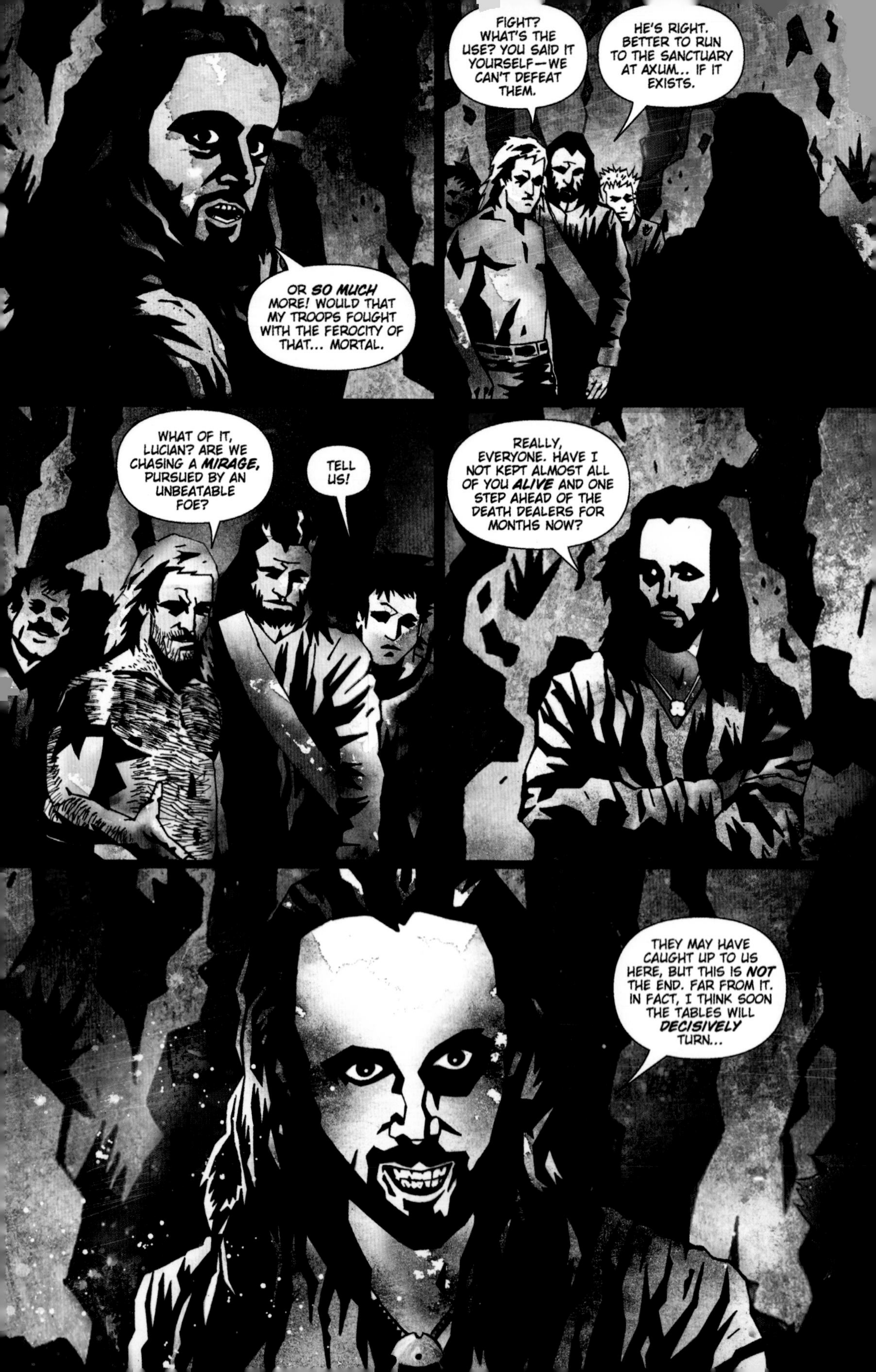
OR *SO MUCH* MORE! WOULD THAT MY TROOPS FOUGHT WITH THE FEROCITY OF THAT... MORTAL.
FIGHT? WHAT'S THE USE? YOU SAID IT YOURSELF—WE CAN'T DEFEAT THEM.
HE'S RIGHT. BETTER TO RUN TO THE SANCTUARY AT AXUM... IF IT EXISTS.
WHAT OF IT, LUCIAN? ARE WE CHASING A *MIRAGE,* PURSUED BY AN UNBEATABLE FOE?
TELL US!
REALLY, EVERYONE. HAVE I NOT KEPT ALMOST ALL OF YOU *ALIVE* AND ONE STEP AHEAD OF THE DEATH DEALERS FOR MONTHS NOW?
THEY MAY HAVE CAUGHT UP TO US HERE, BUT THIS IS *NOT* THE END. FAR FROM IT. IN FACT, I THINK SOON THE TABLES WILL *DECISIVELY* TURN...

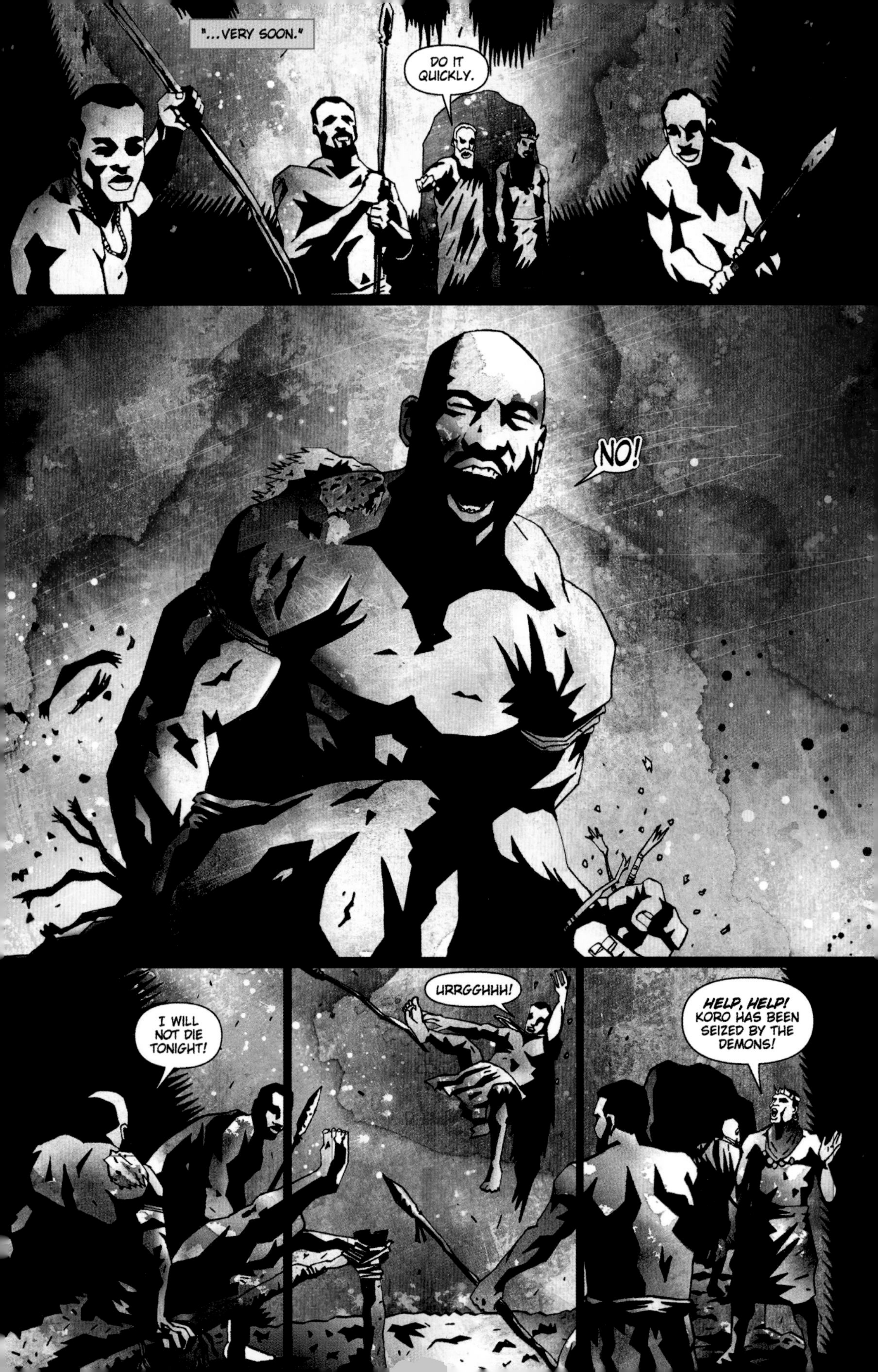
"...VERY SOON."
DO IT QUICKLY.
NO!
I WILL NOT DIE TONIGHT!
URRGGHHH!
HELP, HELP! KORO HAS BEEN SEIZED BY THE DEMONS!

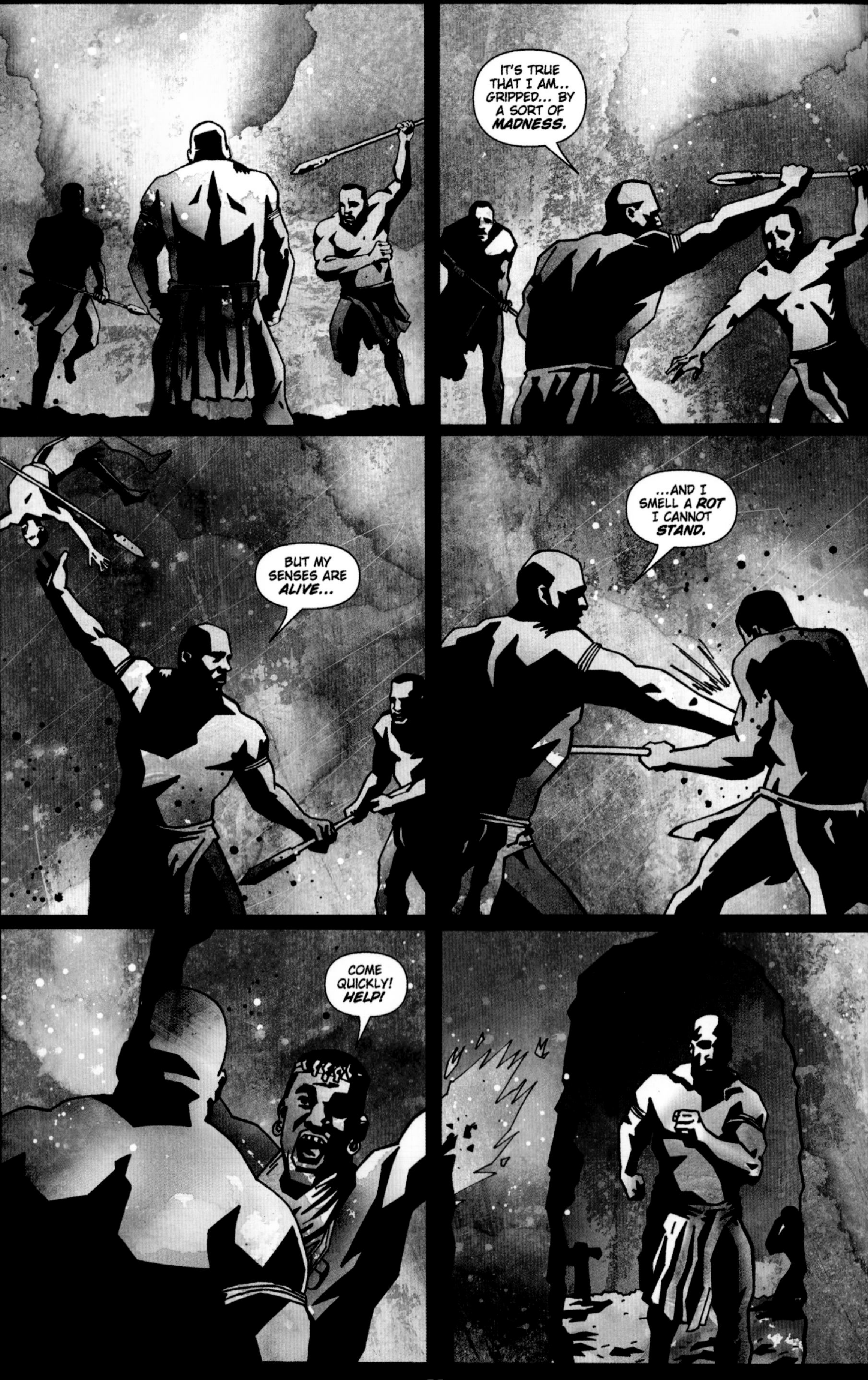
IT'S TRUE THAT I AM... GRIPPED... BY A SORT OF MADNESS.
BUT MY SENSES ARE ALIVE...
...AND I SMELL A ROT I CANNOT STAND.
COME QUICKLY! HELP!

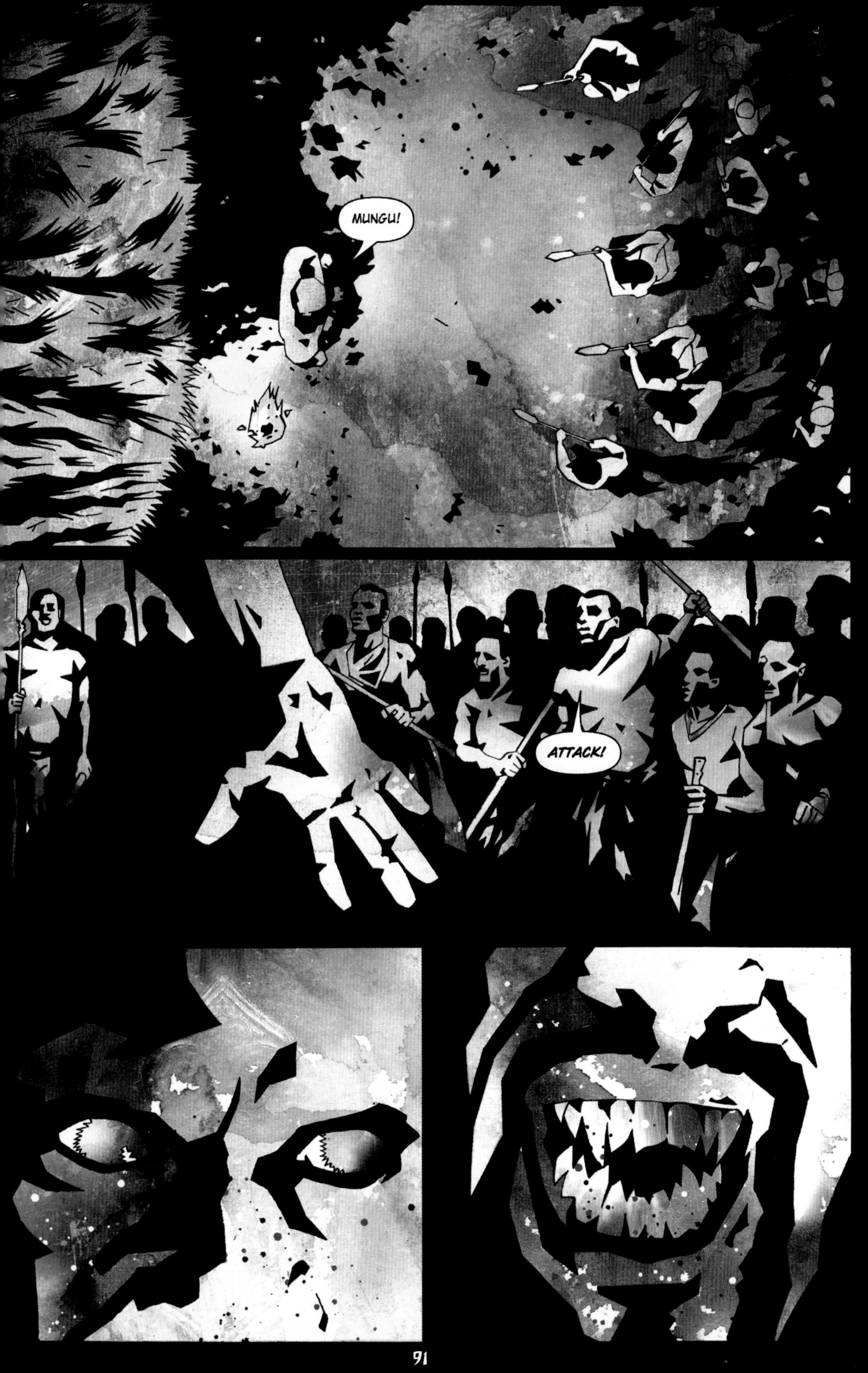
MUNGU!
ATTACK!

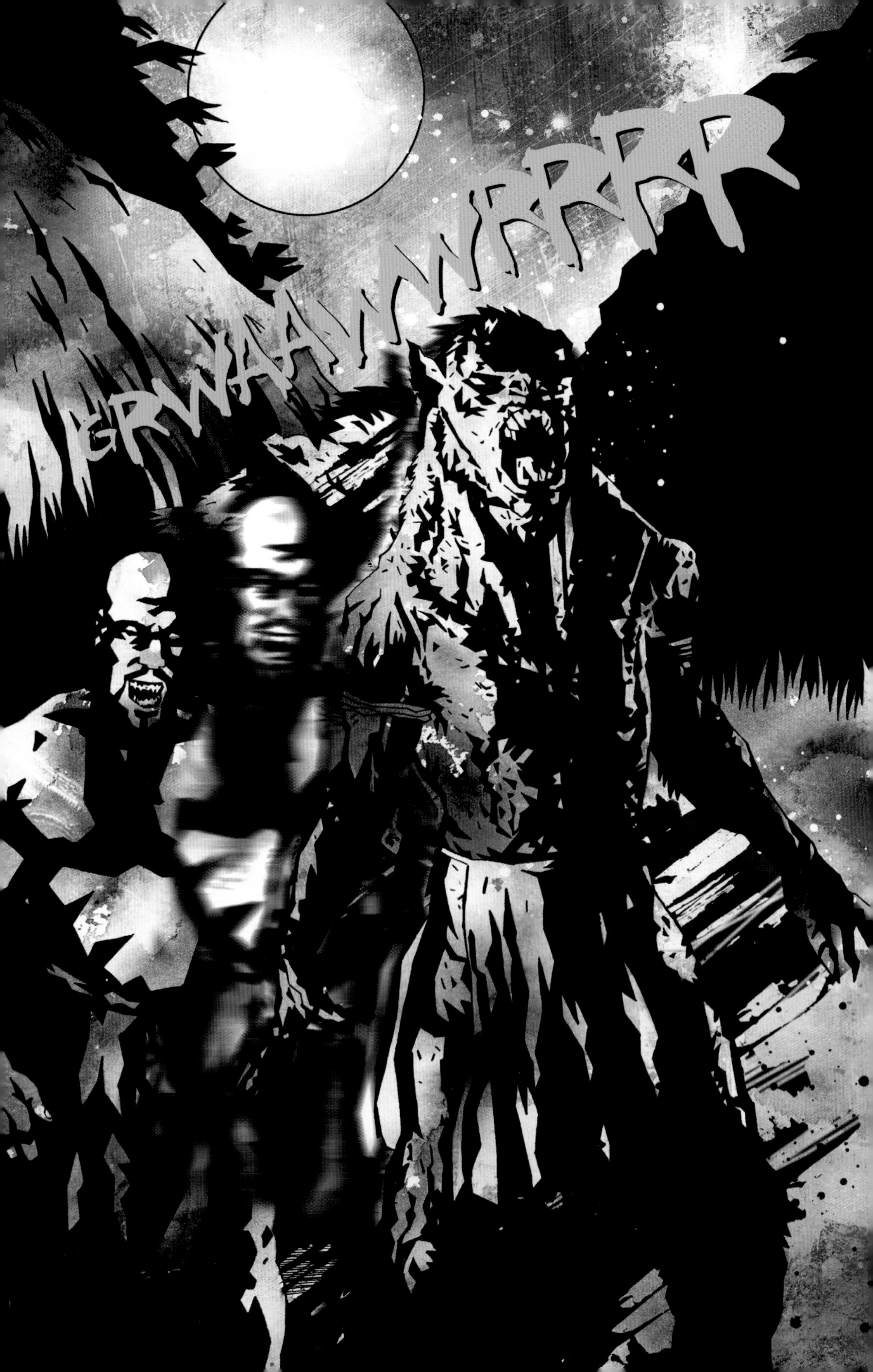
GRWAAWWRRRR

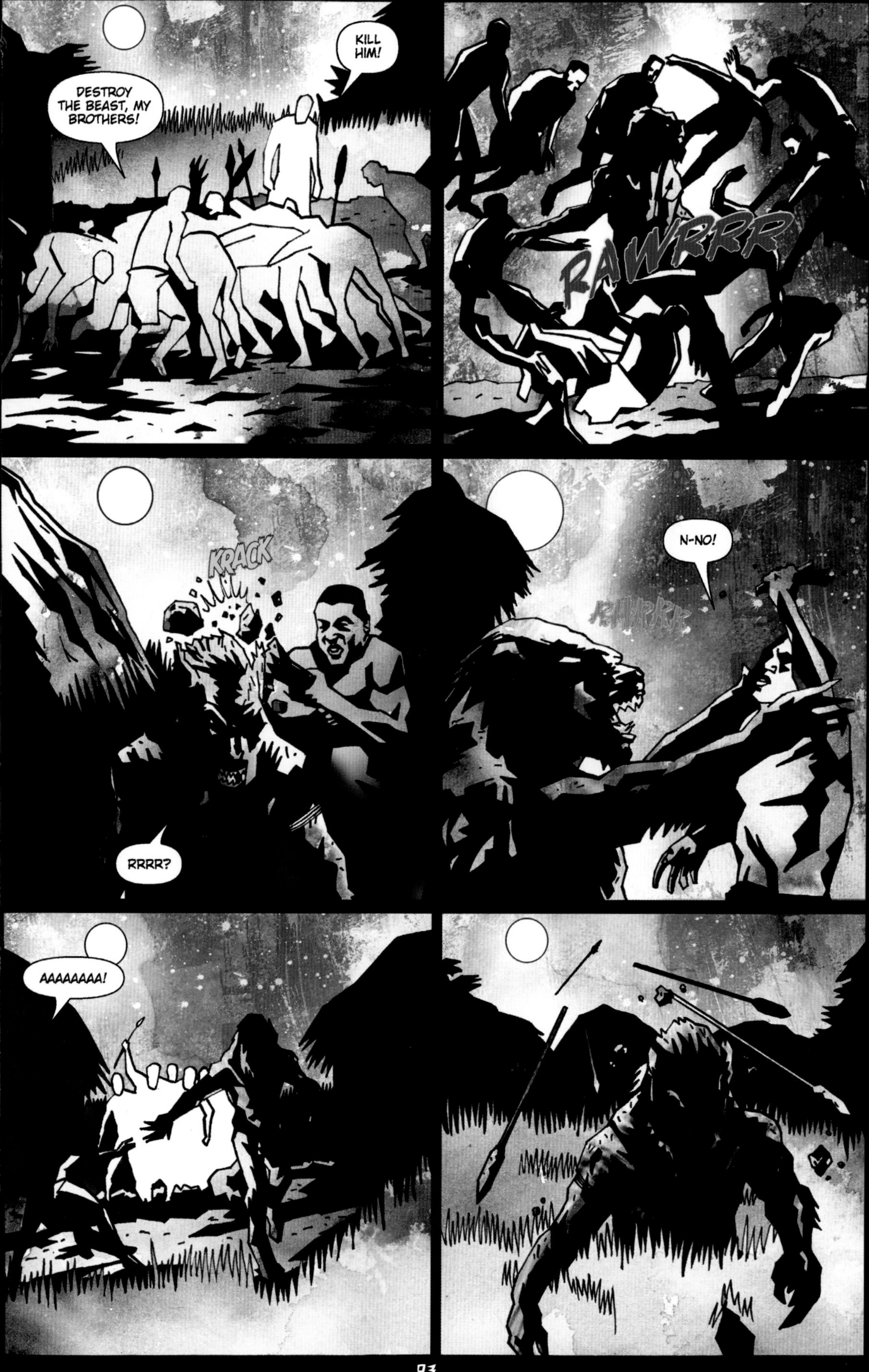
DESTROY THE BEAST, MY BROTHERS!
KILL HIM!
RAWRRR
KRACK
RRRR?
N-NO!
AAAAAAAA!

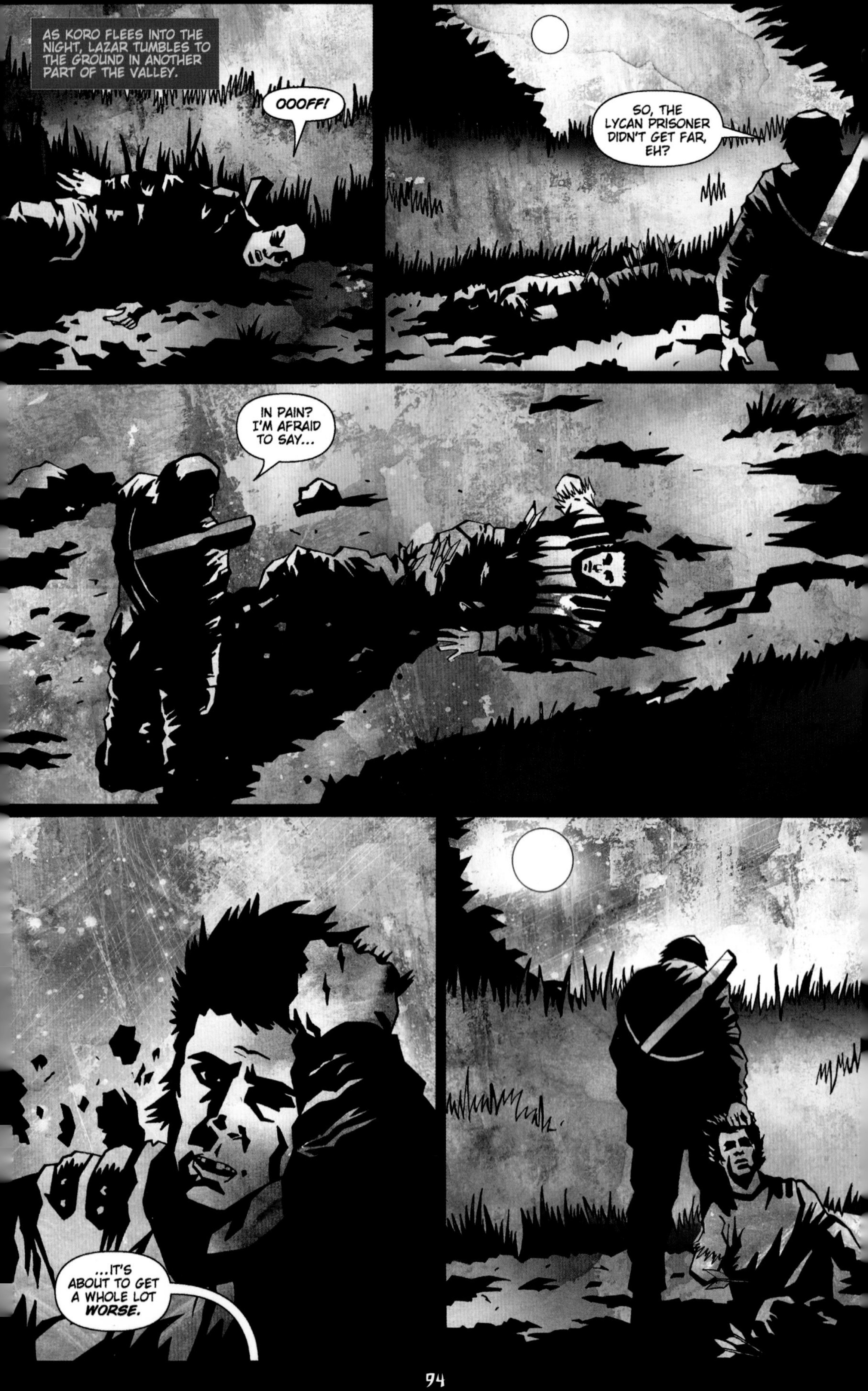
AS KORO FLEES INTO THE NIGHT, LAZAR TUMBLES TO THE GROUND IN ANOTHER PART OF THE VALLEY.
OOOFF!
SO, THE LYCAN PRISONER DIDN'T GET FAR, EH?
IN PAIN? I'M AFRAID TO SAY...
...IT'S ABOUT TO GET A WHOLE LOT WORSE.

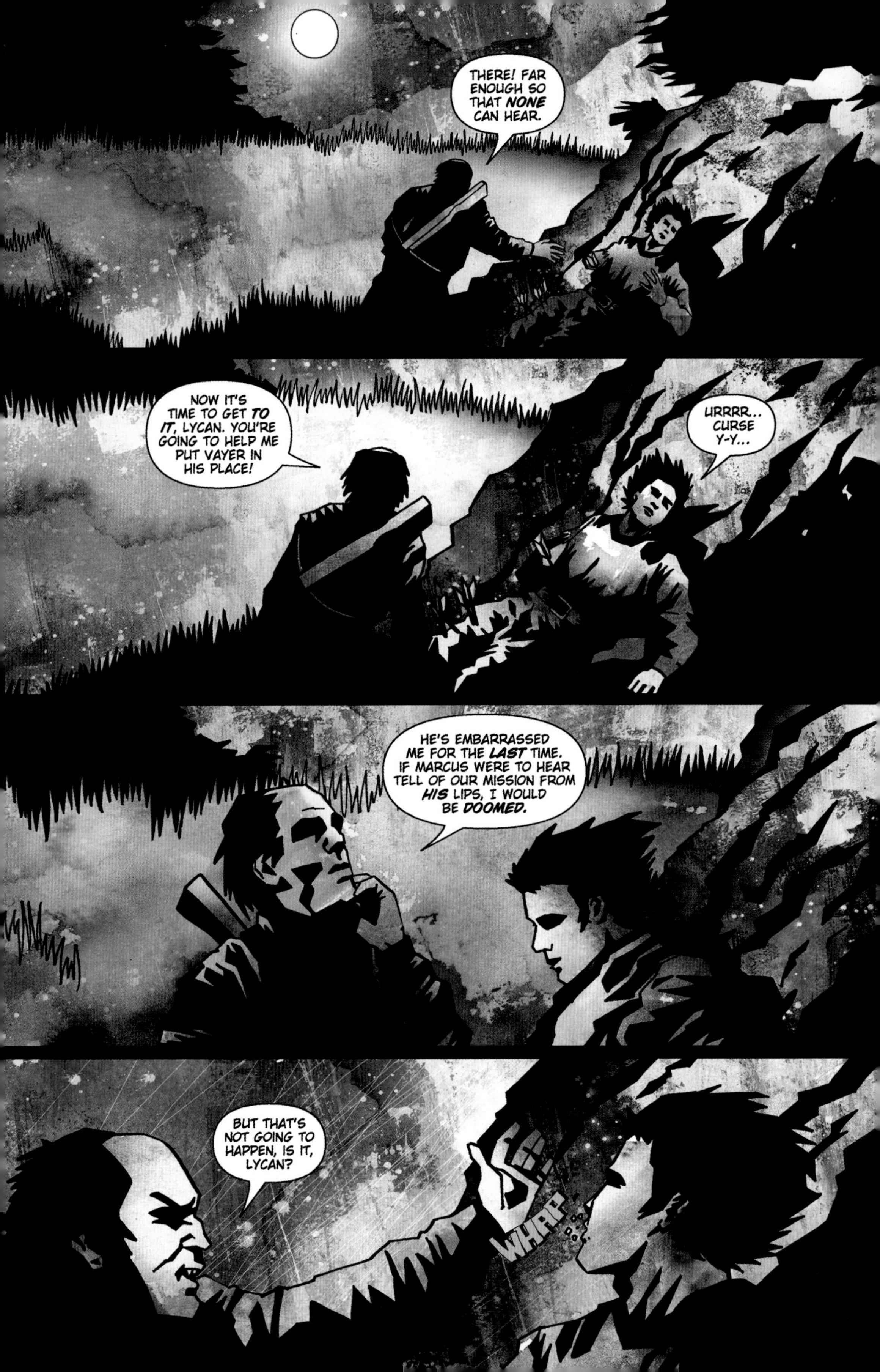
THERE! FAR ENOUGH SO THAT NONE CAN HEAR.
NOW IT'S TIME TO GET TO IT, LYCAN. YOU'RE GOING TO HELP ME PUT VAYER IN HIS PLACE!
URRRR... CURSE Y-Y...
HE'S EMBARRASSED ME FOR THE LAST TIME. IF MARCUS WERE TO HEAR TELL OF OUR MISSION FROM HIS LIPS, I WOULD BE DOOMED.
BUT THAT'S NOT GOING TO HAPPEN, IS IT, LYCAN?

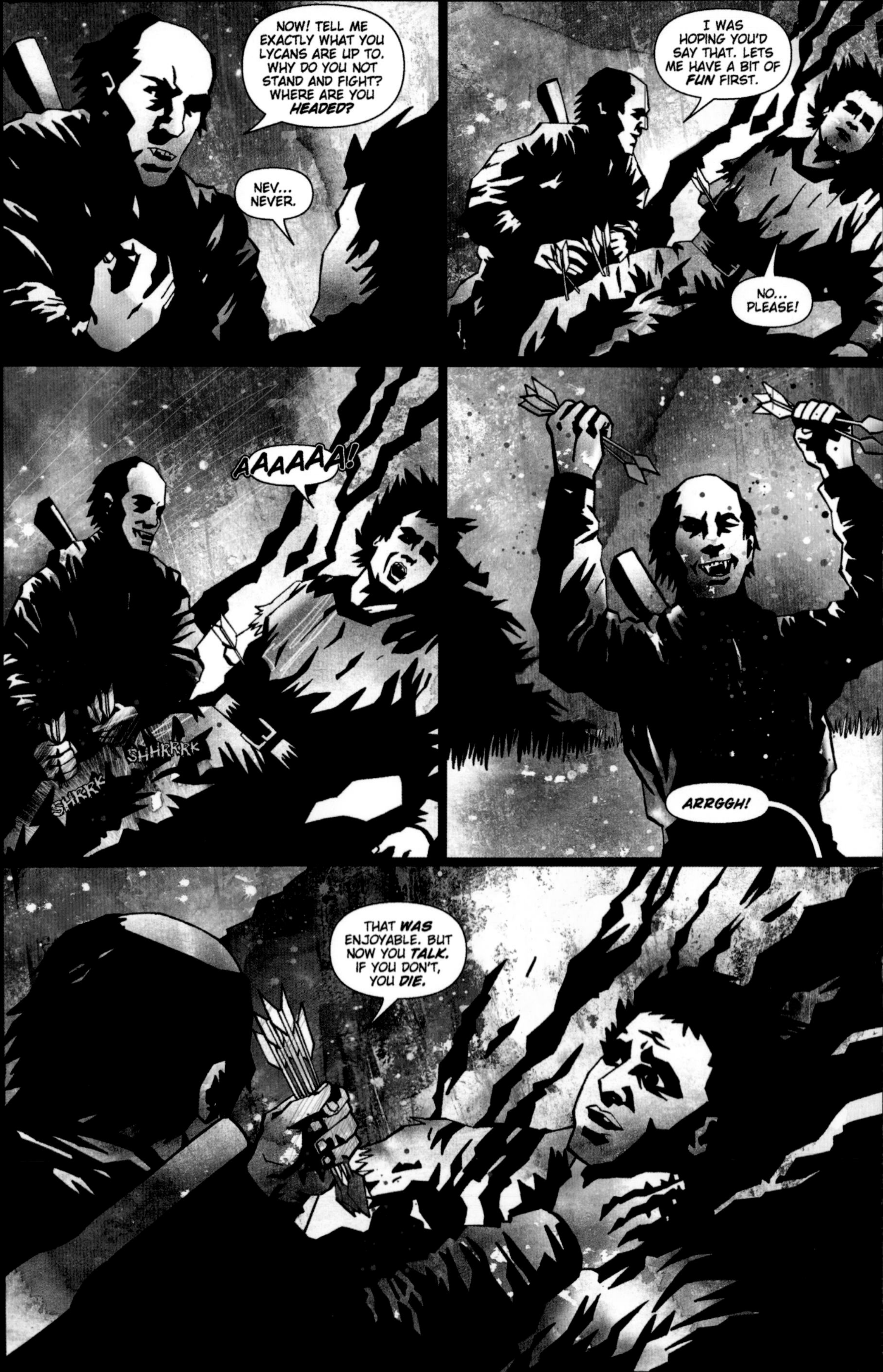
NOW! TELL ME EXACTLY WHAT YOU LYCANS ARE UP TO. WHY DO YOU NOT STAND AND FIGHT? WHERE ARE YOU HEADED?
NEV... NEVER.
I WAS HOPING YOU'D SAY THAT. LETS ME HAVE A BIT OF FUN FIRST.
NO... PLEASE!
AAAAAA!
SHHRRRK
SHRRK
ARRGGH!
THAT WAS ENJOYABLE. BUT NOW YOU TALK. IF YOU DON'T, YOU DIE.

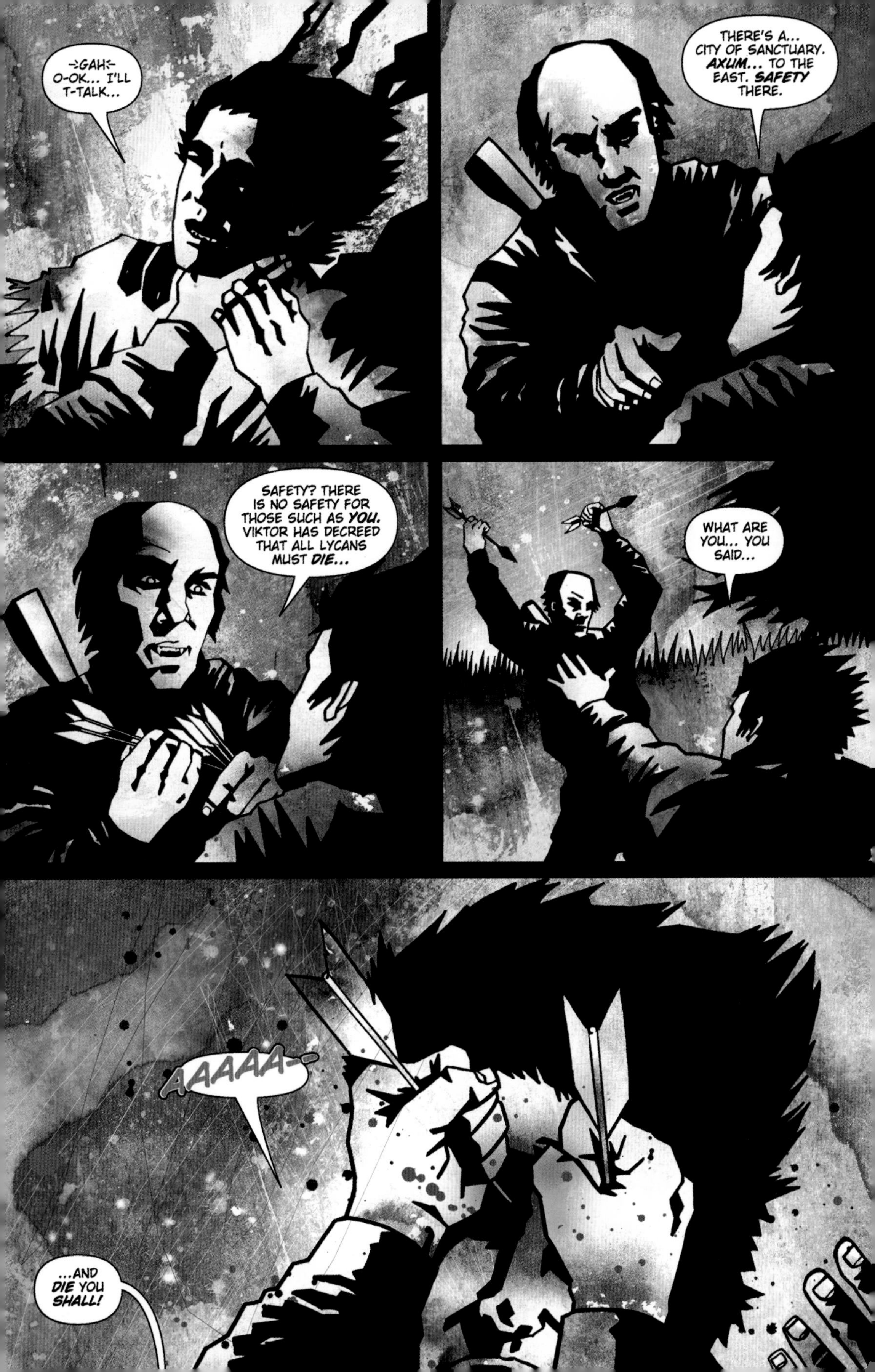

-GAH- O-OK... I'LL T-TALK...
THERE'S A... CITY OF SANCTUARY. AXUM... TO THE EAST. SAFETY THERE.
SAFETY? THERE IS NO SAFETY FOR THOSE SUCH AS YOU. VIKTOR HAS DECREED THAT ALL LYCANS MUST DIE...
WHAT ARE YOU... YOU SAID...
AAAAA-
...AND DIE YOU SHALL!

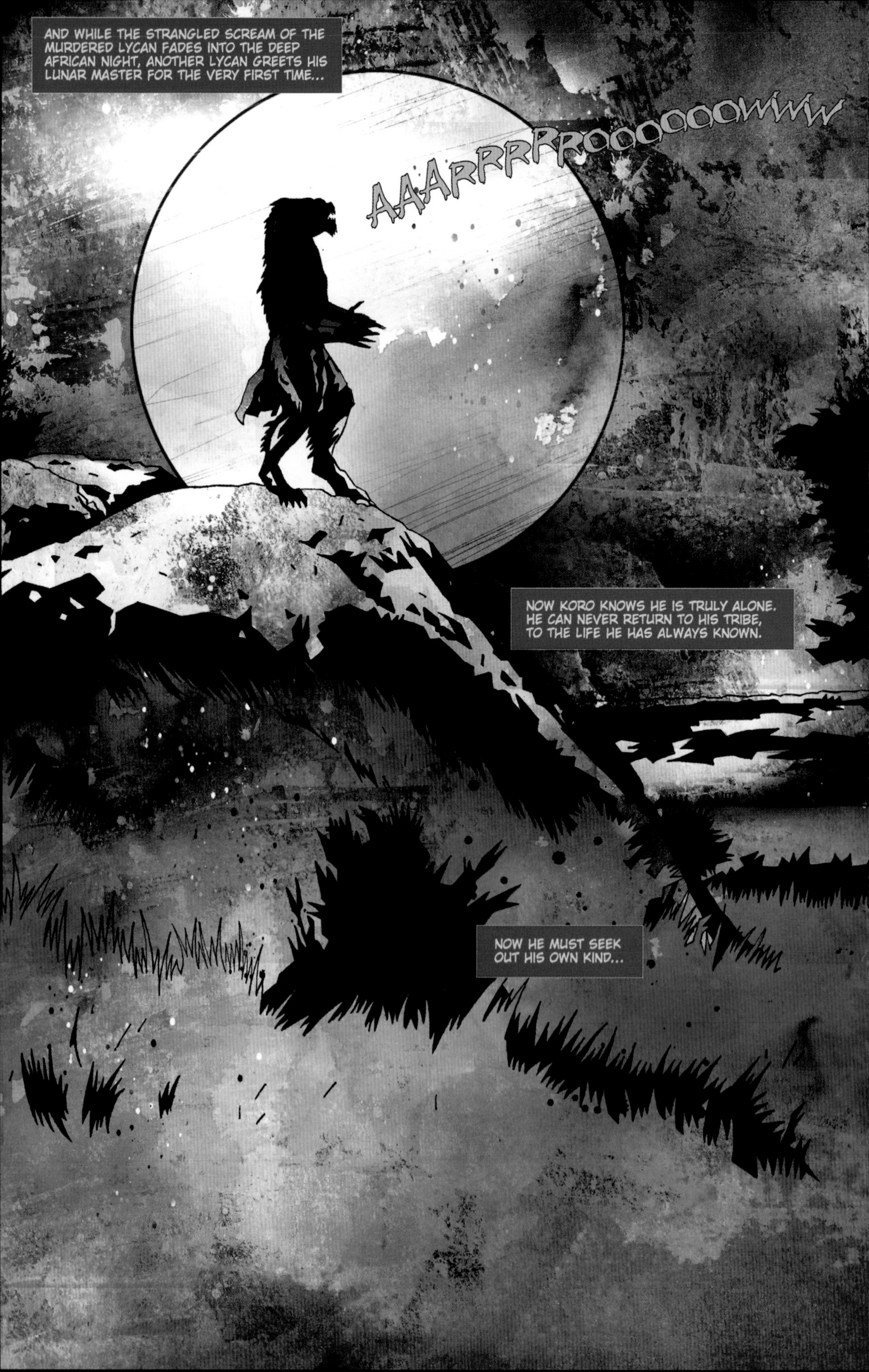
AND WHILE THE STRANGLED SCREAM OF THE MURDERED LYCAN FADES INTO THE DEEP AFRICAN NIGHT, ANOTHER LYCAN GREETS HIS LUNAR MASTER FOR THE VERY FIRST TIME...
AAARRRRROOOOOOOWWW
NOW KORO KNOWS HE IS TRULY ALONE. HE CAN NEVER RETURN TO HIS TRIBE, TO THE LIFE HE HAS ALWAYS KNOWN.
NOW HE MUST SEEK OUT HIS OWN KIND...

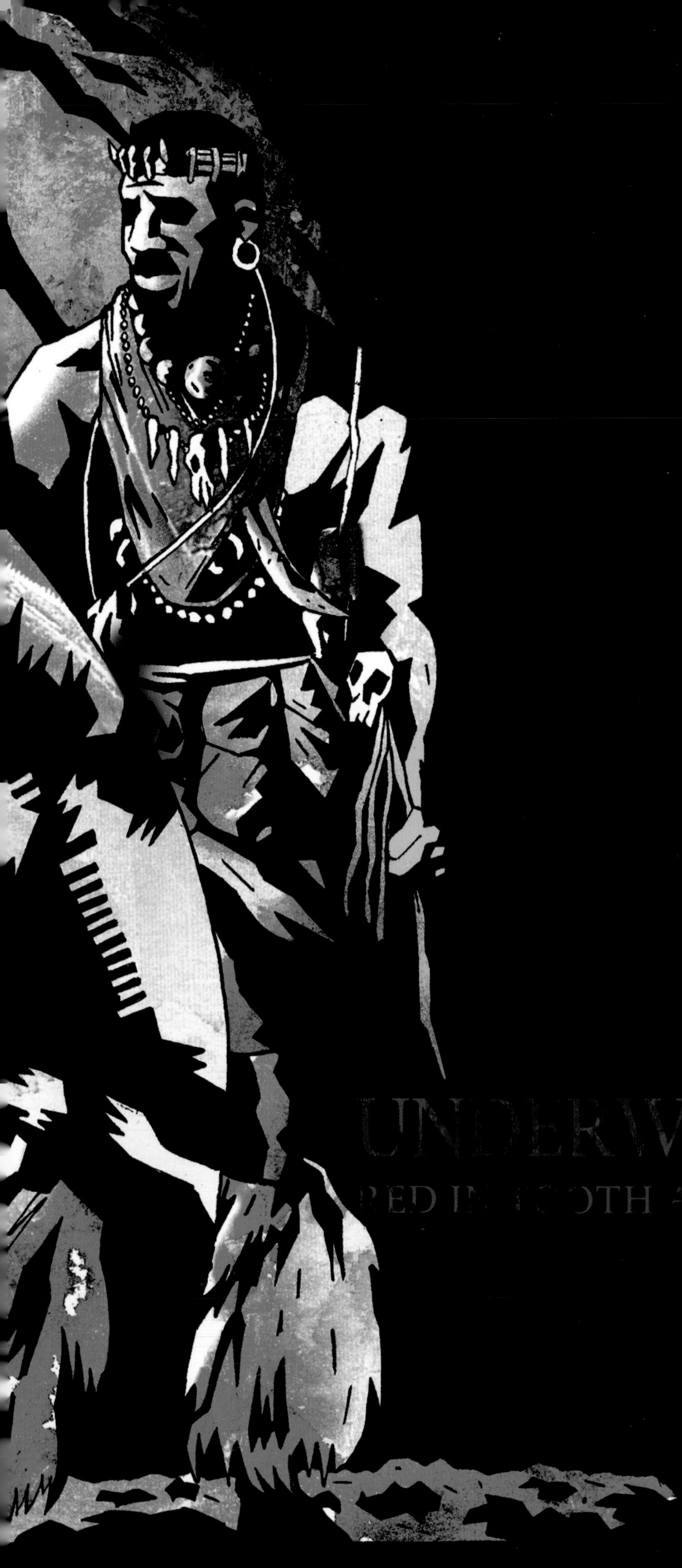

UNDERWORLD™

RED IN TOOTH AND CLAW

CHAPTER 3

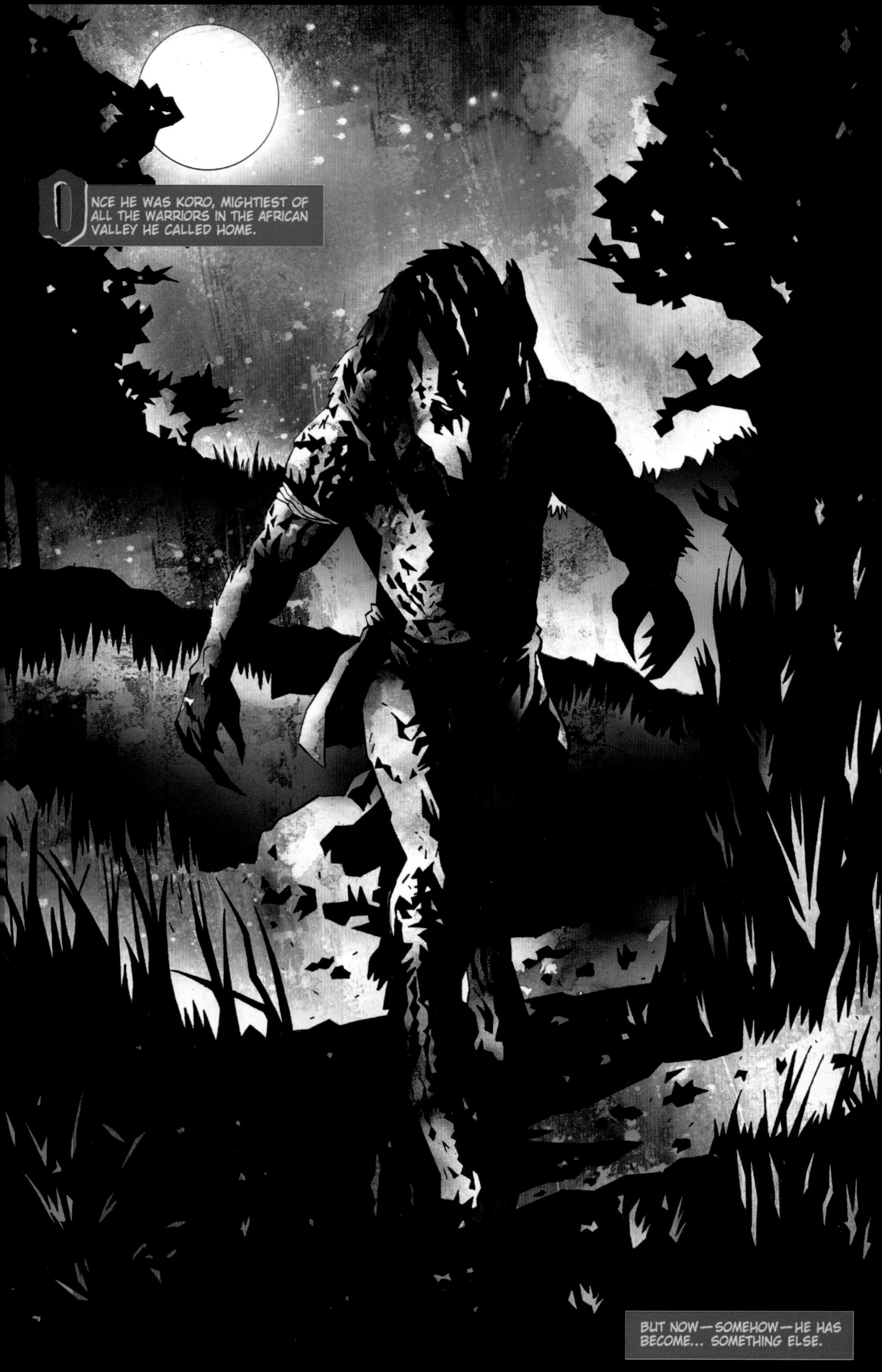
ONCE HE WAS KORO, MIGHTIEST OF ALL THE WARRIORS IN THE AFRICAN VALLEY HE CALLED HOME.
BUT NOW—SOMEHOW—HE HAS BECOME... SOMETHING ELSE.

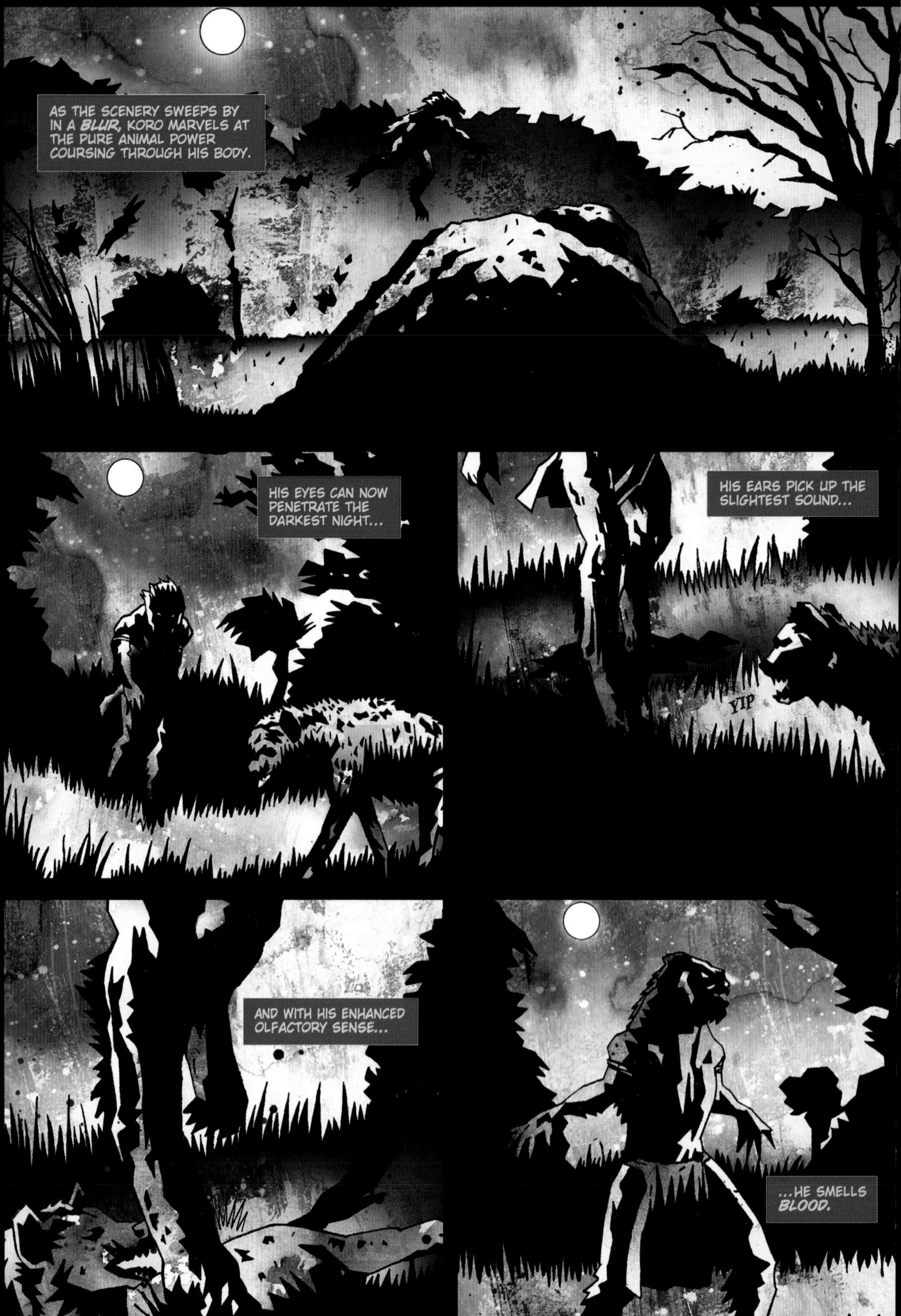
AS THE SCENERY SWEEPS BY IN A *BLUR*, KORO MARVELS AT THE PURE ANIMAL POWER COURSING THROUGH HIS BODY.
HIS EYES CAN NOW PENETRATE THE DARKEST NIGHT...
HIS EARS PICK UP THE SLIGHTEST SOUND...
YIP
AND WITH HIS ENHANCED OLFACTORY SENSE...
AIEE-YI-YI-YI-YI
KRACK
...HE SMELLS *BLOOD*.

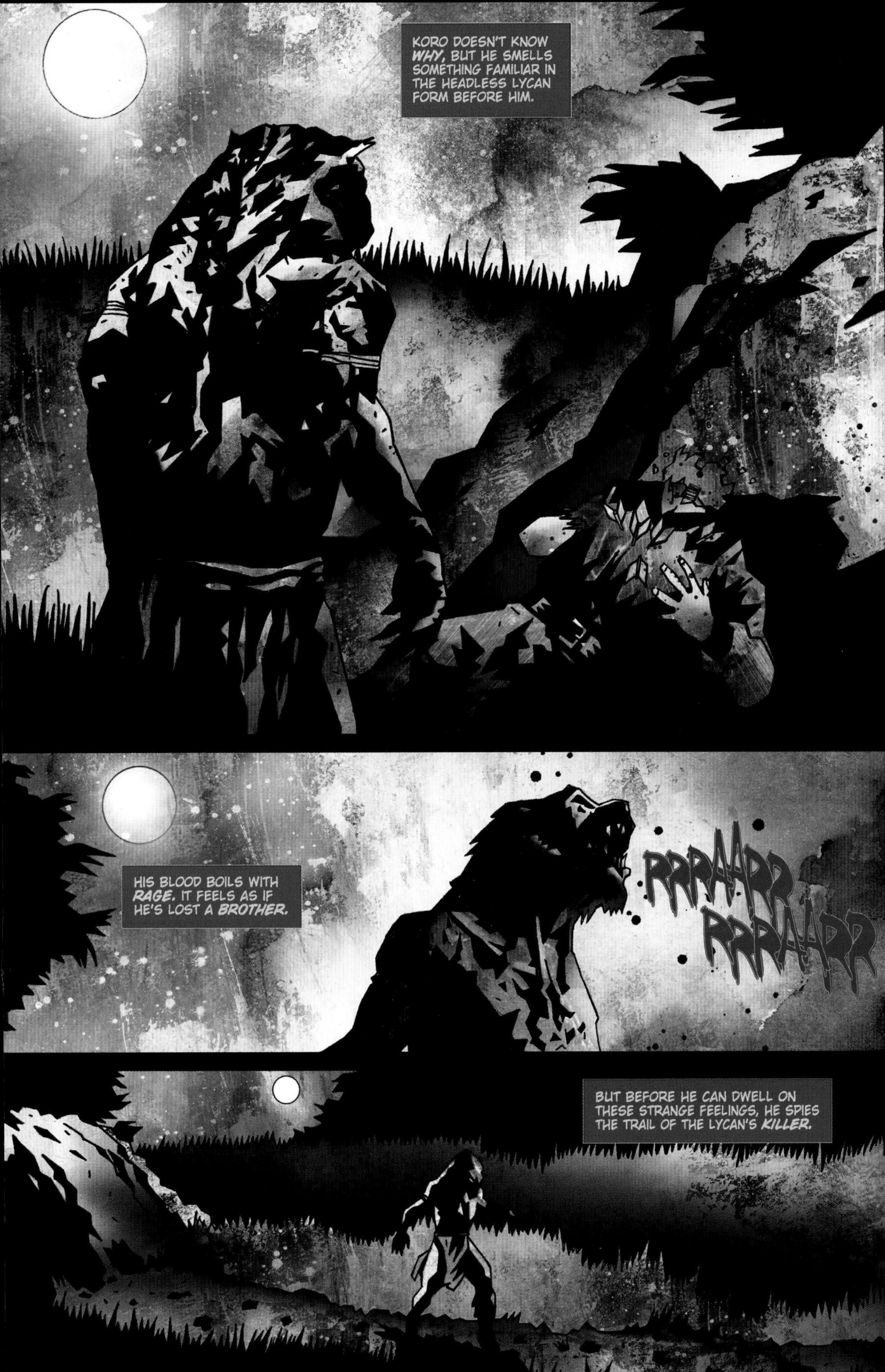
KORO DOESN'T KNOW *WHY,* BUT HE SMELLS SOMETHING FAMILIAR IN THE HEADLESS LYCAN FORM BEFORE HIM.
HIS BLOOD BOILS WITH *RAGE.* IT FEELS AS IF HE'S LOST A *BROTHER.*
RRRAAARR
RRRAAARR
BUT BEFORE HE CAN DWELL ON THESE STRANGE FEELINGS, HE SPIES THE TRAIL OF THE LYCAN'S *KILLER.*

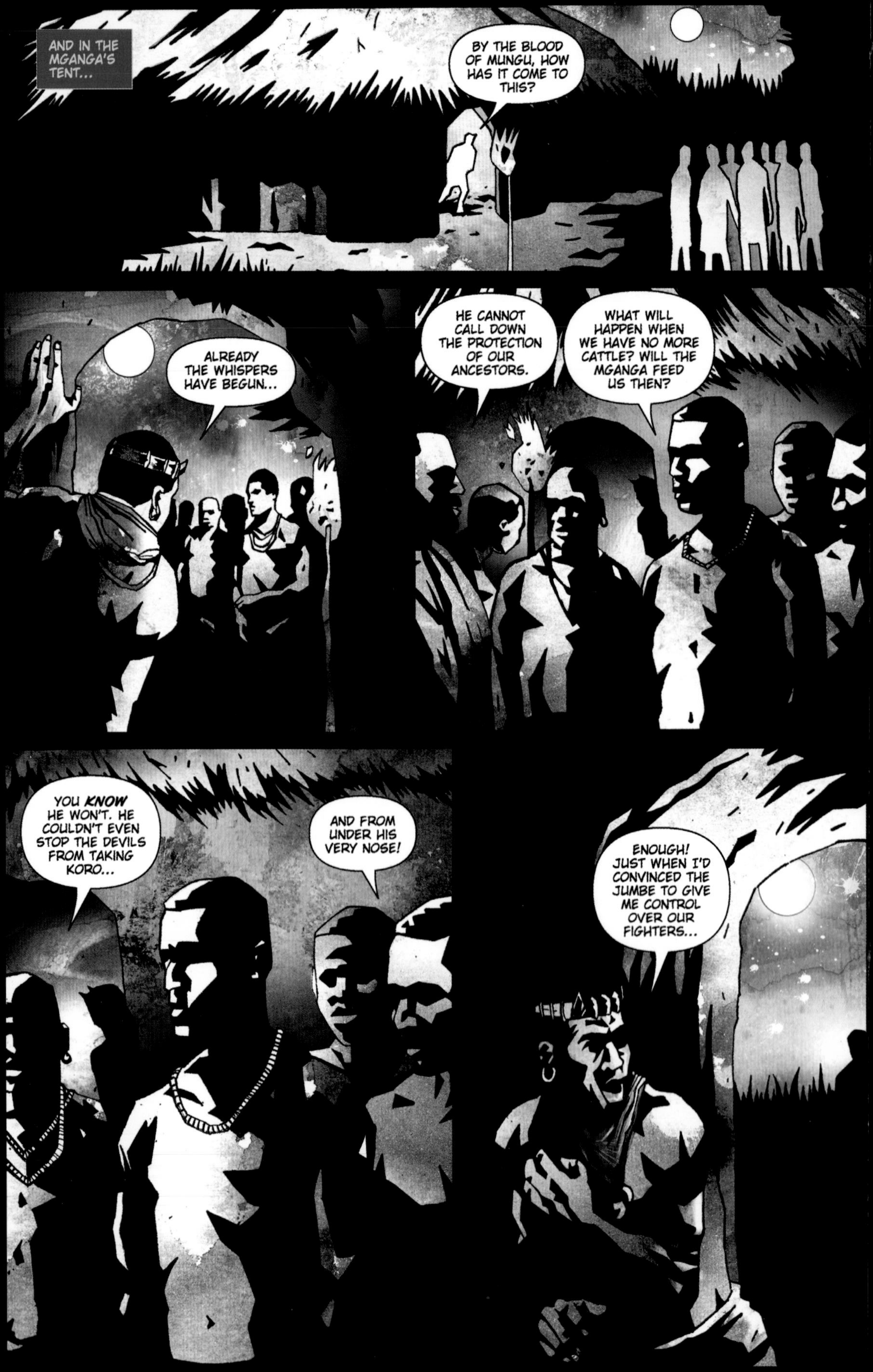
AND IN THE MGANGA'S TENT...
BY THE BLOOD OF MUNGU, HOW HAS IT COME TO THIS?
ALREADY THE WHISPERS HAVE BEGUN...
HE CANNOT CALL DOWN THE PROTECTION OF OUR ANCESTORS.
WHAT WILL HAPPEN WHEN WE HAVE NO MORE CATTLE? WILL THE MGANGA FEED US THEN?
YOU KNOW HE WON'T. HE COULDN'T EVEN STOP THE DEVILS FROM TAKING KORO...
AND FROM UNDER HIS VERY NOSE!
ENOUGH! JUST WHEN I'D CONVINCED THE JUMBE TO GIVE ME CONTROL OVER OUR FIGHTERS...

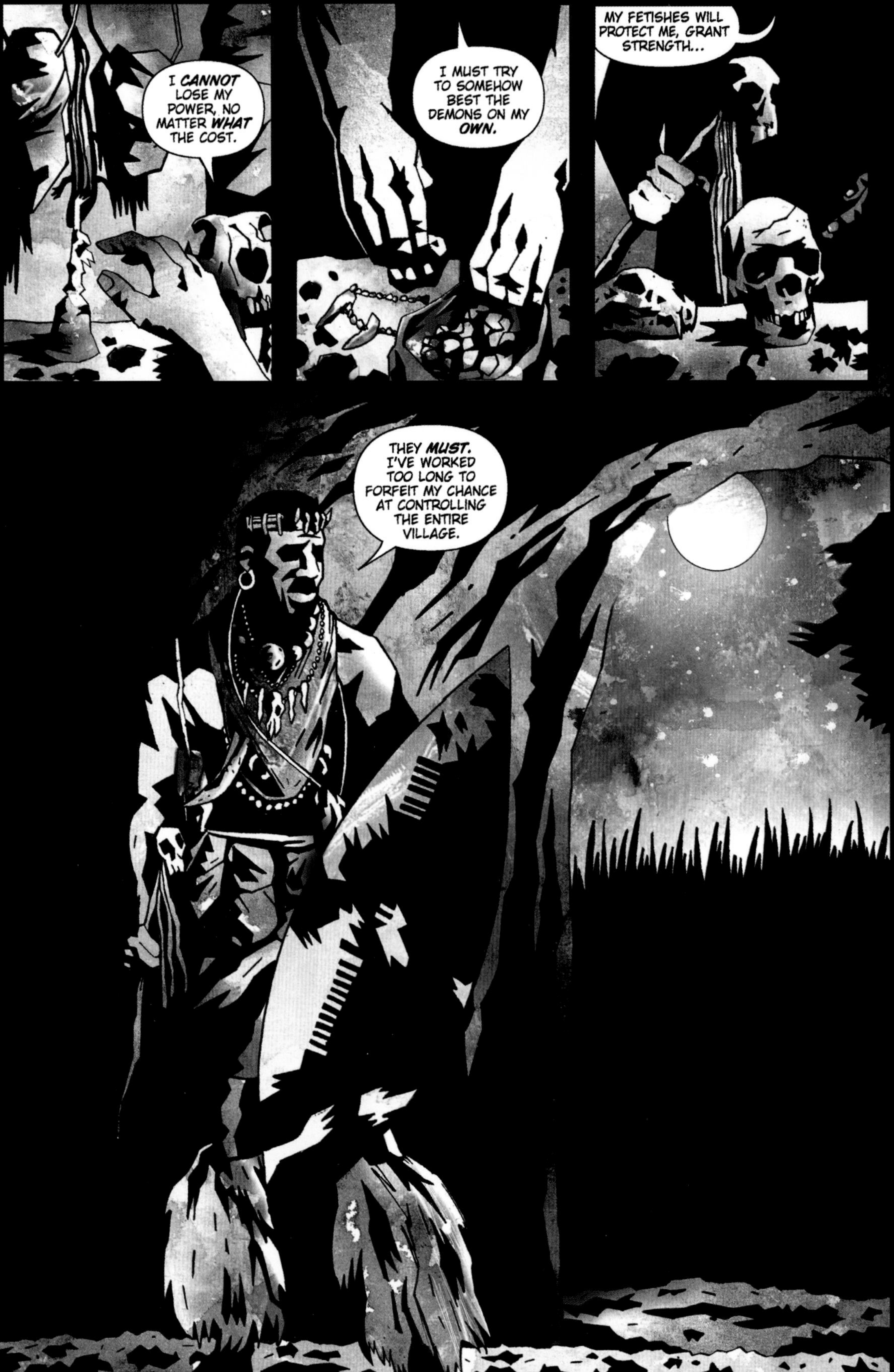
I CANNOT LOSE MY POWER, NO MATTER WHAT THE COST.
I MUST TRY TO SOMEHOW BEST THE DEMONS ON MY OWN.
MY FETISHES WILL PROTECT ME, GRANT STRENGTH...
THEY MUST. I'VE WORKED TOO LONG TO FORFEIT MY CHANCE AT CONTROLLING THE ENTIRE VILLAGE.

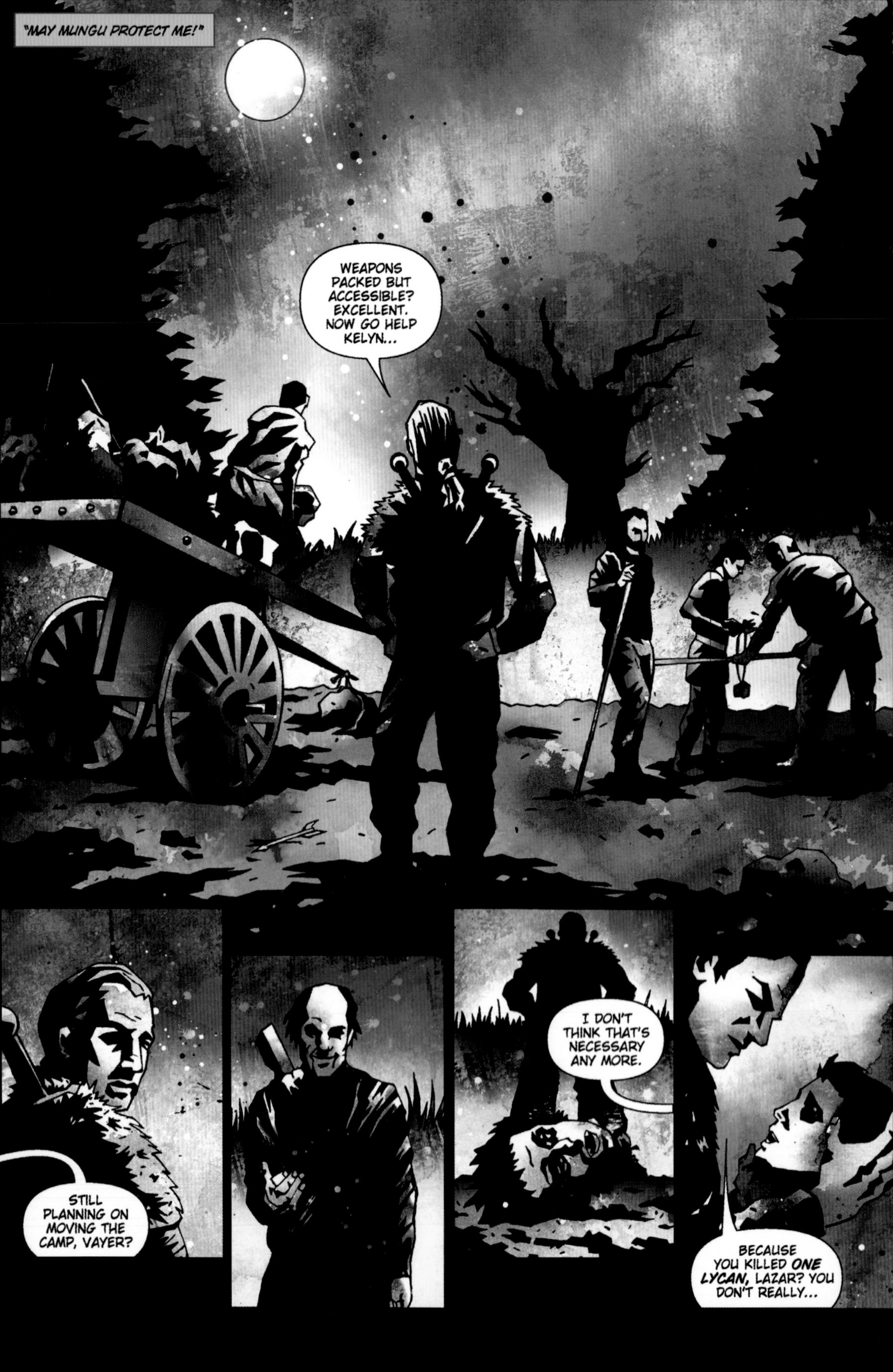
"MAY MUNGU PROTECT ME!"
WEAPONS PACKED BUT ACCESSIBLE? EXCELLENT. NOW GO HELP KELYN...
STILL PLANNING ON MOVING THE CAMP, VAYER?
I DON'T THINK THAT'S NECESSARY ANY MORE.
BECAUSE YOU KILLED ONE LYCAN, LAZAR? YOU DON'T REALLY...

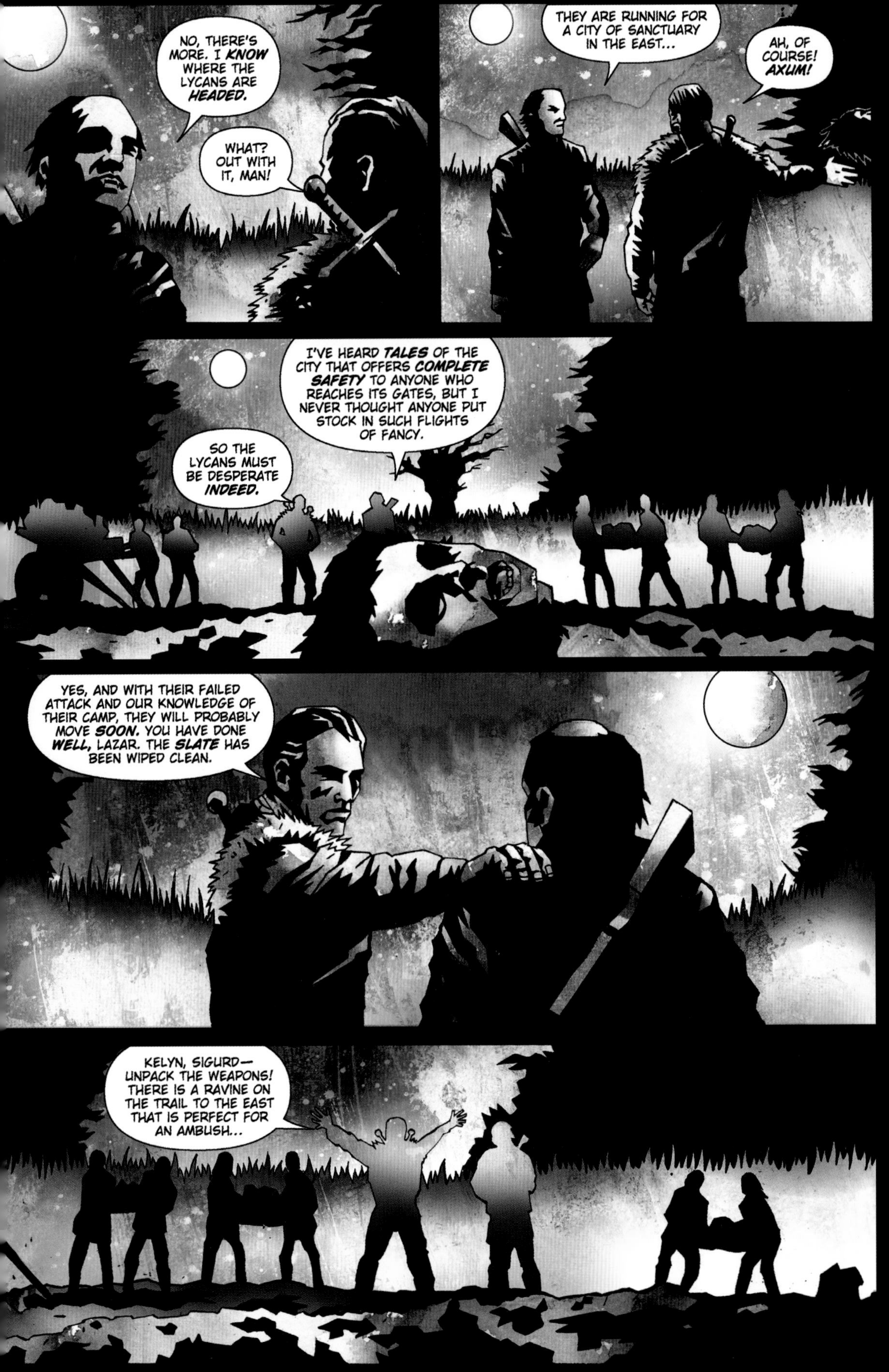
NO, THERE'S MORE. I KNOW WHERE THE LYCANS ARE HEADED.
WHAT? OUT WITH IT, MAN!
THEY ARE RUNNING FOR A CITY OF SANCTUARY IN THE EAST...
AH, OF COURSE! AXUM!
I'VE HEARD TALES OF THE CITY THAT OFFERS COMPLETE SAFETY TO ANYONE WHO REACHES ITS GATES, BUT I NEVER THOUGHT ANYONE PUT STOCK IN SUCH FLIGHTS OF FANCY.
SO THE LYCANS MUST BE DESPERATE INDEED.
YES, AND WITH THEIR FAILED ATTACK AND OUR KNOWLEDGE OF THEIR CAMP, THEY WILL PROBABLY MOVE SOON. YOU HAVE DONE WELL, LAZAR. THE SLATE HAS BEEN WIPED CLEAN.
KELYN, SIGURD— UNPACK THE WEAPONS! THERE IS A RAVINE ON THE TRAIL TO THE EAST THAT IS PERFECT FOR AN AMBUSH...

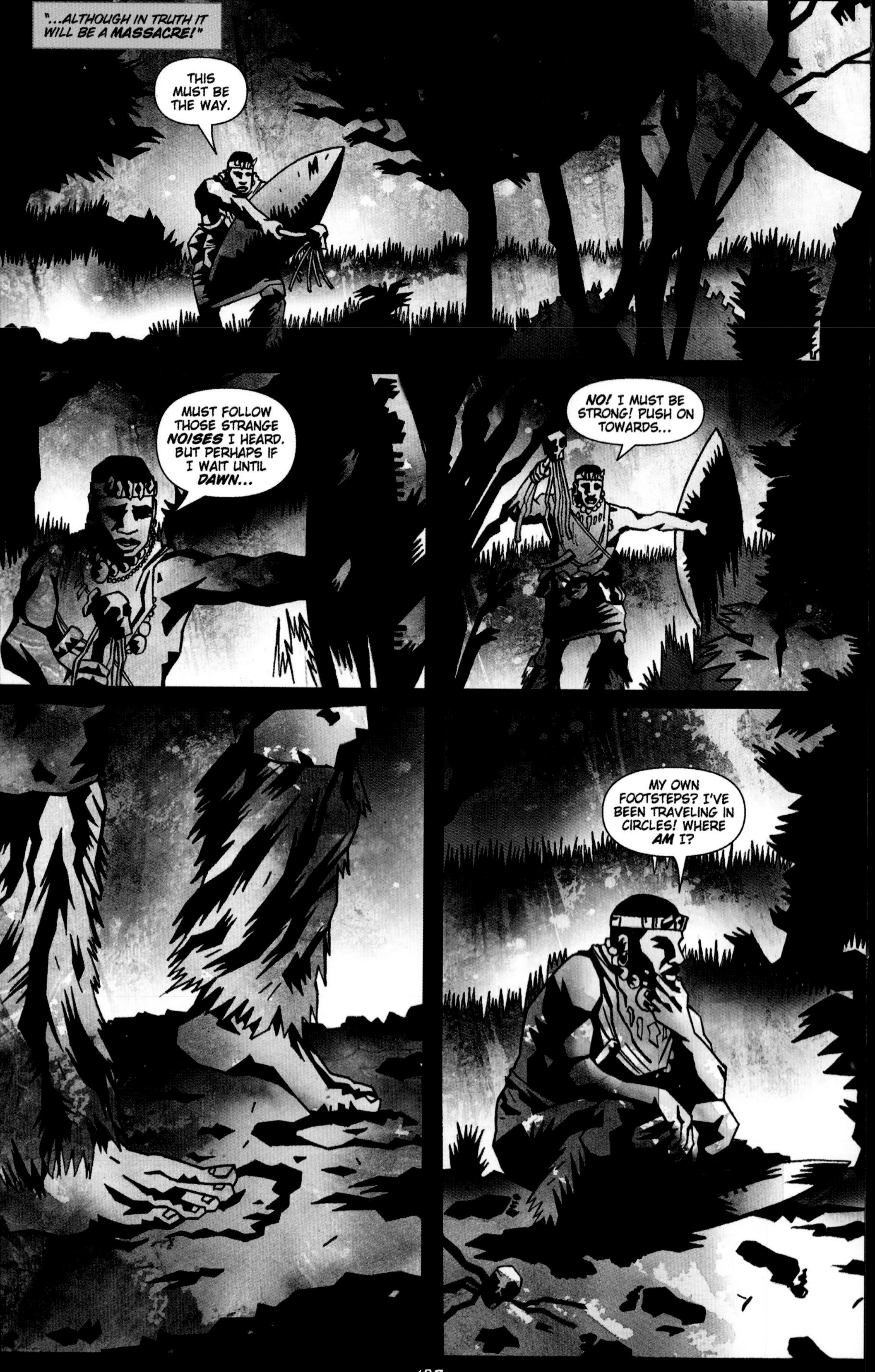
"...ALTHOUGH IN TRUTH IT WILL BE A MASSACRE!"
THIS MUST BE THE WAY.
MUST FOLLOW THOSE STRANGE NOISES I HEARD. BUT PERHAPS IF I WAIT UNTIL DAWN...
NO! I MUST BE STRONG! PUSH ON TOWARDS...
MY OWN FOOTSTEPS? I'VE BEEN TRAVELING IN CIRCLES! WHERE AM I?

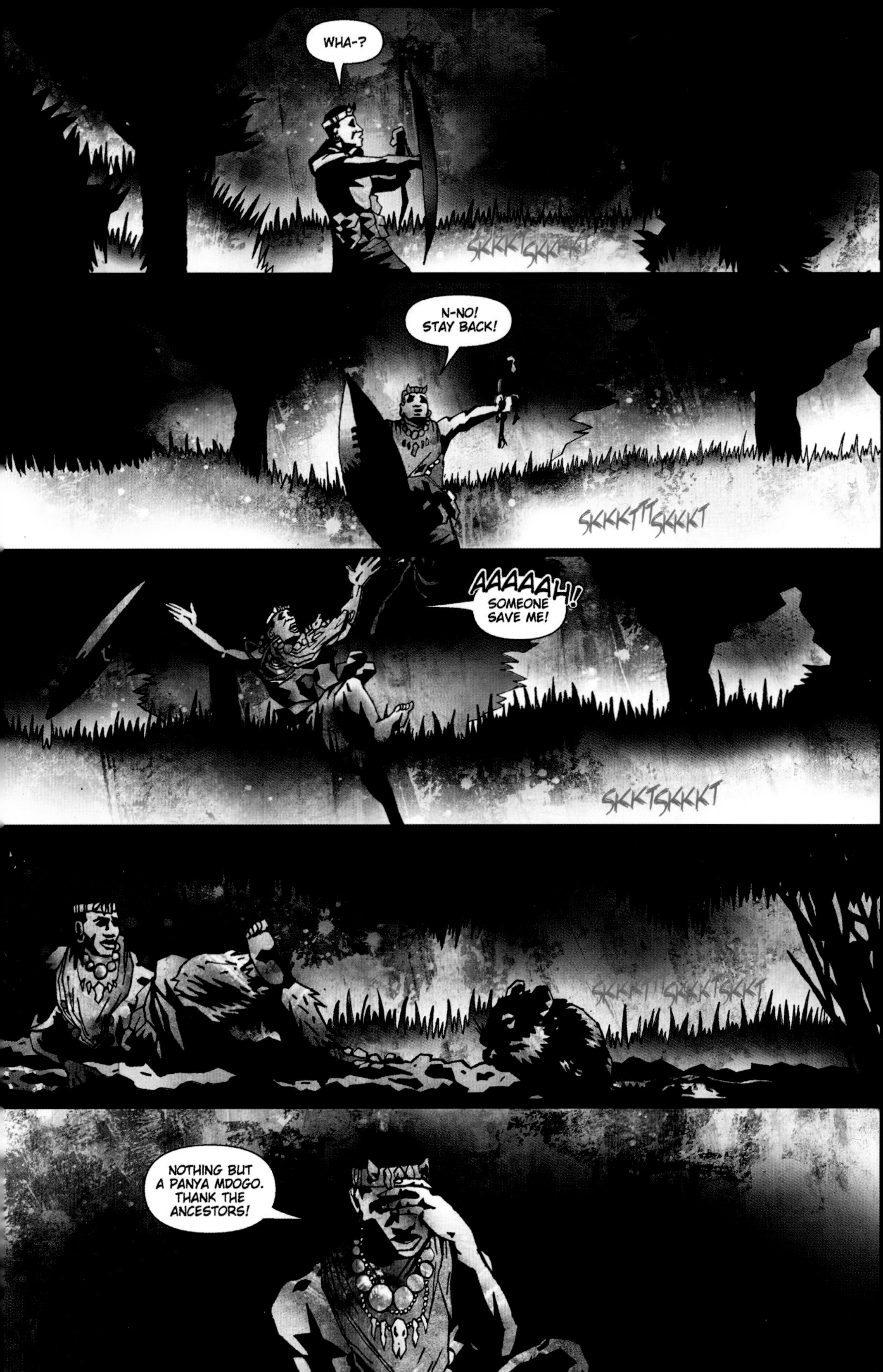
WHA-?
SKKKT
N-NO! STAY BACK!
SKKKTTT SKKKT
AAAAAH!! SOMEONE SAVE ME!
SKKTSKKKT
SKKKTSKKKTSKKT
NOTHING BUT A PANYA MDOGO. THANK THE ANCESTORS!

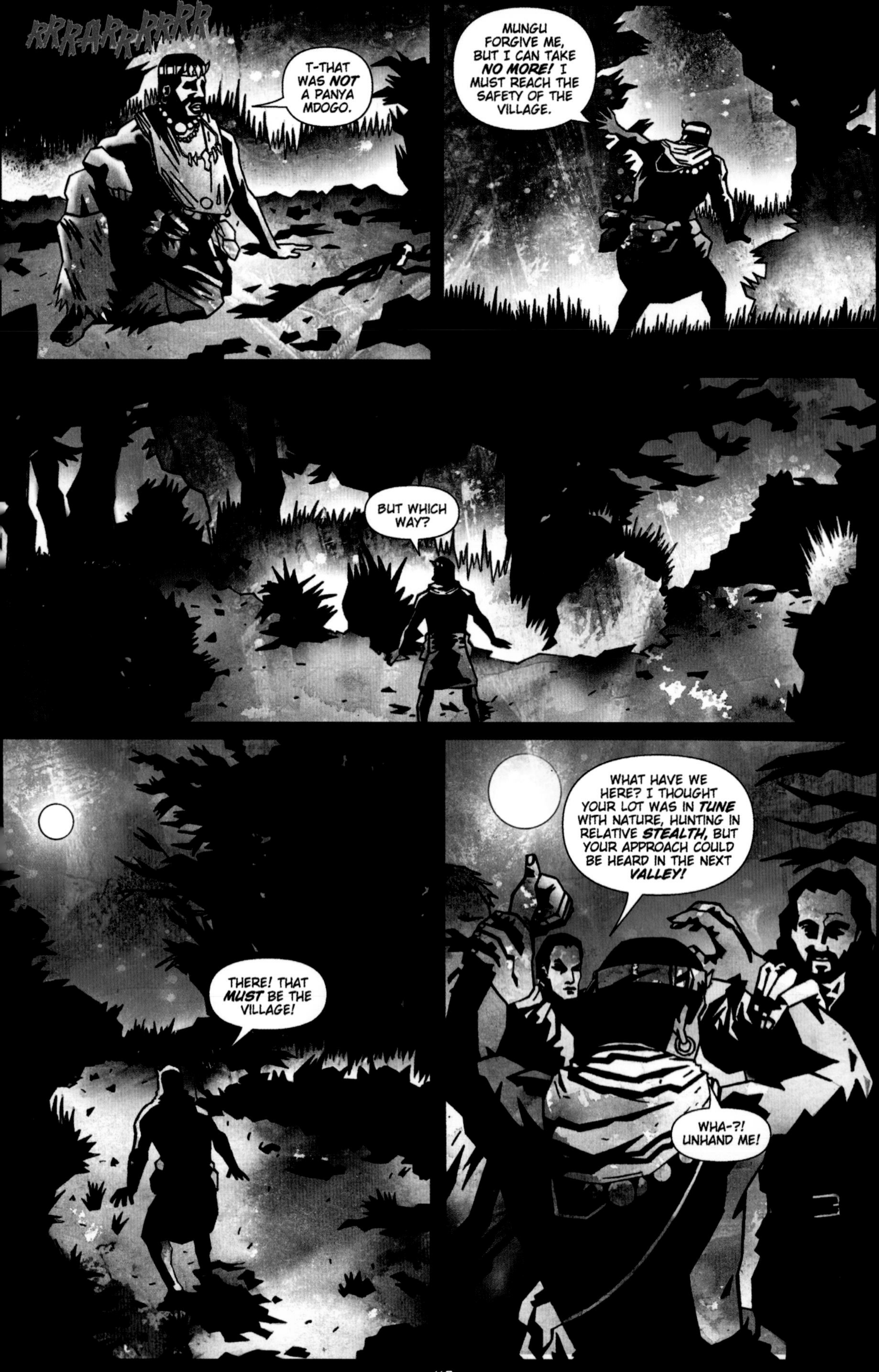
RRRR-ARRRRRRR
T-THAT WAS NOT A PANYA MDOGO.
MUNGU FORGIVE ME, BUT I CAN TAKE NO MORE! I MUST REACH THE SAFETY OF THE VILLAGE.
BUT WHICH WAY?
THERE! THAT MUST BE THE VILLAGE!
WHAT HAVE WE HERE? I THOUGHT YOUR LOT WAS IN TUNE WITH NATURE, HUNTING IN RELATIVE STEALTH, BUT YOUR APPROACH COULD BE HEARD IN THE NEXT VALLEY!
WHA-?! UNHAND ME!

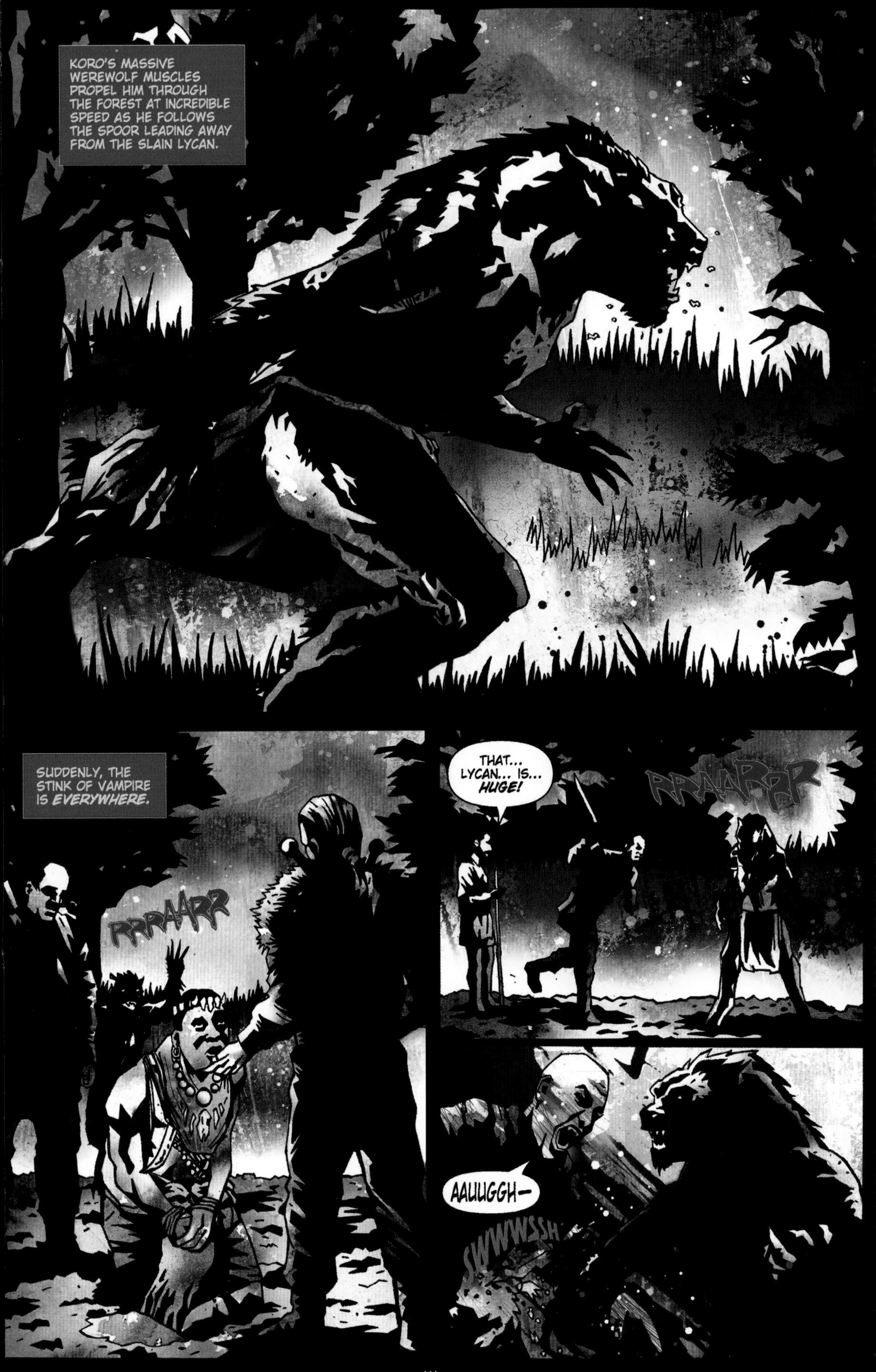
KORO'S MASSIVE WEREWOLF MUSCLES PROPEL HIM THROUGH THE FOREST AT INCREDIBLE SPEED AS HE FOLLOWS THE SPOOR LEADING AWAY FROM THE SLAIN LYCAN.
SUDDENLY, THE STINK OF VAMPIRE IS *EVERYWHERE.*
RRRAARR
THAT... LYCAN... IS... *HUGE!*
RRRAARRR
AAUUGGH—
SWWWSSH

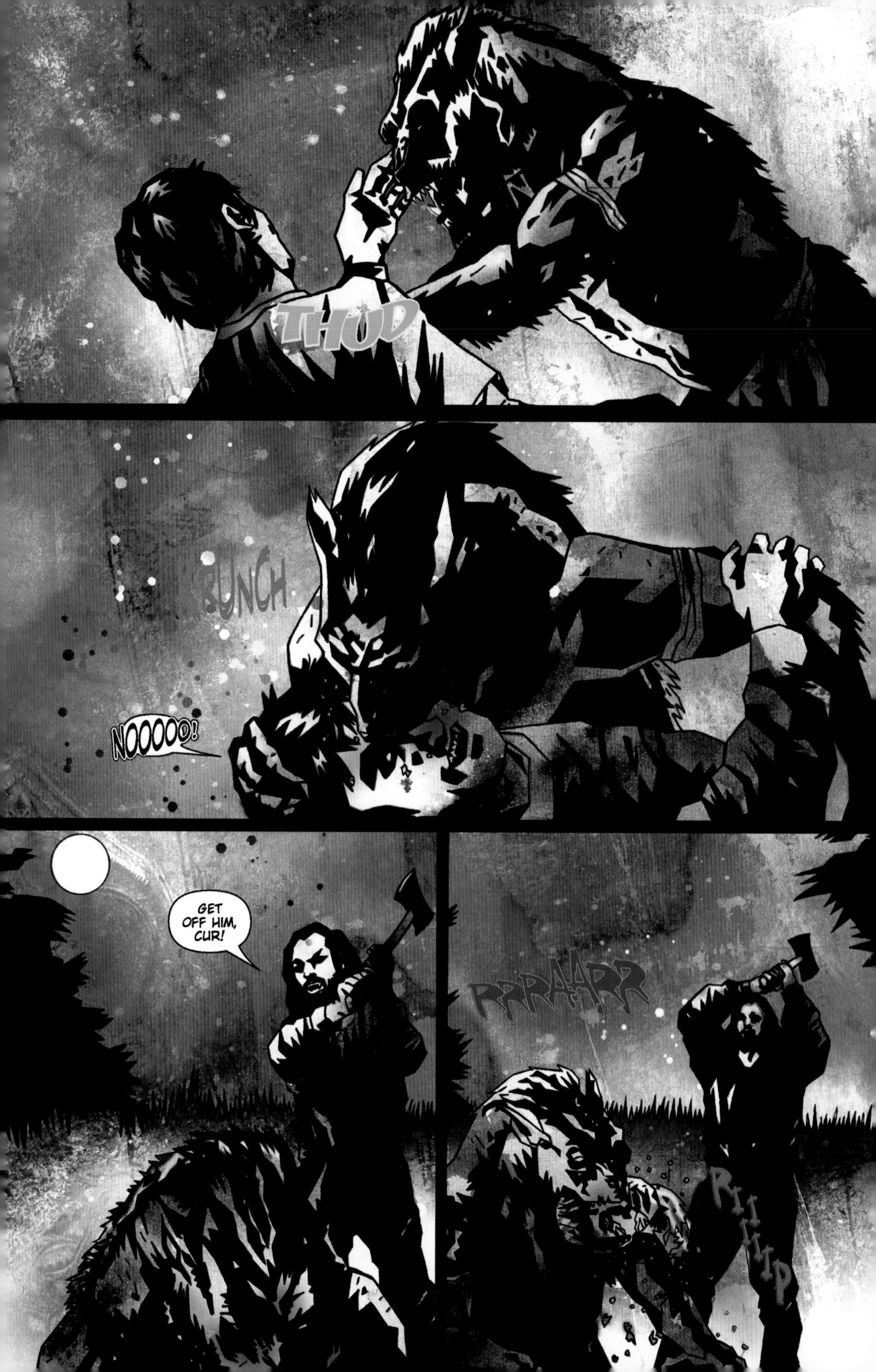
THUD
KRUNCH
NOOOOO!
GET OFF HIM, CUR!
RRRAARR
RIIIIP

PLEASE, I *KNOW* THIS ONE. YOU... YOU ARE NOT THE CREATOR OF THESE DEVILS?

CREATOR? *PLEASE!* WE SEEK NOTHING LESS THAN THE *DESTRUCTION* OF THE FILTHY BEASTS.

THEN... PERHAPS I CAN *HELP.*

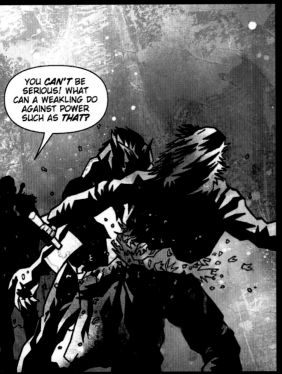

YOU *CAN'T* BE SERIOUS! WHAT CAN A WEAKLING DO AGAINST POWER SUCH AS *THAT?*

THIS ONE IS FROM *MY* TRIBE. HE IS SUBJECT TO THE POWER OF OUR ANCESTORS, WHOSE MIGHT I CAN *USE* TO *DESTROY* HIM.

YOUR TRIBE?

COULD THE LYCANS BE SEEKING TO *INCREASE* THEIR NUMBERS TO *STAVE OFF* EXTINCTION?

OUR ENEMIES ARE THE *SAME.* LET ME *HELP* YOU.

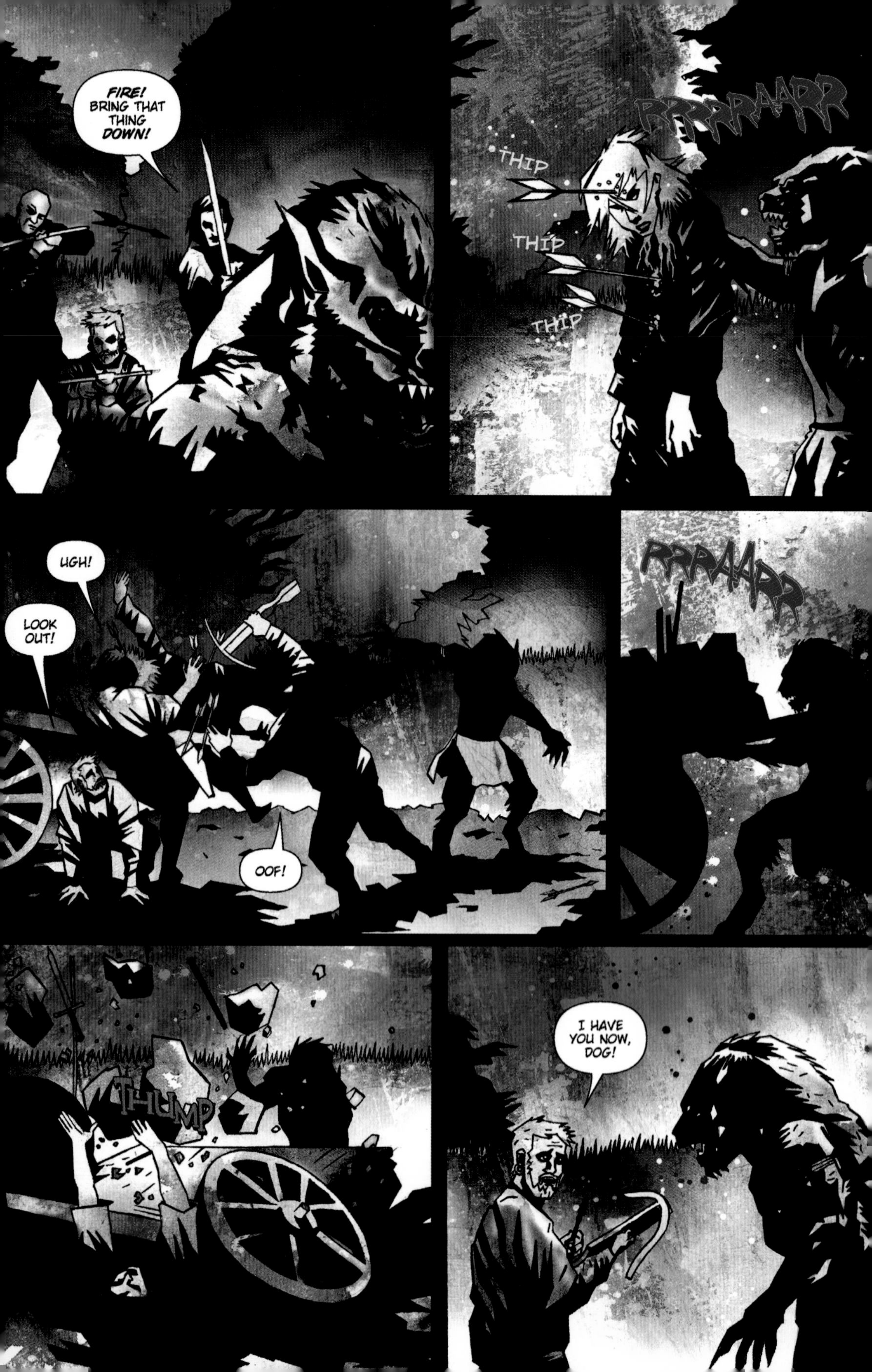
FIRE! BRING THAT THING DOWN!
THIP
THIP
THIP
RRRRRAARR
UGH!
LOOK OUT!
OOF!
RRRAARR
THUMP
I HAVE YOU NOW, DOG!

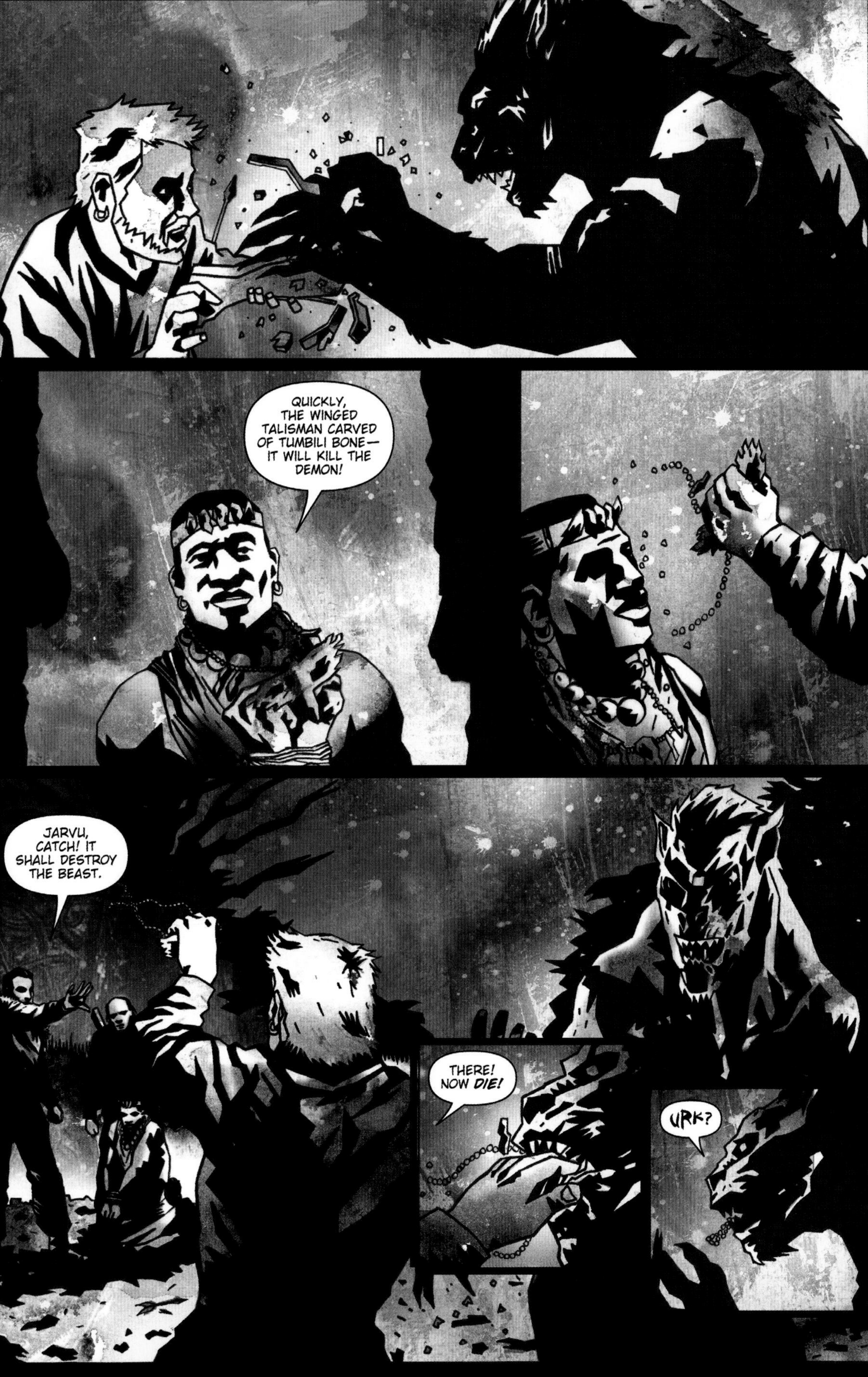
QUICKLY, THE WINGED TALISMAN CARVED OF TUMBILI BONE— IT WILL KILL THE DEMON!
JARVU, CATCH! IT SHALL DESTROY THE BEAST.
THERE! NOW DIE!
URK?

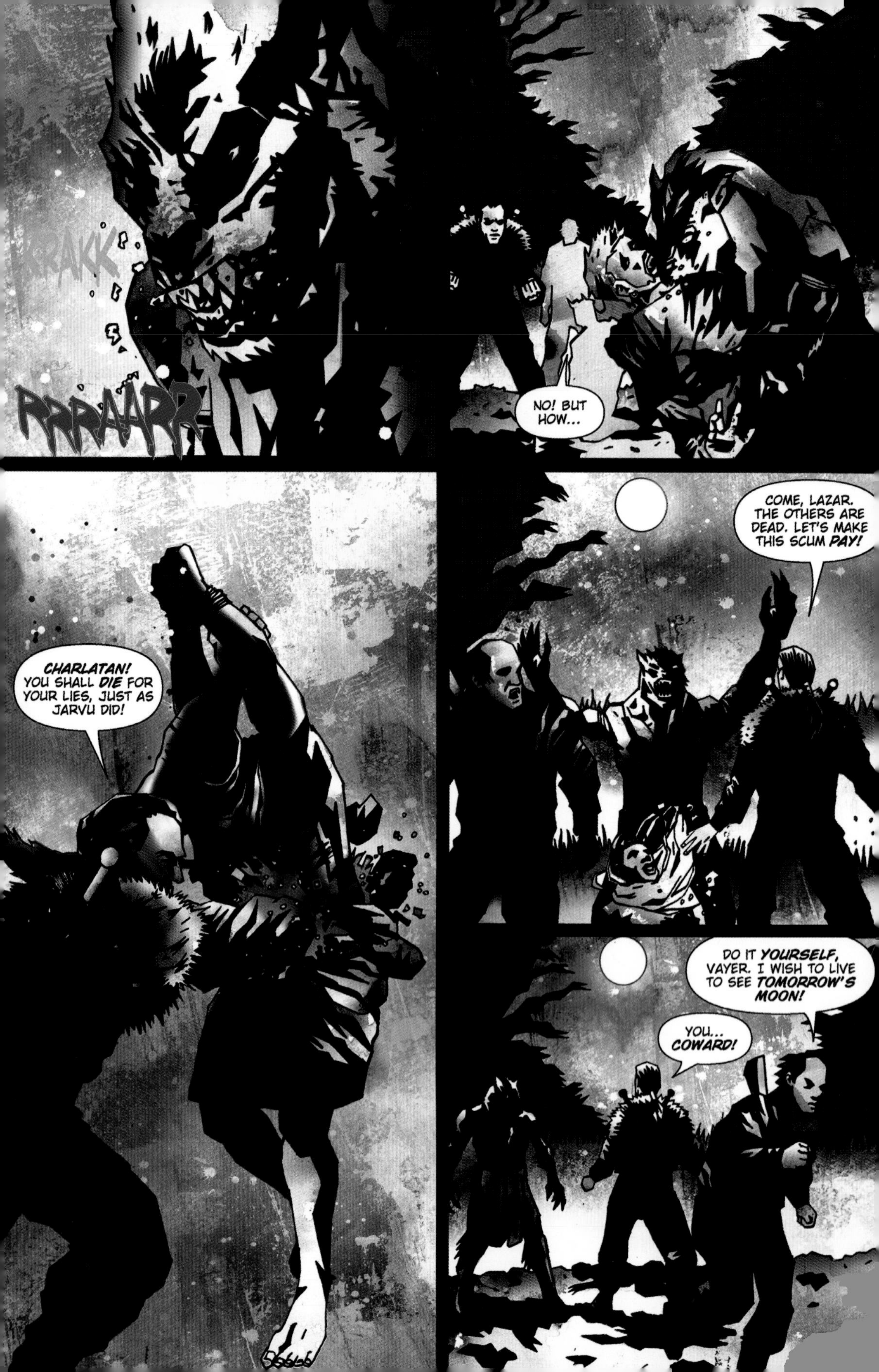
KRAKK
RRRAARR
NO! BUT HOW...
CHARLATAN! YOU SHALL DIE FOR YOUR LIES, JUST AS JARVU DID!
COME, LAZAR. THE OTHERS ARE DEAD. LET'S MAKE THIS SCUM PAY!
DO IT YOURSELF, VAYER. I WISH TO LIVE TO SEE TOMORROW'S MOON!
YOU... COWARD!

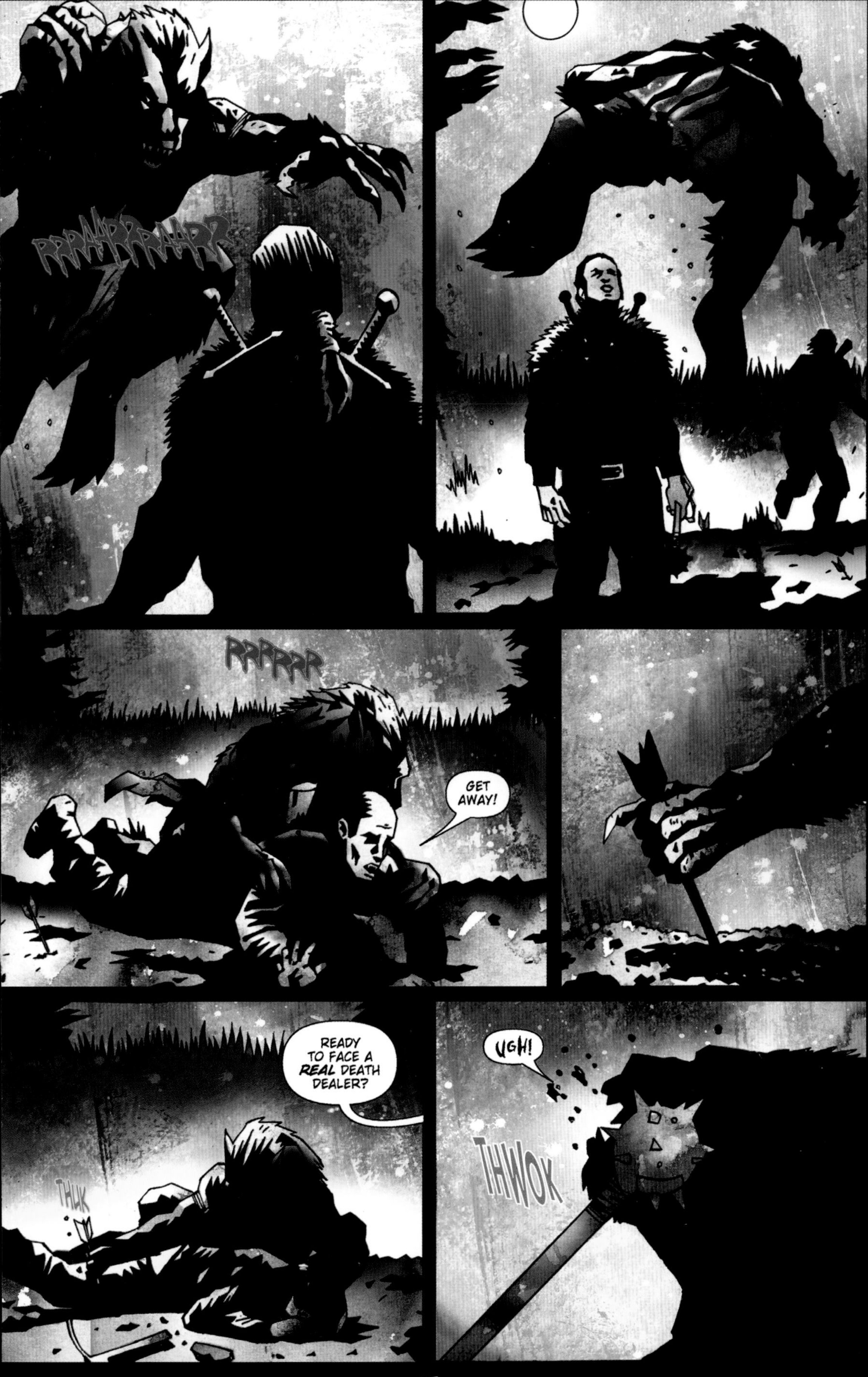
RRRAHRRRAHRR
RRRRRR
GET AWAY!
READY TO FACE A REAL DEATH DEALER?
THUK
UGH!
THWOK

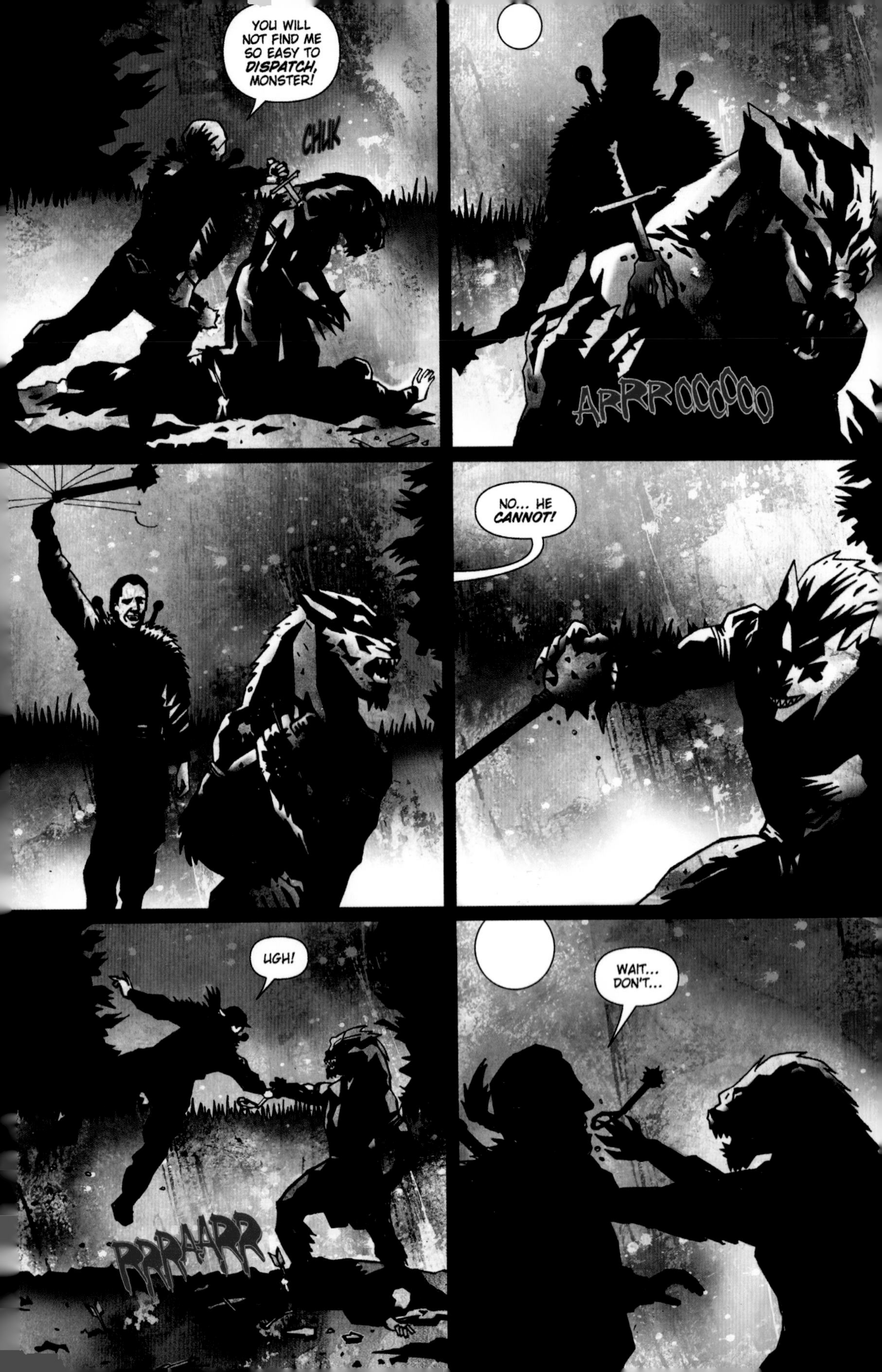
YOU WILL NOT FIND ME SO EASY TO DISPATCH, MONSTER!
CHUK
ARRROOOOOO
NO... HE CANNOT!
UGH!
RRRAARR
WAIT... DON'T...

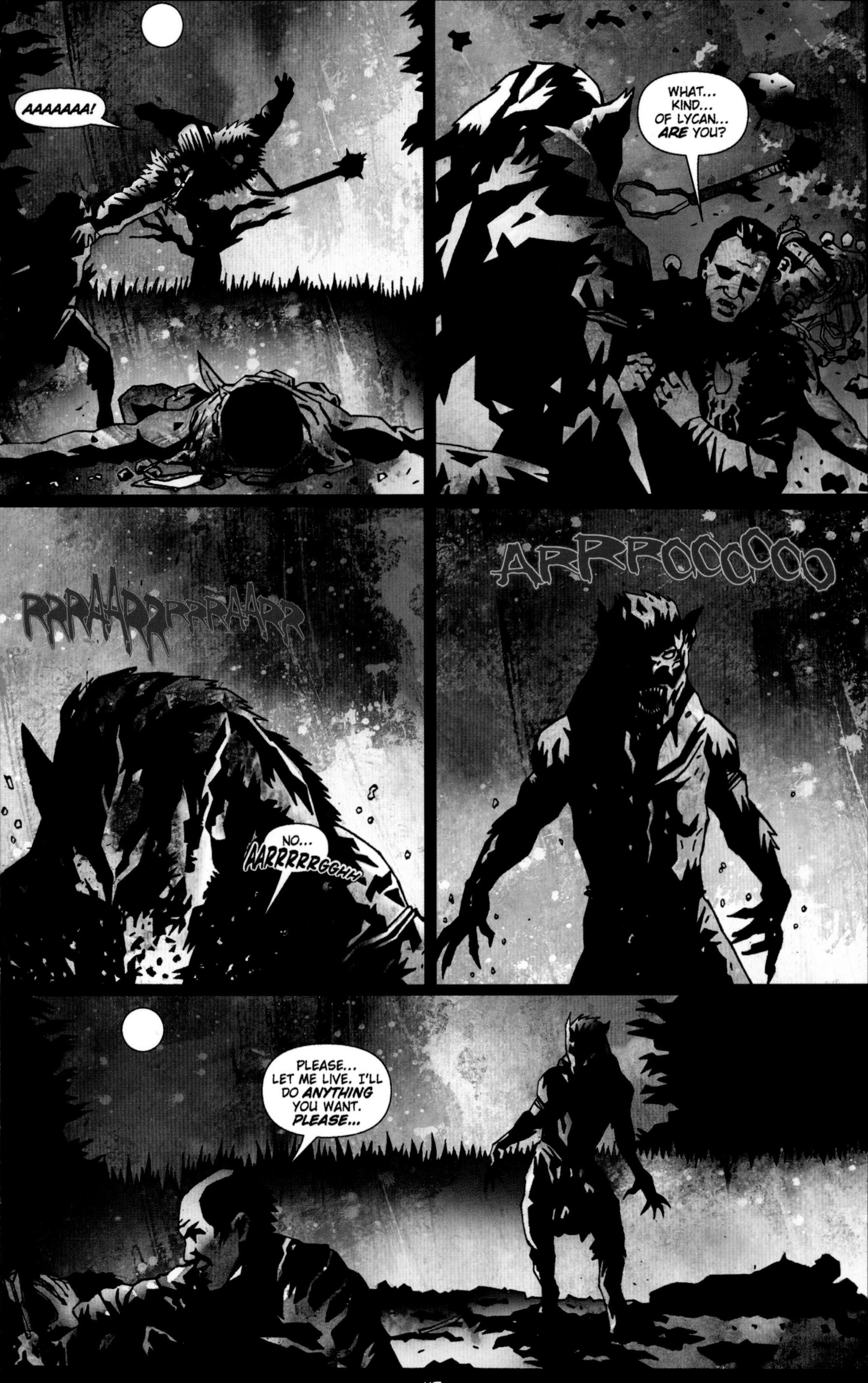
AAAAAAA!
WHAT... KIND... OF LYCAN... ARE YOU?
RRRAARRRRRAARR
NO...
AARRRRRGGHH
ARRROOOOOO
PLEASE... LET ME LIVE. I'LL DO ANYTHING YOU WANT. PLEASE...

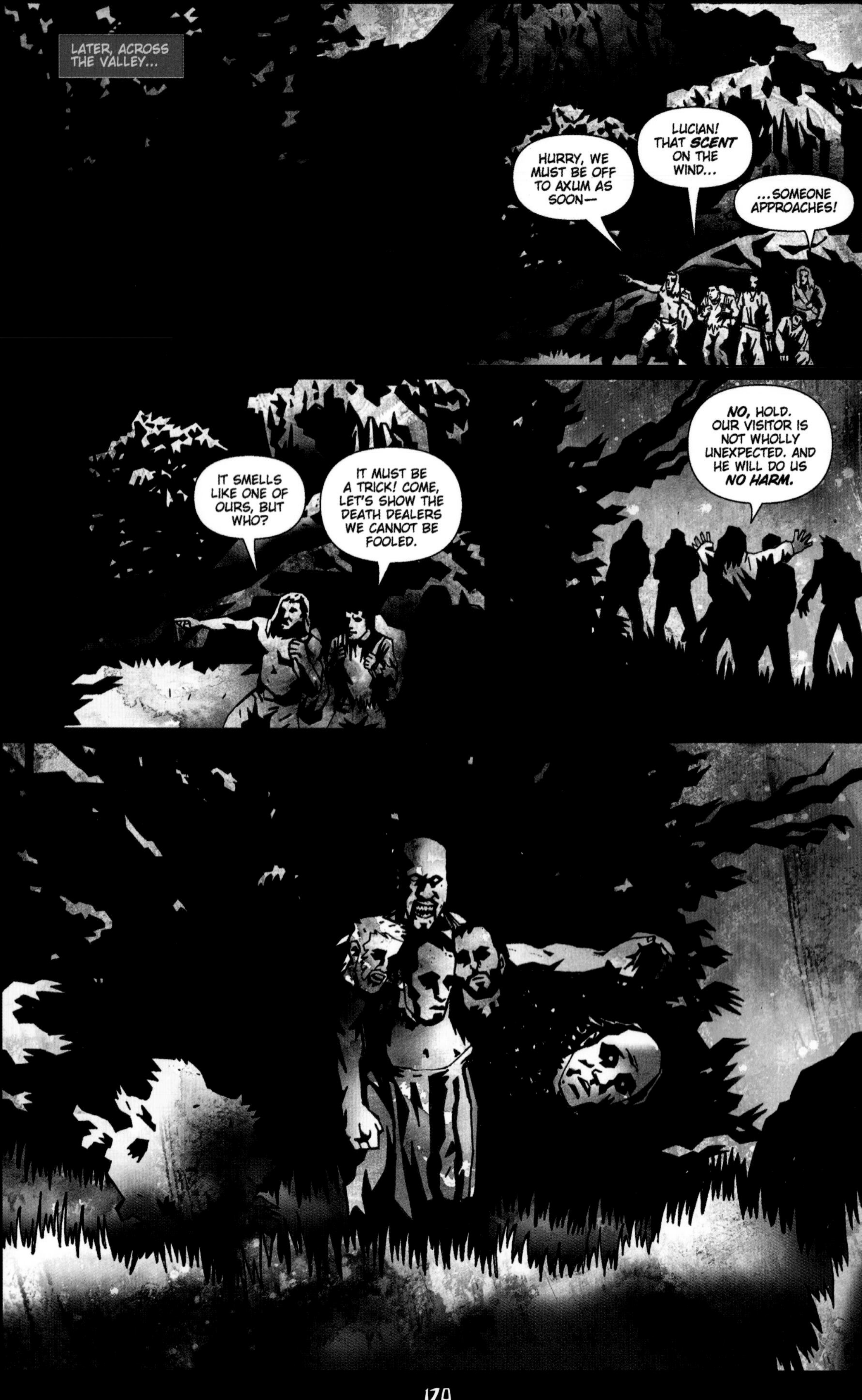
LATER, ACROSS THE VALLEY...
HURRY, WE MUST BE OFF TO AXUM AS SOON—
LUCIAN! THAT SCENT ON THE WIND...
...SOMEONE APPROACHES!
IT SMELLS LIKE ONE OF OURS, BUT WHO?
IT MUST BE A TRICK! COME, LET'S SHOW THE DEATH DEALERS WE CANNOT BE FOOLED.
NO, HOLD. OUR VISITOR IS NOT WHOLLY UNEXPECTED. AND HE WILL DO US NO HARM.

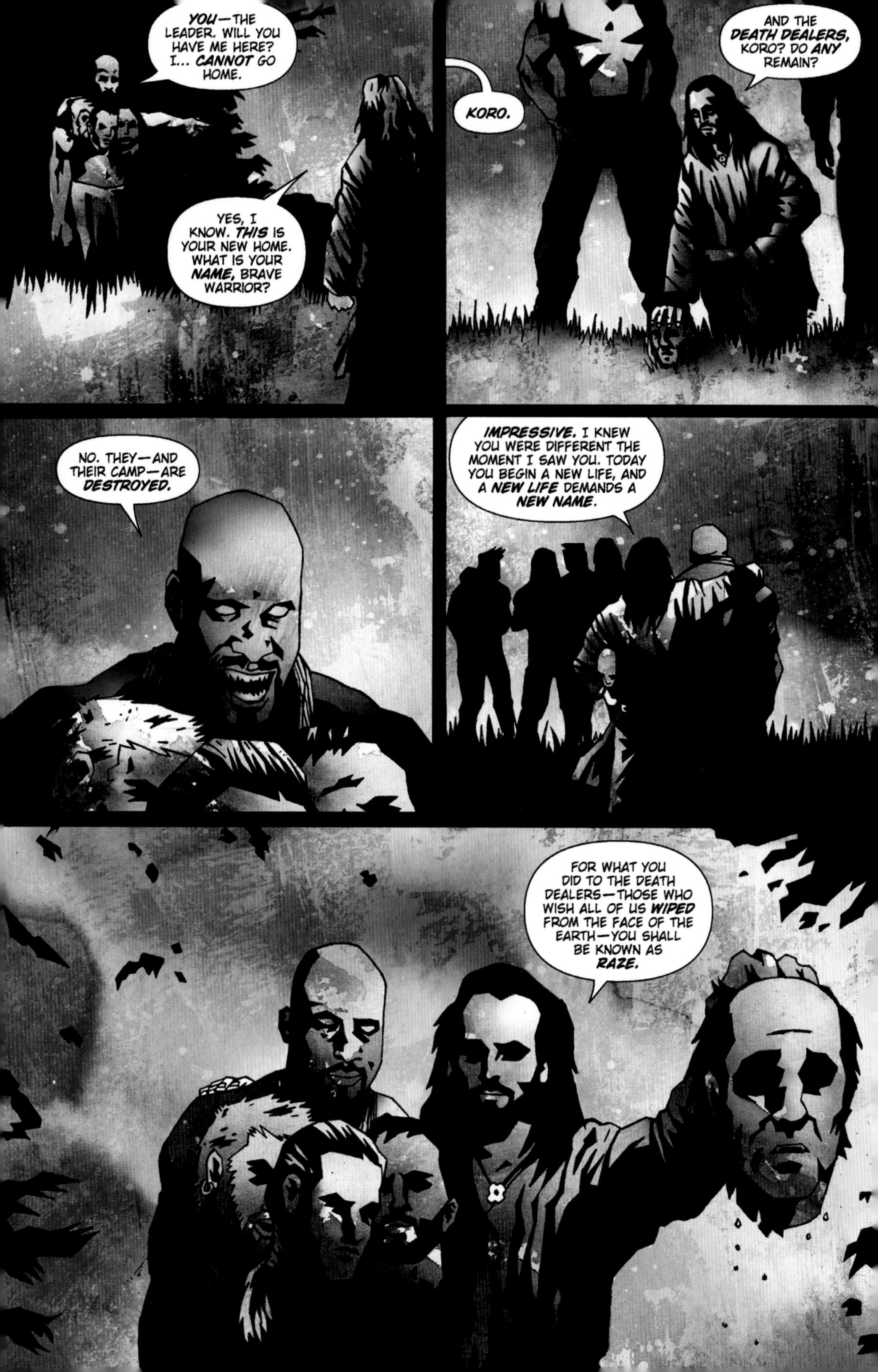
YOU—THE LEADER. WILL YOU HAVE ME HERE? I... CANNOT GO HOME.
YES, I KNOW. THIS IS YOUR NEW HOME. WHAT IS YOUR NAME, BRAVE WARRIOR?
KORO.
AND THE DEATH DEALERS, KORO? DO ANY REMAIN?
NO. THEY—AND THEIR CAMP—ARE DESTROYED.
IMPRESSIVE. I KNEW YOU WERE DIFFERENT THE MOMENT I SAW YOU. TODAY YOU BEGIN A NEW LIFE, AND A NEW LIFE DEMANDS A NEW NAME.
FOR WHAT YOU DID TO THE DEATH DEALERS—THOSE WHO WISH ALL OF US WIPED FROM THE FACE OF THE EARTH—YOU SHALL BE KNOWN AS RAZE.

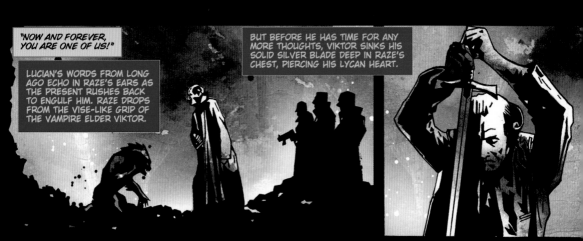

"NOW AND FOREVER, YOU ARE ONE OF US!"

LUCIAN'S WORDS FROM LONG AGO ECHO IN RAZE'S EARS AS THE PRESENT RUSHES BACK TO ENGULF HIM. RAZE DROPS FROM THE VISE-LIKE GRIP OF THE VAMPIRE ELDER VIKTOR.

BUT BEFORE HE HAS TIME FOR ANY MORE THOUGHTS, VIKTOR SINKS HIS SOLID SILVER BLADE DEEP IN RAZE'S CHEST, PIERCING HIS LYCAN HEART.

AFTER ALL THESE CENTURIES, RAZE WILL AGAIN BE KNOWN AS KORO...

...IN THE WORLD OF THE ANCESTORS.

THE END

UNDERWORLD
COVER GALLERY

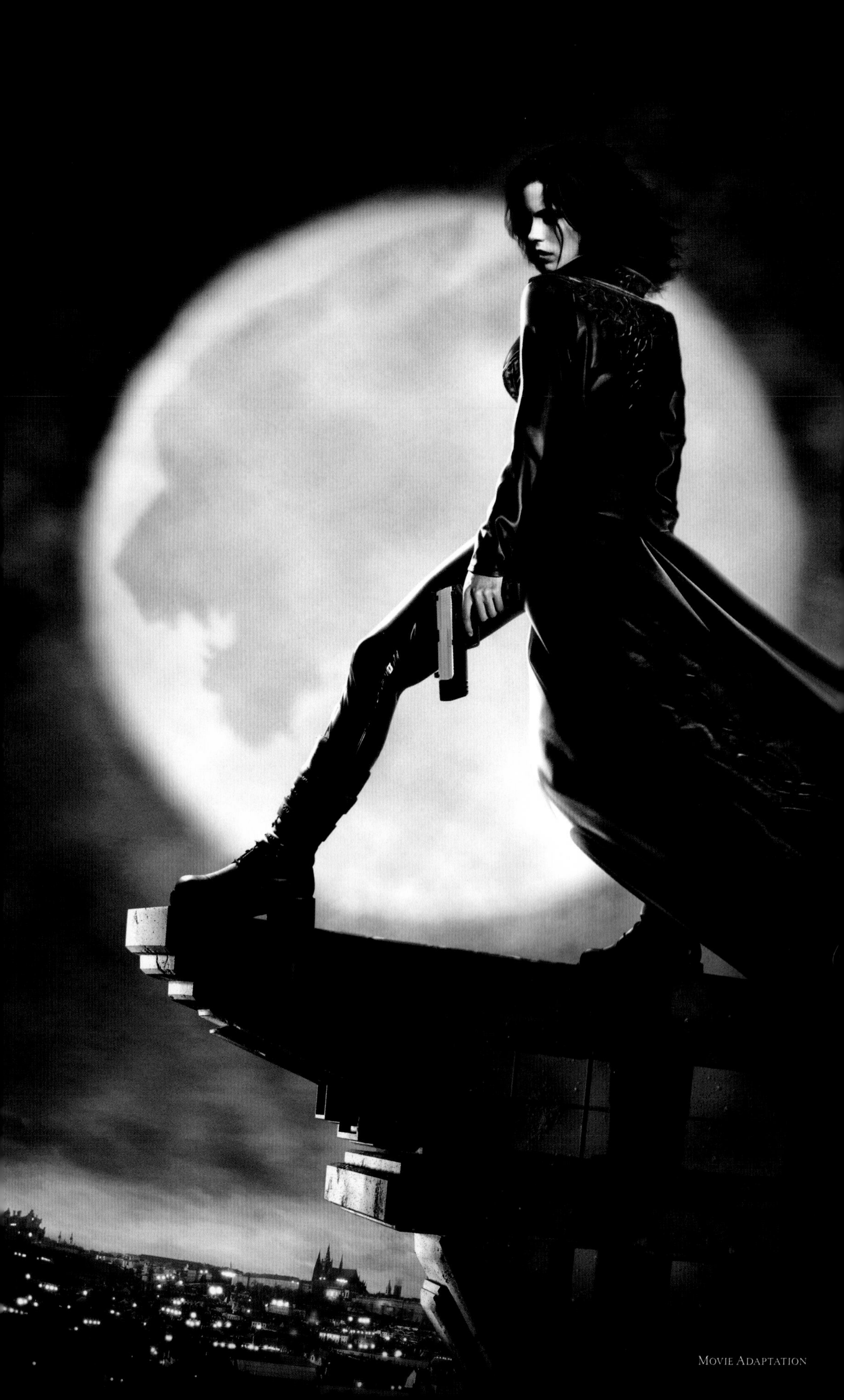

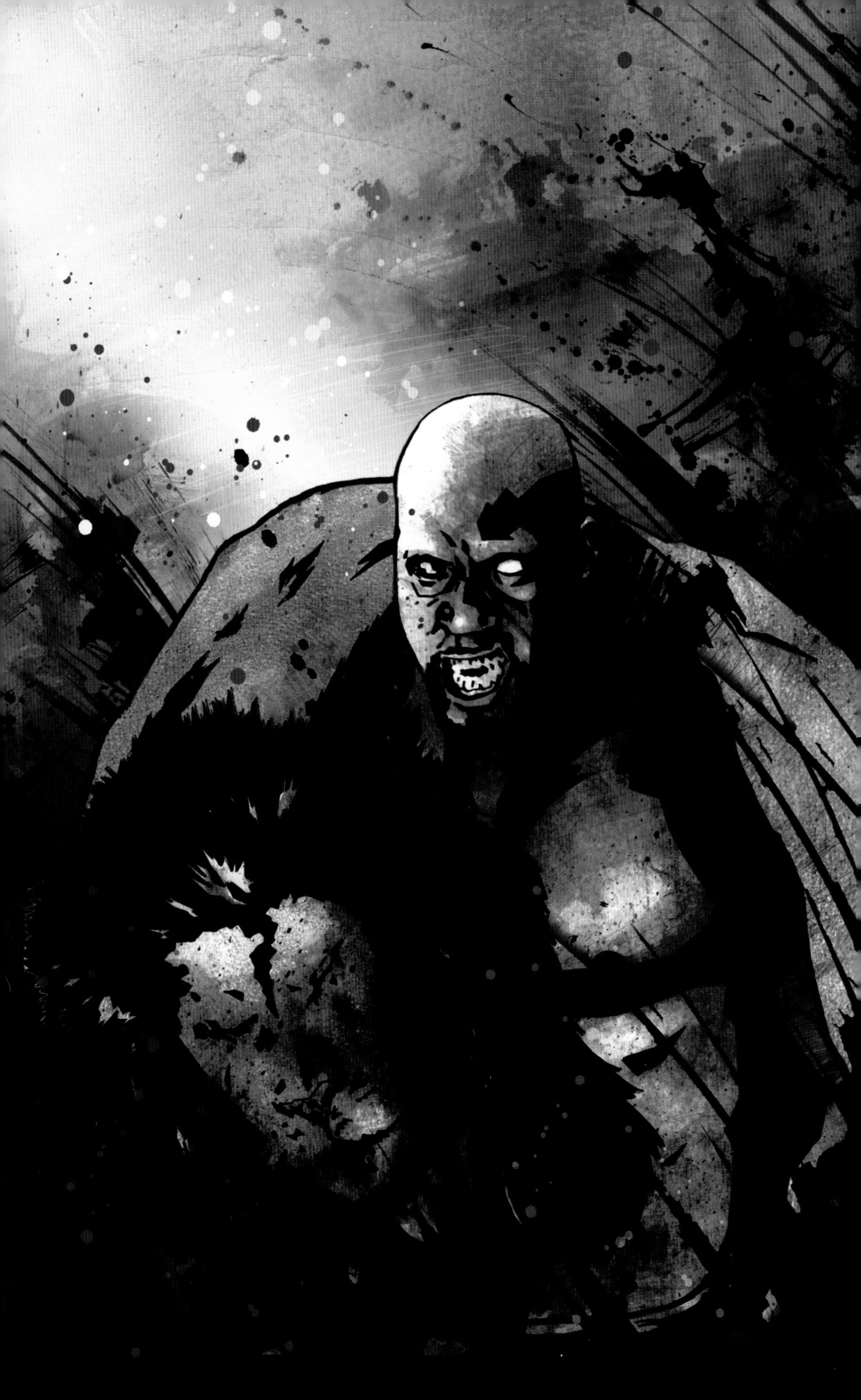

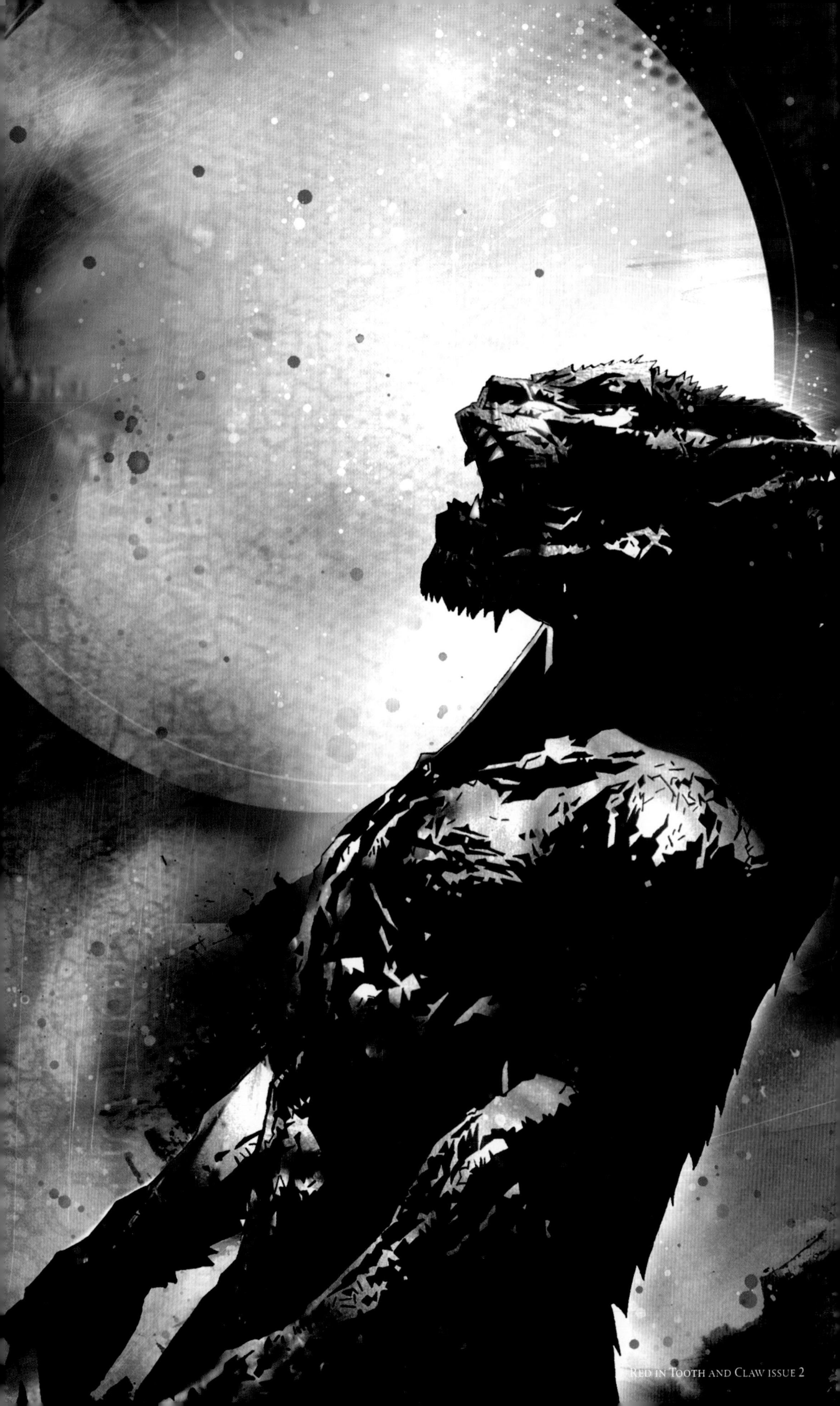

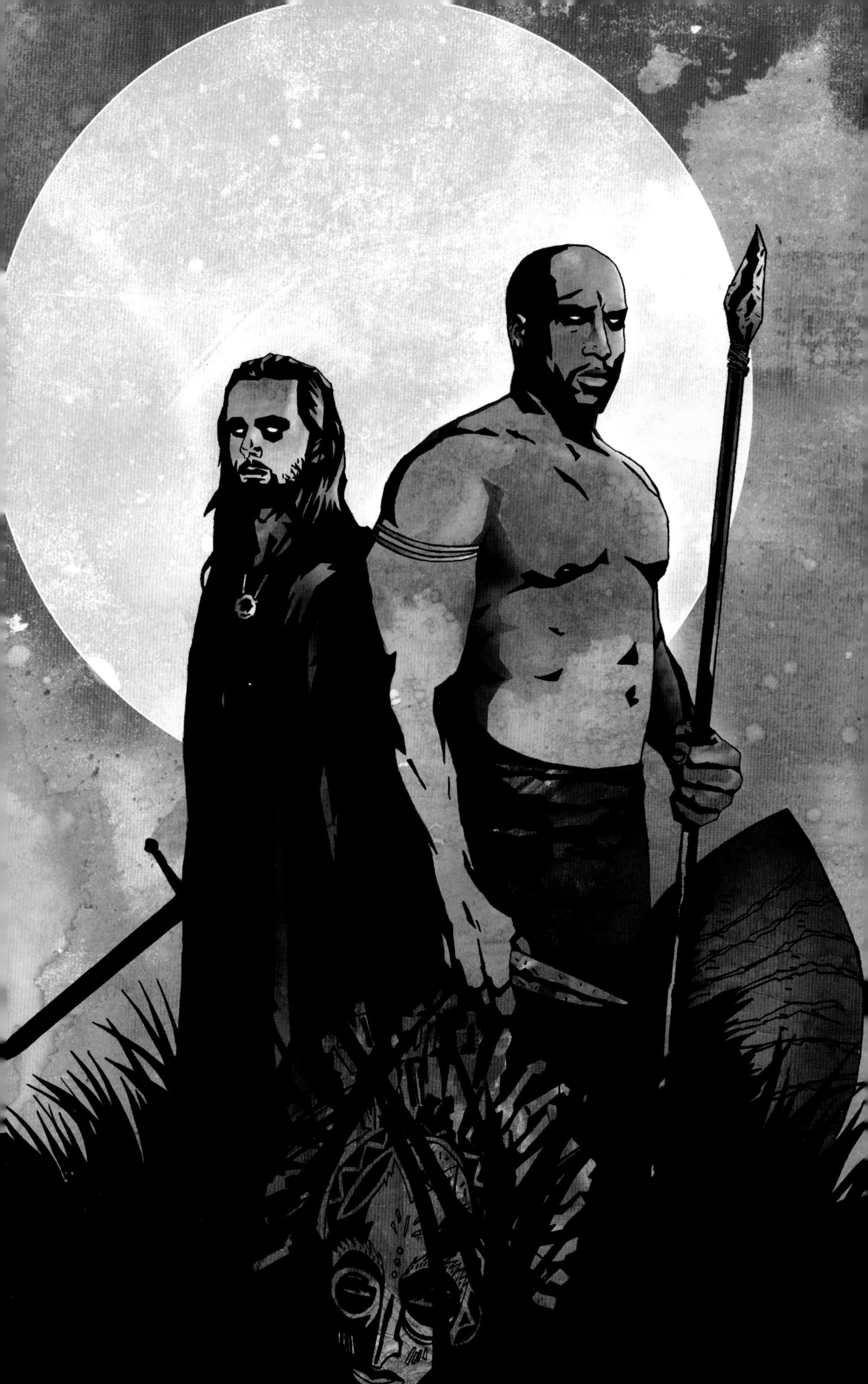

Red in Tooth and Claw issue 3

WWW.IDWPUBLISHING.COM